Popular Culture
and Everyday Life

Popular Culture
and Everyday Life

Toby Miller and Alec McHoul

SAGE Publications
London • Thousand Oaks • New Delhi

SAGE Publications Ltd
6 Bonhill Street
London EC2A 4PU

SAGE Publications Inc
2455 Teller Road
Thousand Oaks, California 91320

SAGE Publications India Pvt Ltd
32, M-Block Market
Greater Kailash – I
New Delhi 110 048

British Library Cataloguing in Publication data

A catalogue record for this book is
available from the British Library.

ISBN 0 7619 5212 8
ISBN 0 7619 5213 6 (pbk)

Library of Congress catalog card number 98-060905

Typeset by Photoprint, Torquay, Devon
Printed in Great Britain by Redwood Books, Trowbridge, Wiltshire

Contents

Acknowledgements

Thanks to Sarah Berry, Elizabeth Botta, Susan Brand, Mary Schmidt Campbell, Sophie Craze, Julia Hall, Mike Innes, Geoff Lawrence, Randy Martin, Bill Mowder, Gillian O'Shaughnessy, John Richardson, Jeff Sammons, Bambi Schieffelin, Kiren Shoman, Grant Stone, Jon Watts, Allen Weiss, the people involved in Sage's development review, and undergraduate and graduate students at Murdoch and New York Universities in related classes. Some of the impetus for this book arose from our involvement in the course H235, Popular Culture and Everyday Life, at Murdoch University with Garry Gillard, Bob Hodge and Alan Mansfield. We owe each of them much gratitude for their inspiration. Particular thanks also to Garry Gillard for his meticulous attention to several drafts of the manuscript.

Parts of Chapter 2 on food were given as a talk to the Rural Social and Economic Research Centre at Central Queensland University. Thanks to the audience for comments. Parts of Chapter 3 on sport have appeared in the *Journal of Sport & Social Issues* and *Competing Allegories*. Parts of Chapter 4 on self-help have appeared in *Social Text*. Parts of Chapter 5 on cultural devices appear in different forms in *Social Semiotics*, *Deny All Knowledge: Reading the X-Files*, and *Pretending to Communicate*. A Junior Faculty Fellowship from NYU allowed the authors to spend time together in 1995.

Preface:
An Interruption in Cultural Studies

The field of popular culture and everyday life is one that's central to the emerging discipline of cultural studies. And, in this book, we want to continue in that tradition – but in a new way. That is, on our reckoning, cultural studies has, for all its internal diversity, taken a very particular tack when it comes to the everyday. First, it has tended to deal with the *spectacular* (pop stars and their sexuality, politically 'hot' topics, youth resistance, and so on). Secondly, it has dealt with these topics in a *speculative* fashion. For example, it has tended to equate mundane transgressions with general social tendencies. Thirdly, and relatedly, it has assumed that everyday cultural objects stand on behalf of, or *represent*, wider social forces.

We can see this at almost every turn in cultural studies. For example, opening an early 1990s cultural studies collection on Madonna at random, we found the following:

> MTV is an important site for the struggle over control of popular memory. Because of their short duration, music videos provide important raw material for the bricolage construction of memory links. The perpetually changing juxtaposition of videos suggests that meaning construction on MTV is more like the montage proposed by Sergei Eisenstein . . . than the narrative trajectory widely accepted as cinerealism. Although there are not yet any comprehensive studies of MTV-watching behavior, it seems more likely that viewers half listen for favorite songs or artists and half watch for visual patterns that signify the style of their favorite musical genres.
> Situated in this panoply of meaning units. . . . (Patton 1993: 91)

Note here how an everyday event, watching TV, becomes *spectacular.* It becomes, that is, a form of 'popular memory', 'meaning construction' and so on, that can be likened to the great artistic feats of early cinema (Eisenstein). In this way, it opens up, for Patton, 'the site of struggle over who will "own" the gender or racial problematic evident in the male-male/racialized stylistics of voguing' (1993: 91). The connection, then, is *speculative*: it is unable to show exactly how a certain kind of watching is actually so deeply and 'hotly' political; or how, exactly, it articulates with the broader sociopolitical agendas of race and sexuality. And it is speculative because it simply assumes that the everyday event *represents* that much broader field of contested sexuality.

Now, it is not our position, in this book, to criticize such endeavours, much as they make up the mainstream 'theology' of cultural studies. They clearly have their place as a kind of theoretical artform. Instead, we would simply point to how Patton's text (and many another like it) makes its moves. Note that the writer begins with a speculation: that MTV is 'an important site for the struggle over control of popular memory'. This speculative claim guides the rest of the 'argument'. From here, it is possible to assume that the text is indeed, factually, made up of a 'panoply of meaning units' for its everyday viewers, regardless of their differences, regardless of their particular histories, and regardless of the *in situ* details of their particular watching events. The critical point in the argument arises where Patton tells us one very definite (if negative) fact: 'there are not yet any comprehensive studies of MTV-watching behavior'.

And this is precisely where we would wish to *interrupt* (rather than criticize) mainstream speculative cultural studies. We would like to stop it in its tracks right there – at those points where it simply does not go and look at the everyday in its *historical particularity* and in its *utterly mundane character*. These, then, are the two things that we want to take up as a quite different approach to the study of culture.

Whether this is still 'cultural studies' is neither here nor there for us – for it is an approach to the study of culture and we're unconcerned about the effects our interruption may or may not have on the cards we're subsequently allowed to carry. All we have to say (or rather, to show) in this book, is that everyday popular culture is too important a social phenomenon to be dealt with speculatively, as the spectacular, and always as a representation of something else. Instead, we want to show how (first, using a *historical* or genealogical approach) everyday cultural objects arise out of local conditions – conditions which are highly specific and far from spectacular. And then (secondly, using some variations on conversation analysis) we want to show what these objects actually look like in their everyday situated places.

What inspires this extremely data-driven double approach is a number of ideas that have arisen in the field of ethnomethodology. Portentous though this term may be, it hides a very simple insight: if you want to know about how people do things in everyday life and how it's possible for them to do those things in regular ways, why speculate? Why not – given that the everyday is everywhere and by no means hard to access – go and have a look at what folks are doing? And in going to look, one may discover properties of everyday events as they are, in their own right, rather than as *representations* of other matters (such as sexuality, race and gender, as conceived from macro-speculative standpoints).

One of us (Toby Miller) has taken this brief – which we refer to via the shorthand of 'EMICS', or ethnomethodologically inspired cultural studies – and gone to look at the specificities of the history of particular cultural fields such as eating, using self-help books and sport. In particular, he focuses on the salient *literatures* on, and the histories of the *public discourses* involved in the production of these fields. The other (Alec McHoul) has used the brief to open typical cultural studies questions – such as 'how do people watch TV?', 'how do people use fast food outlets?' and so on – as everyday accomplishments, by actually going out and collecting relevant data. In particular, he focuses on the kinds of *talk* and *text* used to accomplish everyday cultural order. What we offer, then, is a two-pronged approach, coming at cultural studies from two different directions – the specifically historical and the specifically mundane – in the attempt to interrupt its tripartite reliances on speculation, the spectacular and representationalism.

It's true, therefore, that our different uptakes of EMICS are not always seamless and harmonious. Sometimes they match one another; sometimes they abruptly collide. But this should not be a problem for the field of cultural studies which, in both its methods and its objects of study, has always celebrated the diverse, the 'panoply of meaning units'. Cultural studies, that is, is enormously diverse and interdisciplinary. In fact, it has made its reputation on the basis of diversity and interdisciplinarity. But, for all that, we have to ask about its limitations in this respect. Can it tolerate even more diversity in the form of specific details of everyday phenomena and events? Or is it limited to its attraction to the spectacular?

To find out, we bring you now a series of investigations that insist on being, above all, data-driven. The historical parts are rigorously based in the factual bases of cultural phenomena. The 'analytic' parts are, equally, rigorously based on empirical data. As and where they happen to meet, we will draw tentative conclusions about the relations between the historical and mundane characters of popular culture and everyday life. Where they happen simply to cross one another, we will refrain from speculative conclusions.

So what you are about to read is terribly old (because everyone is involved in everyday life) and also terribly new (because cultural studies has hardly dealt with the fact that everyone is involved in everyday life). A whole new beginning, then, based on the sheer fact that the things called 'popular culture' and 'everyday life' can never be new, that they are always already someone else's beginning.

1

Introduction to Popular Culture and Everyday Life

This book is about people's collective and individual participation in both majority cultures (for example voting, paying taxes, or watching broadcast TV) and minority ones (like watching girlbands, drinking in lesbian bars, or collecting military figurines). We cover a range of topics: sport, food, and self-help/therapy, concluding with audiences to the entertainment media. The intention is to give readers a broad background in approaches to popular culture and the everyday, using tools derived from anthropological, historical, literary, linguistic, screen, and sociological studies. The focus is on subjectivity and power. By 'subjectivity' we mean the ways in which people experience themselves as human: what it means to be, for example, exercised, fed, and counselled; and how individuals move through society inside these and other categories. By 'power' we refer to the exercise of knowledge and agency to construct and police such identities.

This book is written from the perspectives of cultural studies and ethnomethodology. Cultural studies mixes economics, politics, gender and race studies, ethnography, history, textual analysis, and policy studies, focusing on who controls communication and culture and how they do so (Frow and Morris 1993: xvi–xviii). To exemplify the project of cultural studies, we might consider Arthur Danto's argument – in another field of study – that pop drew attention to art history as a series of oversights and erasures, of canonical exclusion rather than obedience to the immanent beauty of certain texts. By its very presence in galleries and museums, pop art made it apparent that in the difference between commercial dross and aesthetic heights lay the power to tell history and control institutional space. Pop art also stressed the democratic potential of everyday life (Danto 1992: 3–7). These are among the tasks of cultural studies.

Ethnomethodology examines social relations via everyday meaning, as it is constructed by talking, listening, moving, exchanging, reading, and so on. Ethnomethodology focuses on how people make sense of their local environment, asking such questions as: is a job interviewer looking for intense precision or broad discursivity? or, when an accident victim is propped up by an ambulance driver, does the look on the helper's face say something different from the look on the face of a passer-by? Ethnomethodologically, the situations that comprise the everyday are a composite of their participants' practices. This is not a voluntarist position, where fully-formed individuals select from a repertoire of actions based on desire or caprice. Rather, it is about selecting from the practices available within the rules of a situationally particular discourse. Ethnomethodology is interested both in the reasoning that informs this selection and in its outcomes. The two are reflexively related: the public display of reasons in the form of accounts is itself a practical action. Ethnomethodology criticizes the notion that society is a pre-formed object which human subjects simply uncover through language, suggesting instead that members of a social formation join it by employing *methods* that produce social facts; these are ethnomethods.

Each chapter of this book begins with a summary of key studies (sometimes cultural studies, sometimes ethnomethodology, sometimes other) on the relevant subject. It then goes on to examine other public discourses that produce these cultural fields, and concludes with one or more original empirical investigations based on ethnomethodologically inspired cultural studies (EMICS). This is our effort to combine the analysis of power and subjectivity provided by cultural studies with the understanding from ethnomethodology of how everyday accomplishments comprise the social. As Alec McHoul and Wendy Grace have put it elsewhere, this links investigations of *making meaning* with studies of how *what can be meant* is controlled (1993: 31). Prior to returning to cultural studies and ethnomethodological approaches in more detail, we shall define the terms of our title.

THE POPULAR

What is the popular? The word denotes 'of the people', 'by the people', and 'for the people'. But if we think this through, it becomes clear that, in an era when most cultural products are subject to mass distribution, there must be a more complicated story. The demotic appeal indicated by the adjective 'popular' is only partly adequate. For popular culture is also related to markets. Markets tell us what people will buy, but not what they will tolerate (such as broadcast television and radio), what they make of what they buy (some people read James Bond novels in search of misogynistic character descriptions), or what happens when markets fail or are irrelevant (if a city's advertising base cannot sustain more than one newspaper).

There are three intersecting discourses or ways of knowing the popular. A discourse about art expects culture to elevate us above the diurnal, transcending body, time, and place. Conversely, a discourse about folk-life expects culture to settle us into a sedimented collectivity through the wellsprings of community. This second discourse situates culture as part of daily existence. Finally, a discourse about pop idealizes fun as the summit of cultural pleasure (Frith 1991: 106–7). The pop discourse brings together the exhilarating loss of self engendered by entertainment and its paradoxical everydayness; a combination of the *wonderment* you may experience the first time you hear Elvis Costello with the *familiarity* of background pop in the kitchen.

The popular is marked by hierarchies of artistic value, with European high art and the philosophical aesthetics of Western ruling classes set against the entertainment that people purchase from the commercial world. Any attempt to transcend this high–low divide must deal with a definitional legacy from neoclassical economics. It assumes that expressions of the desire and capacity to pay for services stimulate the provision of entertainment and hence – when the product is publicly accepted – determine what is 'popular'. This is a processual and quantitative measure, as opposed to the directional and qualitative definitions that seek out originary, organic sites of the popular in the people themselves through 'folk' culture (Frow 1993).

Money is a key component of everyday life. It is both a universal expression of value that allows the comparison and measurement of objects, and a mediating force that cuts off consumption and production as forms of barter exchange via its own signifying power. The price paid for the provision of goods or services (their exchange-value) can be more important than the utility of what is purchased (its use-value). This price expresses the momentary monetary value of that need, rather than its lasting application. Built-in obsolescence becomes the key to commodities, popular or otherwise. They elicit desire by wooing consumers, by smelling or looking nice in ways that are borrowed from romantic love, but then reverse that relationship: people learn about correct forms of romantic love *from* the commodities themselves (Haug 1986: 14, 17, 19). The term 'commodity aesthetics' covers the division between what commodities promise (pleasure) and what animates them (profit) (Haug 1986: 35).

Must value be conferred by price, or should we understand value as the guardianship of heritage that announces certain sites, texts, and practices as indices of how we got to be where and who we are? Is value economic, historical, or ethical? Donald N. McCloskey's standard undergraduate primer on microeconomics proposes that 'the understanding of maximization and markets . . . is one of the great products of the human mind'. By dispensing with 'ersatz economics, the economics of the man in the street', readers will come to know a 'major achievement of Western science, the jewel of the social sciences' (1985: 1–3). For such mainstream neoclassical economics, value is decided through competition between providers to obtain the favour of consumers, with the mutual rationality of the parties producing an equilibrium of social good.

One of us came to own the McCloskey book by rummaging through a garbage bin near Union Square in New York City (researchers frequently get their hands dirty in the field). Someone had tossed it there, just a few feet from the eight miles of second-hand books that can be bought and sold at the Strand Bookstore. What brand of marginal utility, we wonder, produced the decision to dump the volume; which calculation of opportunity cost found *persona economica* throwing away a valuable commodity that claimed the capacity to help 'produce informed citizens, clever economic actors, educated graduates, useful social engineers, or creative economic scientists' (McCloskey 1985: 1)? Had the long-run return on investment in human capital failed to appear for the owner? (Interestingly, McCloskey recently underwent a change of sex, and is now Deirdre McCloskey. In reflecting on her former life as a man, she indicates that denigrating and ignoring social theory was something she took as integral to being a male economist, which she now regrets: Polanyi 1997: 20–21.)

Unlike the balanced conclusion to a classical Hollywood narrative, the lonely hour of the long run rarely arrives for most of us. The catch, of course, is the *ceteris paribus* consumer information that economists put in the small print on their goods: 'other things being equal' is their way out, the sign that there is an alternative. And its alternative is another mechanism for ascribing value: history. For history produces patterns of organization, expectation, and struggle that run counter to the conditions identified by neoclassical economists as prerequisites for their ideas to function effectively and efficiently (for example, the murder of 500,000 Chilean trade unionists in the 1970s by a military regime that hired US professors to advise on economic 'restructuring').

Market-derived senses of value are ironically connected to a more Marxist, processual meaning. In this formulation, popular culture stands opposed to dominant culture. As with neoclassical economics, particular texts have no intrinsic value. But the reactionary model assigns value through supply and demand, while the radical alternative finds it in contingent occasions of internal and external difference from, and struggle with, dominant symbols that attach themselves to working-class and other forms of oppositionality as agents of historical transformation (Frow 1993). These two models of value crop up again and again. As the anecdote about finding the economics book illustrates, whilst we consider the tension between these grand narratives to be productive, we want to understand the everyday in ways that do not reduce every practice to the macro-level favoured by them. The examples we have looked at illustrate the *domain* of the popular and how contested that domain can be in both theory and practice.

CULTURE

There are two common definitions of culture. The first refers to artistic output, defined and valued by aesthetic criteria and emerging from a community of creative people. The second meaning takes culture to be an all-encompassing concept about how we live our lives, the senses of place and person that make us human. These two definitions intertwine: the cultural human subject is both practical/ sensual/active and theoretical/spiritual/judging. This opens up the possibility of culture as ethical and aesthetic self-improvement: a civic programme directed at the spiritual development of the individual. From this point one can speak, for example, of the arts as a civilizing pursuit, as something good in itself. Seemingly disconnected from utility, the body, and facticity, the arts are in fact geared towards quite civic-utilitarian ends: the production and management of a specific kind of human being.

What happens when we put 'popular' and 'culture' back together, with the commercial world binding them? The foremost theorist of popular culture in the cultural studies literature is Antonio Gramsci, whose career as a left activist against Mussolini in the 1920s and 1930s has become an ethical exemplar for progressive intellectuals. Gramsci maintains that each social group creates 'organically, one or more strata of intellectuals which give it homogeneity and an awareness of its own function not only in the economic but also in the social and political fields': the industrial technology, law, economy, and culture of each group (1978: 5). The ' "organic" intellectuals which every new class creates alongside itself and elaborates in the course of its development' assist in the emergence of that class, for example via military expertise (pp. 6–7). Some intellectual types linger on beyond this organic status because of their monopoly stature, in areas such as religion and schooling (p. 6). Intellectuals operate in '[c]ivil society', which denotes 'the ensemble of organisms commonly called "private", that of "political society" or "the State" '. They comprise the ' "hegemony" which the dominant group exercises throughout society' as well as the ' "direct domination" or command exercised through the State and "juridical" government'. Ordinary people give ' "spontaneous" consent' to the 'general direction imposed on social life by the dominant fundamental group' (p. 12). So according to Gramsci, popular culture generates an ideology of legitimacy to a sociopolitical arrangement by eliciting public acceptance of it. But this is not just about politics.

Gramsci refers to industrial divisions of labour and factory production lines as 'Americanism and Fordism . . . [a] chain marking the passage from the old economic individualism to the planned economy' (p. 279). Fordism, named after the car manufacturer, extends to a concern by corporations for the entire lives of their workers, in the interests of moral and physical fitness for labour.

Exhaustion on the production line must not be allowed to diminish 'physical and muscular-nervous efficiency', and so companies intervene off-the-job to save their employees from 'alcohol and sexual depravation' (pp. 303–4). 'Private' life becomes standardized and bureaucratized just like daily exertions in the workplace. This insight could lead us towards a consideration of the popular as itself an industry, whose products encourage agreement with prevailing social relations and whose work practices reflect such agreement.

The idea that cultural industries 'impress . . . the same stamp on everything' derives from Theodor Adorno and Max Horkheimer of the Frankfurt School, an anti-Nazi group of scholars writing around the same time as Gramsci (Adorno 1991; Adorno and Horkheimer 1977). After migrating to the United States, they found a quietude reminiscent of pre-war Germany. Their explanation for this lies in the mass production-line organization of entertainment, where businesses use systems of reproduction that ensure identical offerings; although demand is dispersed, supply is centralized. A unitary administration of cultural output is socially acceptable because it is said to reflect the already established and revealed preferences of consumers, a reaction to their tastes and desires. But for Adorno and Horkheimer, this account denies a cycle of power. They see consumers as manipulated by those at the economic apex of production. 'Domination' masquerades as choice in a 'society alienated from itself'. Coercion is mistaken for free will, and culture becomes just one more industrial process, subordinated to dominant economic forces within society that insist on standardization. For the Frankfurt School, the one element that might stand against this levelling sameness is 'individual consciousness'. In its precapitalist form, this authentic spirit of creativity could produce and appreciate forms of art that both expressed and surpassed the conditions of their existence. But that consciousness, according to Adorno and Horkheimer, has itself been customized to the economy. From a politically more conservative position, 1950s American critic Dwight Macdonald used 'mass' rather than 'popular' culture to describe the output of the culture industries. Once parasitic upon high cultural innovation, by the 1950s mass culture drew on its own dubious archive, integrating the populace into 'political domination' guaranteed by the pre-digested ordering of audience response – something democratic in its constituency, but not its effects (1978: 167–69, 171). Discourses such as that of Macdonald elevate 'true art' by allowing it the virtues of courage, innovation, and energy. The popular, by contrast, is construed as 'lazy and craven in its "contentment" to deal with prefabricated signs and materials' (Gibson 1992: 201).

Mass culture may be implicitly gendered in these critiques. Consider television. Daytime TV-viewing in the home is a crucial point of division between public and private lives, productive and reproductive spheres, and paid and unpaid work. Such distinctions, whether at the level of conversation, wage-fixing, or cultural critique, involve mechanisms of distinction. As Michèle Mattelart puts it:

> It is in the everyday time of domestic life that the fundamental discrimination of sex rôles is expressed. . . . The hierarchy of values finds expression through the positive value attached to masculine time (defined by action, change and history) and the negative value attached to feminine time which, for all its potential richness, is implicitly discriminated against in our society, interiorized and lived through as the time of banal everyday life, repetition and monotony. (1986: 65)

Here, everyday television – especially soap opera – is deemed inferior because it inscribes passivity and emotiveness. Conversely, 'quality' television – especially the 'literary' mini-series – is superior because it encourages active and objective viewing. These active/passive high/low distinctions made by critics of mass culture predate television by a century (Huyssen 1988: 46–47).

Whilst much of this dismay is shared by conservatives, for some 1960s theorists mass culture represents the apex of modernity. Rather than encouraging alienation, it stands for the expansion of civil society, the moment in history when central political organs and agendas became receptive to, and part of, the general community. The population is now part of the social, rather than excluded from the means and politics of political calculation. It is claimed that the number of people classed as outsiders is diminished in mass society; and that mass society also brings a lessening of authority, the promulgation of individual rights and respect, and the intensely interpersonal, large-scale human interaction necessitated by industrialization and aided by systems of mass communication. The spread of advertising is a model for the breakdown of the social barriers that separate high from low culture (Shils 1966: 505–6, 511).

Because of its complex conjunctions with commerce, the popular, and the mass, the concept of culture is notoriously difficult to pin down. But it seems to be formed in the tensions and debates between two distinct forms of self that we have called practical/sensual/active and theoretical/spiritual/judging. The values that we, as cultural analysts, attach to these different selves will, in many respects, define our theoretical allegiances and, in turn, our preferred definitions of culture. But regardless of any analyst's particular variations, the field of culture today appears to be bounded by this double conception of the self. This might be as close as we get to a non-evaluative definition of culture – an activity of the self.

THE EVERYDAY

Where does all this activity actually 'happen'? The popular takes place in the everyday, which is also where we move between repetitive sides of life, which are formulaic and mechanical, and the peculiarities of spirituality and aesthetics. The everyday is invisible but ever-present. It is full of contradictions, and it can be transcended, passed over, and gone beyond, as when the drudgery of the workday is said to be transformed via popular cultural forms and flings. But even the enactment of the everyday is a 'business' that 'takes work, as any other business does' (Sacks 1995b: 216–17). It requires watching, training, and self-monitoring for us to get on with others. If 'individuals are to reproduce society, they must reproduce themselves as individuals' (Heller 1984: 3–4). To someone suddenly thrust into prison life, this might mean learning to examine the corner of a ceiling as a nightly activity, as against a former pastime like examining the diegesis of a film on TV. In the aggregate, such productive tasks manufacture everyday life, manipulating the material conditions of existence and coexistence.

French social theorist Henri Lefebvre, who wrote at the same time as Adorno and Horkheimer, gives us a history of the everyday. In Europe until the nineteenth century, forms of life were diffused across classes, places, religions, resources, and times. Standardized dress, housing, and food accompanied modern capitalism and statehood. From that point, sign value was given to these items and practices, according to the status of those who could afford them.

The everyday became subject to factory-like production and distribution systems via manufacturing and advertising. Today, objects 'speak out' about their function in a way that apparently signals utility: they must publicize themselves rather than simply fitting into everyday life (remember the sexualized commodity). Replaceables become tied to durables, as food is linked to costly household white goods. The everyday is remade by controllers of capital, but in the space of ordinary people. It is 'the most universal and the most unique condition, the most social and the most individuated, the most obvious and the best hidden'. There is a 'collapse of the referent' in the latter half of the twentieth century's planned abundance and waste. Lefebvre argues that intellectuals look in all the wrong places for referentiality: in language and politics. They ought to be examining the everyday and how power emerges there. 'Why should the study of the banal itself be banal? . . . Why wouldn't the concept of everydayness reveal the extraordinary in the ordinary?' The everyday can be found 'at the intersection of two modes of repetition: the cyclical, which dominates in nature, and the linear, which dominates in processes known as "rational" '. The principal sectors of the everyday are work, family, leisure, and privateness: passivity and/or/as consumption (Lefebvre 1987: 7–10). That division – minus the notion of passivity – is in keeping with the logic that animates this book, with one important revision: the cultural-commodity version of everyday life lacks ethnomethodology's sense of how members actually shape their world.

The everyday is a space and time that is materially invisible but ever-present and obvious (ethnomethodology refers to this as what is seen but unnoticed): vital even as it necessitates obedience and repetition; unchanging yet offering the prospect of transcendence through the play of opposites: 'activity and passivity', 'creativity and addiction', 'public' and 'private', 'dependence' and 'independence', and 'consumption and production', a play that occurs across space, time, and technology. In keeping with these multiple meanings, theorists propose three ways of understanding the everyday: (1) as alienated and reified life under capitalism; (2) as pleasure and resistance by members of a community; and (3) as psychic relationships between objects and persons. Capitalism must make people both obedient as employees and independently desiring as consumers; or at least give the appearance that this latter freedom is real. Nevertheless, the everyday can be a space for resisting incorporation into the wheels of production that holds out the possibility of autonomy. And yet the everyday is achieved, or made to happen, in a dynamic manner that does more than play out already determined social structures, texts, and tastes (Silverstone 1994: 159–61, 165, 22).

Michel de Certeau is the most significant contemporary cultural theorist of the everyday. He takes developments since Lefebvre, notably the contribution of ethnomethodology, to redefine popular culture as a series of ' "arts of making" ' that amount to 'combinatory . . . modes of consumption': how people use a 'formal structure of practice' that engages with goods and services to produce 'everyday creativity' (1988: xiv–xvi). De Certeau borrows from ethnomethodology to oppose strategies and tactics in the everyday. Strategies belong to 'a subject of will and power (a proprietor, an enterprise, a city, a scientific institution)' at a particular site, to exercise power and generate well-ordered relationships with others. Tactics, on the other hand, belong to the less powerful, who do not control any specific site on an ongoing basis. Tactics are organized by time and motion rather than space. In place of ongoing rules enforced through a strategy (the architectural drawings of a supermarket), tactics are mobile and conflictual (calculating the cost of goods on the way to the checkout counter in terms of family tastes) (de Certeau 1988: xix, xxii, 116). Unlike de Certeau, however, ethnomethodology declines to place a comparative value on such practices: they are ethically equal, and equal too in sign value (Garfinkel and Sacks 1970).

Clearly, human interaction is a critical part of everyday life. There are several options for engaging with it. We could follow the psy-complexes (depth psychology, psychiatry, ego psychology, psychoanalysis, and psychotherapy), an area engaged with in our chapter on self-help and therapy. For the moment, we want to distance ourselves from the teleological and universal narratives they use to measure human development and engagement. Instead, we shall turn to symbolic interactionism and the work of Erving Goffman, which is more attuned to the proxemics of daily intersubjectivity and is frequently – if wrongly – conflated with ethnomethodology (Sharrock 1987: 149–52; Watson 1992). It is worth outlining his position briefly, prior to developing a perspective in dialogue with both cultural studies and ethnomethodology.

Goffman begins from the understanding that when individuals meet, they try to retrieve information about each other – such things as socioeconomic position, self-conception, attitudes towards people, trustworthiness, and decency. These are sought out of interest and as practical issues for making do in the everyday: knowing the kind of social situation one is in, what is expected of the participants, and how to communicate. Two exchanges of information characterize each person: 'the expression that he *gives*, and the expression that he *gives off*'. The former is verbally communicative and explicit, whereas the latter encourages symptomatic readings. Goffman is principally concerned with the second type, which tends to be non-verbal and theatrical, but unintentional (1959: 1–2, 4).

Goffman looks for a 'social establishment' with 'fixed barriers to perception'. Activities within these barriers give an implicitly agreed impression to onlookers. These establishments can be analysed (1) in terms of how efficiently and effectively they produce desired impressions, (2) in terms of how power and control are exercised over others, (3) in terms of vertical and horizontal structures inside the family, (4) in terms of what it [the family] tolerates or rejects as behaviour by its members, and finally (5) Goffman's preference – in terms of a dramaturgical analysis. Individuals appearing before others always give off a form of analysis/definition (what ethnomethodology calls a formulation) of the establishment they are in. If events take place that contradict this understanding, three outcomes may occur: social interaction, such as dialogue, may stall in the face of an assumed closeness brought into question; individuals may be entirely rethought, shifted into different categories by participants from their original location, making a new minisocial structure; and individuals may do this to themselves, dislocating their own sense of self. Goffman calls these 'performance disruptions' (1959: 238, 242–43). He understands individuals as performers and characters: the first category attempts to evoke the second, but each is only partly within the control of a given individual, because of the different cultural competences brought to bear by others. The self is a construct, deriving not merely 'from its possessor, but from the whole scene of his action' (1959: 252). Going beyond Goffman, we understand this self as comprising practices that may be radically disarticulated from one another. No static, totalizing category, such as role theory, can capture the forces that generate conduct. They operate beyond even custom and subjectivity, in everyday modes of, for example, turn-taking and informational exchange.

QUESTIONS OF MEANING, QUESTIONS OF METHOD

What is the 'whole scene' that Goffman sought? How do we go looking for it, and what should be our means of description when we get there? That set of queries turns our attention to cultural materialism, a position usually associated with Raymond Williams, a founding figure in cultural studies. Williams is critical of idealist conceptions which assume that culture is a march towards human perfection as determined by universal values that are basic to the human condition, as if these were timeless rather than empirically grounded in particular conditions of possibility. He also questions documentary conceptions of culture, which seek to record artistic work so as to preserve specific insights and highlight them through criticism. Instead, Williams proposes that we concentrate on record-ing the way of life and values of particular communities at particular times, noting benefits and costs in representativeness (1975: 57).

Cultural materialism works with Marx's insight that people manufacture their own conditions of existence, but without a neces-sarily conscious, consistent, or even enabling agency (equally a precept of ethnomethodology, though with important variations). Social activity, not nature, genius, or individuality, makes a way of life and changes it over time. This insight directs us away from any view of historical and contemporary culture that privileges aesthetic civilization, the experiences of rulers, or the impact of religion delivered from on high (Williams 1977: 19).

Instead, we should engage culture by reading its products and considering their circumstances of creation and circulation. Art and society – Williams calls them 'project' and 'formation' respectively – intertwine, with no conceptual or chronological primacy accorded to either term. The relations of culture, their twists and turns, the often violent and volatile way in which they change, are part of the material life of society. For example, language neither precedes nor follows the social world, but is part of it. That means allowing something, namely intellectual work, an autonomy from the prevailing mode of economic production, but not from its own micro-economies of person, place, and power (Williams 1989: 151–52, 164–66). There can be no notion here of an organic community that produces a culture of artworks, or a culture of artworks that reflects an organic community, for both have their internal, non-epiphenomenal politics.

Cultural materialism refers, then, to the specifics of material culture (buildings, film, cars, fashion, sculpture, and so on) within the dynamics of historical change. Hierarchies of taste are established by co-opting and reordering the popular culture produced *by* ordinary people and repackaging it as mass culture delivered *to* them. Williams' method involves a further three-part division of culture into *dominant* versus *residual* and *emergent* cultural forms, as per Gramsci's idea of hegemony. Hegemony involves a contest of meanings, allowing dominant groups to gain popular assent by making it appear normal and natural. Residual cultures comprise old meanings and practices, no longer dominant but still influential. Emergent cultural practices are either propagated by a new class or incorporated by the dominant, as part of hegemony. These manoeuvres are best expressed in the notion of a structure of feeling: the intangibles of an era that remain with those who have lived through it, indicators that explain or develop the quality of life. Such indicators often involve a contest – or at least dissonance – between official culture and practical consciousness (Johnson 1987: 169–73).

In short, Williams' view of culture insists on the importance of collective, community life; the conflicts in any cultural formation; the social nature of culture; and the cultural nature of society. But he is clearly working with descriptions that, whilst they are both neat methodologically and flexible enough to accommodate difference, are of little use in explaining how people make their own meanings. Williams continues to depend on the presumption that ethically competent critics can comprehend the way of life of unseeing, ordinary people, despite his romantic faith in the goodness of the everyday and his suspicion of institutions.

The role of the cultural critic in revealing the 'true' valency of cultural practices is exemplified in cultural studies' investment in subcultures, a shift away from culture as a tool of domination and towards culture as a tool of empowerment. Subculture signifies a space under culture, simultaneously opposed to, derivative of, and informing the official, dominant, governmental, commercial, bureaucratically organized forms of life. According to this logic, the socially disadvantaged use culture to express opposition to structural forms of their oppression. Historical and contemporary studies conducted in the 1960s and 1970s on slaves, crowds, pirates, bandits, and the working class work with this understanding in their emphasis on day-to-day non-compliance with authority: dragging your feet, stealing pencils, sabotaging faculty members' payslips, and so on – in short, making do with the available forms of expressiveness. The Centre for Contemporary Cultural Studies at Birmingham University, where much early cultural studies work was done, concentrated at this time on teddy boys, mods, bikers, skinheads, punks, school students, teen girls and Rastas. Its magical agents of history were truants, drop-outs, and magazine readers – people who 'deviated' from the norms of school and the transition to work by 'appropriating' cultural styles.

The deviance thesis examines structural underpinnings to collective style, whereas the appropriation thesis assumes that subcultures involve subversive bricolage. This research and its political agenda are opposed to the achievement-oriented, materialistic, educationally driven values and appearance of the middle class. The working assumption is that subordinate groups adopt and adapt signs and objects of the dominant culture, reorganizing them to manufacture new meanings. Consumption becomes the epicentre of subcultures; and it also, paradoxically, reverses their status as groups of consumers. They become producers of new fashions, inscribing alienation, difference, and powerlessness on their bodies. The decline of the British economy and state during the 1970s is said to be exemplified in punk's use of rubbish as adornment: bag-liners, lavatory appliances, and ripped and torn clothing. But then commodified fashion and convention take over when capitalism appropriates the appropriator; even as the media announce folk devils via moral panics, the fashion and music industries are sending out spies in search of new trends to market (Leong 1992).

Understanding subcultures requires us to move beyond accounts of the economy or interpersonal conduct and into textual reading, via semiotics. Semiotics' stress on the arbitrariness of meaning dispenses with elevations of high over popular culture. In addition, the media-studies component of cultural studies concentrates on technical forms and possibilities of meaning, distancing its work from the hypodermic or effects model of television. The latter asserts a quasi-chemical, or at least instantaneously behavioural, connection between media texts and audience responses: TV can rot your mind or give you grand new insights via its electronic–neural interface. The move away from such scientism, towards how texts function and what they foreground, is critical, in a paradoxical way, to legitimizing different reading protocols by audiences and the notion of subcultural power. The arbitrariness of the sign positions interpretative competences even as it concentrates on the text. Culture is seen not so much to reflect ideas, but to be itself a clump of signifying practices, with its own determinations of meaning. The shift is one from *what* is signified to *how* it is signified – and what is left out of the account.

Myth, denotation, and connotation are three key terms. Myths provide information about a culture in a non-self-reflexive way: they give no account of their own conditions of existence. Roland Barthes describes myth as '*a type of speech*' that 'transforms history into nature' (1973: 109, 129). Myths become natural parts of language, rather than contestable norms that have histories and produce political effects. Myths are not defined by the objects they describe, but by their mode of utterance, how they signify as photography, painting, writing, or the audiovisual. Semiotics argues that while myths appear to be statements of fact, they stand in for something else. When we analyse the process of making myths, we are taking material forms of language and interrogating their history – how they came to have that meaning – even as we ask questions about them as ideology in the here and now (Barthes 1973: 109–12, 115). Roland Barthes offers seven systems by which myths function. *Inoculation* warns of 'accidental evil' without acknowledging its inevitability as part of a social system (think of coal disasters). The *privation of history* dematerializes the past, permitting objects to be valued apolitically in an aesthetic way (the Pyramids). *Identification* permits dominant social forces to naturalize their power, failing to 'imagine the Other' and the impact on others of one's actions ('we won!' – for which see a different form of analysis, in Chapter 3 on sport). *Tautology* involves the unitary restatement of authority ('this is so because it is so', 'this is real baseball'). *Neither-norism* is the fence-sitting gesture that avoids responsibility (economic growth is necessary; so is environmental protection). *Quantifying quality* takes away the contingent nature of taste as a classificatory system by adding up allegedly similar items (TV violence). And *statements of fact* see myths become proverbial, ahistorical common sense (myth analysis is resistive) (Barthes 1973: 150–54).

Examining myths about a society requires unpacking them, however implicitly, into *how* they signify and *what* they signify. The first and most obvious meaning comes at a *denotative* level, of apparently literal significance. Looking for what is excluded, prioritized, or distorted occurs at a *connotative* level. Connotation offers a contest between multiple meanings. Barthes' classic example is from a cover of *Paris-Match* magazine that shows a young African man in a French military uniform, saluting and looking at the French flag. The denotative code explains that a soldier is obeying the routine of his workplace. The connotative code, the deeper myth, is about the allegedly colour-blind, beneficent nature of French imperial rule (1973: 116). Barthes goes on to describe the difference between Spanish-Basque architecture in its original surroundings, where it has an organic quality, a unity, and an ethnicity, and the same physical form translated to Paris. There, it calls him up as an observer, expecting to be noticed as a style, a quotation, a 'magical object', to which he must respond by interpreting (1973: 125). In Chapter 2 we see traces of this in the circulation of various cuisines as multicultural exotica.

This is a process of encoding and decoding: *en*coding at the point of cultural production and *de*coding at the point of cultural reception (Hall 1980). Both involve making sense of the obvious and doing something about its other, which is to say moving between denotation and connotation – an uneasy negotiation between dominant cultural meanings inscribed by encoders, which may refer to very orthodox forms of life, and possibly aberrant decodings by viewers, which may derive from more heterodox situations. We favour this sense of negotiation, but want to move beyond a literary/linguistic/mythemic mode of analysis, towards social scientific accounts of the everyday, notably ethnomethodology.

Both cultural studies and ethnomethodology began around the same time, in the mid-1960s, and there was some initial dialogue between them. For example, an early issue of the Birmingham Centre's *Working Papers in Cultural Studies* contains an ethnomethodological account of a motor-car race fatality that is explicitly connected to emerging cultural studies work on subcultures. But even then, there was a clear distance between the site-specific interest associated with ethnomethodology and cultural studies' claim to understand entire ways of life. In this instance, ethnomethodology assumed it was quite normal for the public-address system at such an event to euphemize death. For cultural studies, on the other hand, this would be a spectacular absence (Watson 1973: 7). Discussion across the two fields did not continue, partly because cultural studies increasingly took its lead from an engagement with connotative readings from Marxism and structuralism, whereas ethnomethodology developed from an amalgam and critique of phenomenology, Parsonian sociological functionalism, and Wittgensteinian ordinary-language philosophy – more denotative influences. This separation was mutually disabling. Cultural studies has become a major intellectual movement across continents, but its claims to empower 'the people' are often based on textual analysis or ethnography that gets extended to more and more instances, without a full conversation with the social and cultural theory that details and explicates those sites. For its part, ethnomethodology remains a marginal enterprise in the social sciences, and has set up boundaries between itself and the politics of the everyday. If cultural studies has a politics but no clear method, then ethnomethodology has a method but no politics.

As we have seen, cultural studies often accounts for human practices in terms of 'magical' properties that seem to be imposed from the top down. Ethnomethodology declines to make such moves, turning instead to the properties of ordinary occasions. We argue here that large categories such as the nation, the economy, or gender are anchored by, and produced in, such mundane sites. Our book offers cultural studies a means of analysing the everyday, by both surveying the relevant literature across the human sciences and taking specific sites and subjecting them to EMICS. Each chapter focuses on a routine practice and takes one or more specific instances of it based on a scene, event, or object. In this sense, like ethnomethodology, we depart from cultural studies, taking language as an achievement, activity, or practice, rather than a source of representation or reference. Where necessary and appropriate, such ordinary activities as exercising, eating, or watching are contrasted with claims made about sport, diet, or TV audiences in cultural studies. The idea is for readers to take away with them both a political understanding and a method for comprehending and negotiating the everyday that is supple enough to find every text 'both special, i.e., a product of all its immediate circumstances, and general, i.e., sequentially organized' (Moerman 1988: 22): EMICS at work (and play). Our decision to focus on what people do as players, eaters, clients, and viewers moves the agenda away from a singular focus on either language (ethnomethodology) or the media (cultural studies).

ETHNOMETHODOLOGY AND EVERYDAY LIFE

You find they all begin by saying something like this, 'About the thing I'm going to talk about, people think they know, but they don't. They still walk around like they know although they are walking in a dreamworld.' Darwin begins this way. Freud begins in a similar way. Bloomfield's analysis of language begins in a similar way, and I could provide a much larger list. What we are interested in is, what is it that people seem to know and use? (Harvey Sacks, in Hill and Crittenden 1968: 13)

Ethnomethodology began in the late 1950s and came to prominence with the publication of Harold Garfinkel's *Studies in Ethnomethodology* in 1967. Etymologically, the term refers to the methods by which members (from the Greek *ethnos*) go about everyday practices and make them *intelligible*. Garfinkel's crucial contribution to social theory is simply this: the two sets of methods are identical. How people make things happen (for example, parties, flower displays, or musical evenings) is identical with how they make those things intelligible as audiovisual, material events taking place within local scenes. This is the crucial ethnomethodological principle of reflexivity – not to be confused with uses of the same term that refer to critical self-reflection.

A study of convict codes in a house for rehabilitating drug offenders provides an instance of reflexivity. Instead of collecting instances of a code and breaking them down into their formal semiotic or structural properties, the analysis concentrates on the mundane work accomplished by specific instances of telling the code. Hence, when an inmate says to a guard, 'You know I won't snitch', the meaning of that utterance is given by its place in an event known as 'telling the code'. And reflexively, the event is structured by this utterance and others like it. So, 'You know I won't snitch', for example, turns the guard's prior question (something like 'Who was around last night?') into a request for what is, by the code, illicit insider information as opposed to, say, a friendly opening line. It turns code-telling into a confrontation (which it may or may not have been for the guard). The utterance helps produce an everyday occasion as a convict–guard confrontation. And the occasion gives the utterance, and the one before it, their meaning: 'Go any further along this line of inquiry and we won't get along; in fact there may be violence'. Interestingly, no amount of traditional semiotic or structural-linguistic inspection of 'You know I won't snitch' could find such semantic richness or explain how it was accomplished (Wieder 1974).

So, utterances derive their meanings from the actual, practical situations in which they arise; and those situations, in their turn, have social import (as confrontations, drinking nights, requests for goods and services, and so on) by virtue of the practices that compose them. This is reflexivity and, in a sense, it's all that need be said about ethnomethodology: empirical studies that look for the methods people use to go about their ordinary affairs, which are identical to the methods they use that make those affairs *intelligible* and *accountable*. Garfinkel sometimes calls this 'incarnateness'. This may seem dull and uninteresting, as though the investigator would just find the same thing over and over again: reflexivity. Yet it is every ethnomethodologist's experience (and this is its abiding fascination) that when you go looking for that general property, you find intricate local ways in which it is accomplished as a universal property of everyday scenes. How 'You know I won't snitch' works in, and as, a case of telling the convict code is quite distinct from the ways in which placing a particular file in a given place in a filing cabinet works as an instance of bureaucratic labour. And this, in turn, is quite different from how an interruption in a conversation works to produce controversy in radio talk. General reflexivity turns out to have complex and manifold local properties. Only ethnomethodology has given any attention to those properties, and yet ethnomethodology itself has just begun to scratch the surface of that quotidian richness. And this richness suggests that society is ordered in everyday action: in getting out of a car, making a sandwich, walking down the street, and the (infinite) rest.

Ethnomethodology's take on the everyday is quite different from most others. It begins with a general idea (reflexivity) but its focus is on what works, and how people make it work, in quite local instances. As Harvey Sacks notes, ethnomethodology is probably unique in this respect: it takes the mundane seriously – *as* the mundane and not as an instance of something else, such as 'the economy', 'the *Zeitgeist*', or whatever. It wants to know what people know and use (their methods) in going about (and hence producing) everyday events, and the intelligibility of those events. Almost every other form of attention to the everyday in the humanities and social sciences (as common sense, ideology, folk wisdom, or what have you) begins in a different way. Such approaches claim deep insights into everyday life, which ordinary people are thought to lack. In effect, Sacks is asking: how can you find out what everyday knowledge is if you begin by assuming that it's wrong? This shows two things about non-ethnomethodological approaches to everyday life. First, that they almost uniformly adopt an ironic stance towards their objects of analysis (popular culture, everyday actors, and so on). Secondly, that they have gone looking for everyday knowledge in the wrong place, in substantive, constative knowledge: knowledge of what. By contrast, ethnomethodology's first study principle is to turn to practical knowledge: knowledge of how (see Ryle 1984). This non-propositional knowledge is not right or wrong, true or false; it either works or it does not. Ethnomethodology does not judge everyday practical knowledge: the principle (often misunderstood) of 'ethnomethodological indifference' (Garfinkel and Sacks 1970). Here 'indifference' does not mean being uncaring or uncritical. It means that the objects of ethnomethodology's interest are practical or technical knowledges (how things are accomplished) which cannot be judged as to their veracity or otherwise. Knowing how to ride a bicycle is never right or wrong, true or false. It is a practical action, knowledge of which is displayed – in fact exists – in its doing.

Cultural studies has run its course differently from ethnomethodology over the question of practical versus substantive knowledge. Cultural studies has taken knowledge to be ideology, by and large, or at least a variation on the theme. Ideology has been interpreted in a number of ways. But it is always thought of as substantive knowledge; something like how an everyday person thinks of, or relates to, his or her 'real' situation. The problem with this formulation is that the 'real' situation has to be given by an analysis outside that person's actual knowledge; usually by a claim to science and, in the case of Marxism, a science of supposedly 'real' economic relations which are by and large unavailable to everyday actors. More recently, cultural studies has rejected this strict interpretation of ideology and has come to think, instead, of everyday knowledge in terms of resistance to dominant power formations. Cultural studies has begun to abandon its ironic stance towards everyday cultures and celebrate them as containing alternative knowledges to the dominant. But there is still a sense, in a great deal of cultural studies, that everyday actors don't know this dominant, which is a topic for a 'higher' or 'deeper' form of knowledge than theirs; and that the supposed resistance of everyday knowledge happens on the basis of a misty, general, but native form of intelligence about what may be wrong with the world and what might be done about it by, for example, watching television programmes in a way that is different and distinct from the way they are 'meant' to be read. An instance would be the pleasure white critics have gained from pointing to a few instances of aberrant decoding of US TV programmes by Australian Aborigines (Fiske 1988, 1989, 1993; Hay 1992; Hebdige 1994; Newcomb 1994a, 1994b; Tomlinson 1991).

Ethnomethodology is now dominated by the analysis of a particular everyday object: conversations. Conversation analysis has proved fruitful in finding the second-by-second properties of naturally occurring conversations by attending to such things as the accomplishment of paired parts (for example questions and answers), turns at talk, corrections and repairs, interruptions, pauses and silences, and the insertion of such short sounds as 'um' and 'eh'. For the most part, it has been able to find regular ways in which these accomplishments are achieved. Borrowing from some versions of linguistics, it has even proposed general rules for such linguistic-pragmatic activities. But with some exceptions, such as John Heritage and Rod Watson's (1979, 1980) analyses of formulations (how conversationalists say and show what they are doing, through such items as 'Are you accusing me?', 'Is that a threat or a promise?' and so on), conversation analysis has forgotten ethnomethodology's initial social-theoretical principle: reflexivity. It has isolated what people know and use to accomplish conversations (and components of conversations) and treated that as practical-technical knowledge. But it has ceased to ask how certain social activities are carried out by talking in a particular way; that is, social activities other than conversations-as-such. Instead, shouldn't we assume that conversations routinely have some purpose? They get lessons conducted in schools, produce boardroom decisions, express aesthetic judgements about films, and so on. A form of ethnomethodology oriented towards popular culture may have to return to the question of reflexivity (see Ashmore 1989), if only to ask how people achieve such routine accomplishments as doing crosswords, having sex, choosing fast food at a counter, and the rest of the 'business' (to repeat Sacks' descriptor).

Some recent ethnomethodology has returned to that question. For example, there is now a school which proposes a non-analytic ethnomethodology (for example Lynch and Bogen 1991, 1994; Livingston 1986). In such cases, investigators are not interested in technical knowledge for its own sake. Rather, like Sacks before them, they are concerned with what might be called local cultures. As often as not, their work is oriented towards perspicuous displays of how those local cultures work. A good example is Dusan Bjelic and Michael Lynch's (1992) demonstration of Goethe's colour theorem. Their paper requires the reader, in a way we've seen nowhere before, to have ready (and use) a particular prism. The paper doesn't argue for a position in the history and philosophy of science; nor does it analyse physicists' theoretical knowledge. Instead it 'seeks to make perspicuous the embodied work of a (scientific) demonstration'. The authors show how a colour theorem might work (in fact how it must work) as an everyday achievement. If we add to this some recent attempts to rethink ethnomethodology's general contribution to the human sciences (Anderson et al. 1988; Button 1991) by asking questions not just about practical moralities and politics, but also about ethnomethodology's necessary imbrication in such practical affairs (Jayyusi 1991; McHoul 1994), we can see that the field may be ready to deal with a range of cultural-studies-based interests in popular culture, subjectivity, and power.

Finally, something must be said about ethnomethodology's 'outside'. In the earliest days, ethnomethodology's detractors were many and diverse. The criticisms called it everything from out-and-out positivism to Californian hippy nonsense, and most things in between. It has been (mis)associated with social phenomenology, dramaturgy, symbolic interactionism, ethnography, and functionalism. Naturally enough, ethnomethodological practitioners have become less than welcoming of inquiries from without. Some have argued for complete independence (Watson 1992). Yet Garfinkel himself, at least at conferences, is happy to talk about 'hybrid disciplines': situations where ethnomethodology does not so much analyse as actually contribute to another discipline (for which see Livingston 1986 on mathematics). Strict ethnomethodological separatists will find problems with our idea of EMICS, but we have nothing more in mind than forming a kind of Garfinkelian hybrid. For as Garfinkel once said of the term 'ethnomethodology', 'whatever you want it for, go ahead and take it' (in Hill and Crittenden 1968: 10). This hybrid is on all fours with his initial insights about the inevitability of reflexivity. And, at the same time, we hope to be able to extend cultural studies and offer it a descriptive-analytic footing for discovering the practical, technical, and – above all – reflexive properties of popular culture *and* everyday life.

ETHNOMETHODOLOGICALLY INSPIRED CULTURAL STUDIES

Janet Wolff differentiates ethnomethodology from cultural studies because whilst ethnomethodologists 'emphasize the constructed and constitutive role of language', they are 'very positivistic'. In other words, ethnomethodology is 'not concerned with the way in which language operates as ideology, or the ways in which forms of representation – literary, visual, and other – construct gender, for example' (1992: 718). Similarly, the parts of cultural studies that share with anthropology the aim of understanding whole ways of life frequently deride ethnomethodology for reducing sociocultural systems to the performance of particular actions, disarticulated from each other. This is said to trivialize political and economic power and miss the motors of social change (Myers and Brenneis 1984: 7; Collins 1992: xiv).

Ethnomethodology must be doing some interestingly contradictory things to be accused of positivism as well as this other extreme. Not only do these critiques deny the notion of a practical uptake of texts as part of the process of design, transmission, and reception, but they fail to argue why the design *or* reception of a text or rule should be its defining characteristic, unless we accept counter-indicative, hermeneutic interpretation (aka representational paranoia) as our norm. Ethnomethodology is not outside the diurnal operation of the social, economic, or customary: it is simply disinterested in theoretical claims that imagine their objects or methods of inquiry to be so (Garfinkel and Sacks 1970). Ethnomethodology understands language as a mode of action in its own right, rather than as the representation or transmission of other, more authentic, messages. The interactive site of conversational or physical exchange is the most collective everyday moment for most people, whether it takes the form of routine work in the home or on the job, or casual encounters in either space: the labour of domestic childcare or the leisure of racing gossip in the office. In each case, the assumption that information is handled in ways that can be read off from members' positions in the social order (class, race, gender, age, and so on) is brought into question by the specificity of the site and the occasionality of the exchange. In short, ethnomethodology is concerned above all with how human engagement happens as a series of activities that tell us – analysts *or* members – something about social organization's dynamic, interactive, and locally managed properties (Drew and Heritage 1992: 3, 6, 17).

Alec McHoul and Tom O'Regan (1992) have introduced the notion of 'textual technologies' to cultural studies as a means of reconfiguring and combining politics, reading, and the everyday. They criticize the idea that 'local instances' of popular-culture audiences refusing the dominant interpretations supposedly preferred by global producers can 'guarantee any general statement about textual meaning'. The urgent hunt (characteristic of cultural studies) for resistive readers who can delegate their wildness to researchers, tends to identify unruly reading with both originary texts and exegetical academics. Aberrant decoding becomes a professorial passport to the popular and a means, ironically, of making the output of the culture industries isomorphic with a demotic, anti-capitalist, anti-patriarchal, anti-racist politics. McHoul and O'Regan propose a shift away from this system of delegation and all-encompassing politics. In its place, they commend 'discursive analysis of particular actor networks, technologies of textual exchange, circuits of communicational and textual effectivity, traditions of exegesis, commentary and critical practice'. In other words, the specific, empirically located 'uptake' of a text by a community should be our analytic referent; but not because this is guaranteed to reveal something essential to the properties of that object or its likely uptake elsewhere or at any time. Instead of a general model of the political, they direct our attention to the 'general outline' of 'interests'. Such an outline can only be applied to specific cases 'upon a piecemeal and local inspection' that may in turn influence the wider model. Politics and textuality are the means of communication that function along a continuum of time and space (McHoul and O'Regan 1992: 5–6, 8–9).

A founding parent of cultural studies, Stuart Hall, acknowledges the virtue of a 'concern for the strategies involved in the understandings of everyday situations, the form of practical accounting by means of which societal members produced the social knowledge they used to make themselves understood', which ethnomethodology brings to what he thinks of as the grounding of ideology (1988: 67). Far from being positivistic, ethnomethodology locates empiricism and positivism as rule-governed practices like any others: the difference is their metalinguistic claim to probe meaning via a non-signifying observation and reporting. In addition to its attempt to unpack the reasons people give for, and display in, their actions (jury service or coronial duties, for example), ethnomethodology explains *post facto* rationalizations of decisions as the products of summation and accounting as much as the actual process of coming to a decision. This could certainly be connected to critiques that see instrumental rationality as cloaking other activities (Brown 1992: 75). Similarly, ethnomethodology's attempt to describe the conditions of existence behind each statement or form of reasoning – the how and where of enunciation – helps in identifying how myths deny their conditions of appearance (Jenks 1993: 8–9). Dorothy Smith's search for a feminist social theory and action takes up ethnomethodology's focus on the way people cooperate, compete, and simply 'are' in the everyday as means of organizing themselves and each other (1987: 123–24). Hall's redefinition by queer anthology editors takes its lead from his early deviancy work, which drew *its* lead in part from the ethnomethodological insight that practical definitions of situational logic become retroactively endorsed absolutes (Hall 1993: 71). Ethnomethodology's founding figure, Garfinkel, was amongst the first to point to the complex liminal space occupied by gay sexuality on the cross-benches of gender. He continues to be cited in recent cultural and queer theory on this basis (Evans 1993: 136, 177; Warner 1993: xiii, xxx n. 16).

And of course, the cultural studies *donnée* that the people should not be considered 'cultural dopes', frequently attributed to Hall, in fact derives from Garfinkel. In addition, ethnomethodology has contributed a vast amount to knowledge about the politics of taking turns in conversation as applied to gender relations and patient–doctor encounters (Kessler and McKenna 1978; Lynch 1993: 240).

Ethnomethodology's great strength lies in its effort to treat all social facts as local, material accomplishments. This means they can be understood as human activities ordered at the moment of their achievement by the members who undertake them, not mere epi-phenomena of externally imposed, top-down registers of meaning and organization. In this sense, everyday actions are locally pro-duced. The reference points of language and action are not only locations alongside other words, correspondences with specific objects being described, or macro-political determinations, but the occasions of their use, the settings in which they appear, the uses to which they are put, and the means of their reception. The docu-mentary validity of reference is often achieved through complex methods of analysis by members, who take the signs handed them and derive meaning from a process of familiar narration that affords those signs indexical accuracy (Cuff and Payne 1984: 157–61).

In a sense, what we are trying to do in this book is to shuttle between very broad inclusive surveys of cultural theory and highly specific applications of ethnomethodology. Following surveys of relevant sociocultural literature, and the public discourses that inform particular cultural fields, each chapter focuses on empirical instances, the devices that produce and recognize them, and some of the other cultural objects those devices generate: the processes that make the everyday. So the chapters take a routine practice, marked by predicates such as eating and based in a routine daily scene or object, located inside a broad field of social and cultural theoriza-tion, and subject it to EMICS. We hope to avoid the risks of economic and textual reductionism, but also their obverse, whereby practices in the everyday can *only* be analysed from a perspective that finds them mere components of a politics that takes place elsewhere. We conclude Chapter 4, on therapy, with an account of how everyday life is composed of devices for making sense of cultural practices. Our final chapter is dedicated to such devices.

2

Food/Eating

STORY ONE: Food riots were 'a form of popular protest generally held to have been common between the seventeenth century and the eighteenth and early nineteenth centuries. Food riots were a reactionary form of collective action – spontaneous and impulsive in nature, purely local in focus, apolitical and communally based – in protest of shortages and/ or an unacceptable inflation in the price of basic necessities.' With the rise of a centralized sovereign-state and a free press, both national and non-governmental forms of information and control made for a different politics, with access to formalized chains of propaganda, critique, and policy formation. No functioning democracy/state with a free press has *ever* had a famine (i.e. no famines in Zimbabwe, Australia, Botswana, or India).

Source: Taylor 1996: 483; Sen 1996

STORY TWO 1988: The US National Heart Savers Association takes out advertisements criticizing McDonald's for serving food with dangerously high levels of cholesterol and fat. McDonald's criticizes these texts as 'reckless, misleading, the worst kind of sensationalism'. 1990: The Association pays for full-page advertisements in twenty-two major newspapers, entitled 'The Poisoning of America' and 'McDonald's, Your Hamburgers *Still* Have Too Much Fat! And Your French Fries *Still* Are Cooked with Beef Tallow'. At the same time, the Citizens Clearinghouse on Hazardous Waste organizes a national campaign against the company's use of plastic foam containers. 1990–91: Fast-food sales figures go down for the first time. July 1991: McDonald's, Wendy's, and Burger King advise they will cook fries in vegetable oil from now on. McDonald's retains public-relations firm the Environmental Defense Fund, promises to recycle, and funds the 'Keep America Beautiful' campaign to support the notion that pollution is a matter of individual responsibility.

Source: Ritzer 1993: 164; Stauber and Rampton 1995: 129, 133

These short stories encapsulate the differences of opinion on popular culture we outlined in Chapter 1. In debates about food, the right criticizes redistribution of wealth that makes public eating across classes a fact of everyday, visible existence, cheapening the élite status of restaurant-dining. The left complains that standardized food infantilizes the masses, in keeping with the fact that in industrial societies working-class people eat less nutritious foods than those further up the social hierarchy. On this score, there has been a fascinating shift in the incidence of coronary heart disease in the UK. Up to the 1960s, this was almost entirely a ruling-class phenomenon because of smoking and high fatty-meat intake; now the figures are down for socially powerful groups and up for manual labourers (Lunt and Livingstone 1992: 17; Steele et al. 1991: 286). (A third of Australia's health costs are attributed to diet, and in 1989 it was estimated that 30,000 Americans would perish from cancer in the year 2000 unless their diets changed: Lupton 1994: 665.) Somewhere between these positions lie the cultural sociologist Pierre Bourdieu's 'paradoxes of the taste of necessity':

> Some simply sweep it aside, making practice a direct product of economic necessity (workers eat beans because they cannot afford anything else), failing to realize that necessity can only be fulfilled . . . because the agents are inclined to fulfil it. . . . Others turn it into a taste of freedom, forgetting the conditionings of which it is the product. . . . Taste is *amor fati*, the choice of destiny, but a forced choice. (1994: 178)

In the first short story, the right would view the emergence of markets as the panacea that ended food riots and contemporary famine relief as a necessary response to the corruption and inefficiency of the Third World. The left would see the food riots as nascent class conflicts prevented by the rise of the welfare state, which recur with reductions in government relief to the poor; while famine's link to charity would be seen as pointlessly reactive and failing to address the underlying causes of underdevelopment. In the second instance, the right would see McDonald's as undermining individuated restaurant space and flattening out gourmet taste. The left would see it as duping customers with unhealthy food and exploiting employees through poor pay and conditions. Proponents of the market would say the alternative consumer information presented by a public-interest group forced large corporations to mend their ways – nutritional and environmental responsibility via supply and demand (and as Geoffrey Lawrence (1995: 10) says, green consumer movements gather pace wherever wealth is distributed, notably in the newly industrializing countries of South-East Asia). Other critics would regard this as Bourdieu's 'ethic of convivial indulgence', a working people's challenge to 'the legitimate art of living', with its 'ethic of sobriety for the sake of slimness' (1994: 179).

Sacks has a relevant fragment, open to conversational rather than political-economic interpretation. Person A invites person B to lunch. B rejects, offering to take A out at some point. A rejects this and repeats the request. B consents but says 'I'm tryina get slim.' We could explain this in several ways. A conventional account would see the dialogue as politeness, a series of refusals that appear to be acceptances. A radical account might focus on the slimming remark, noting the intense pressure on Americans, notably women, to be thin. Sacks, however, looks at the specific properties of the inter-action: each party appears to recognize 'that the invitation was generated out of the interaction', not from a call motivated by the wish to ask someone out. In that sense, the invitation may be phatic: a general expression of goodwill rather than a first move to strike agreement to meet. The exchange becomes an exercise in testing whether the invitation is meant to die with the conversation, or survive and translate into another event (Sacks 1995a: 792). So, in place of the moralities of eating mentioned above, Sacks turns to its incarnation in the pragmatics of everyday life. We shall see the importance of this later.

At a certain level, the issues of public health raised in the first and second anecdotes are clearly of greater import than the chance of misunderstanding raised in the third; but when it comes to the everyday management of interaction, the latter is of great significance. The stories have something in common other than food: each is about deferral. Dietary anxieties are concerned with what will happen in the future as a consequence of what we put in our mouths (lighted bits of paper, kippers, raw onions, or whatever). Making dates for meals is similarly about deferral: establishing that the arrangement being made now is not a phatic by-product of a conversation about something else, but a serious commitment that will produce labour, consumption, talk, and perhaps reciprocity, with no initial certainty about what is being called for or when it will properly finish.

This chapter begins with some theoretical remarks about the meaning of food and its history, the mix of taste and political economy that gives us our daily bread. The second part is about what we do with that bread: how people consume food. One of our assumptions, here as elsewhere, is that everyday life has routine grounds. Eating cannot be done in just any way. This does not mean there are hard and fast rules, but what we might call 'orientationals': templates of techniques that exist, that people know, for doing very ordinary things. Food and the body are intimately related: parts of a cycle of production and reproduction on both macro- and micro-scales that see the body entered and altered. The entering and altering are not precise calculations, but are subject to risk and unforeseen consequences. What the body does to itself is therefore bound up with the pragmatics of everyday life. The bigger picture ('what this will do to me') can never be the subject of an exact science, if only because the body is more than physiology, anatomy, physics, and chemistry – it is also and equally composed of numerous mundane daily self-operations. The body cannot be fully governed in this sense, even though food (and other) producers have made many industries out of claiming that it *can*, trying to allay consumers' fears of contingencies beyond their control.

The trust between providers and eaters may be problematized by an awareness of deceptive conduct by producers, such as the use of artificial flavour and colour. Culinary knowledge is vitally linked to control of bodily parts through a need to constrain human passions in line with prevailing norms of social order. Diet is critical for religious/spiritual and medical forms of bodily regulation and understanding, expressed through dietary tables, exercise manuals, and food charts. Food not only maintains, develops, and diminishes the body; it helps us to define the self in terms of mastering that body as a social sign of our ability to exercise authority. Personal diet is a model for industry and government. No wonder: Swedish studies suggest that shopping, cooking, and cleaning up take half as much time again as paid work (Fine and Leopold 1993: 149; Turner 1982: 24; Foucault 1986: 97–139; Warde and Hetherington 1994: 759).

The period since the 1970s has seen the development of commercial speech as free speech, as the US Supreme Court has increasingly protected businesses so that they can say whatever they want (as if their corporate, promotional speech were the individual liberty theorized by the Founding Parents). Ludicrous claims about the health benefits of foods, reminiscent of the 'snake-oil' merchants of nineteenth-century North America, are allowable following the 'principle of epistemological humility' (although many other Courts differ on this point, as does the Food and Drug Administration). This fascinating principle holds that scientific truth-claims are essentially nominalist. Shifts in orthodoxy in science routinely hold up previous nostrums as ludicrous, so any remark is authoritative only at the time and place it is made; hence the famous finding that 'there is no such thing as a false idea' under the First Amendment. The 'truth' of statements is found in the number and profession of people who subscribe to them. Emboldened by this, food manufacturers are now offering cancer prevention literally at breakfast time, to the point where more than US $1 billion per year is spent on food advertisements making health claims (Redish 1993: 18; Cooper et al. 1993: 51, 66). To understand such developments, one needs both political economy and cultural analysis. The result is not always appetizing. As Otto von Bismarck said, 'those who love sausage and the law should never watch either being made' (quoted in Stauber and Rampton 1995: 99).

The 1990s brought the TV Food Network to US cable, plus numerous cooking programmes to British television, including an exported game show. It principally addresses women audiences (the commercials are mainly for women's health and beauty culture), stressing that the presentational norms promoted apply to professional chefs, hosts entertaining, or the solitary but discriminating home cook. The common *theme* is that food can be fun. The common *requirement* for programmes to be included on the channel is that they be paid for in full by food companies. Like many forms of fun, the provision, circulation, distribution, and interdiction of food are part of everyday life, crucially linked to the working lives of others, both distant and nearby.

MEANINGS

[T]he reason Japanese people are so short and have yellow skins is because they have eaten nothing but fish and rice for 2,000 years. If we eat McDonald's hamburgers and potatoes for a thousand years, we will become taller, our skin will become white and our hair blond. (Den Fujita, McDonald's partner in Japan, 1987, quoted in Reiter 1996: 169)

Most nutrition-based accounts list four main food practices: growing, allocating/storing, cooking, and eating. Each area has its own
fractions of production, distribution, preparation, and consumption,
along with associated spaces for these practices to take place. Other
disciplines divide food into the physical, the social, and the physiological. The physical covers geography, seasons, and economics. The
social covers religion, custom, class, health education, advertising,
age, gender, and race. The physiological deals with genes, allergies,
diets, needs, and biochemical reactions.

In keeping with this division, food stands at the gateway of nature
and culture: it involves the choice made to penetrate the body with
otherness, the point where a *biological given* – hunger – meets and
becomes indistinguishable from a *cultural marker* – appetite. It was
the cause of the Fall from Eden, as the apple's temptation drew
disobedience to the Father's word. In keeping with that lineage, food
continues to present complex dividing lines between public and
private conduct: increasingly, alcohol consumption and/or moderate
inebriation is acceptable in bars but not cars, as is tobacco smoking
in bars but not restaurants. Such historical changes are crucial
determinants of the distinction between private and public spheres:
the very word 'pub' in English refers to a *'public house'*, a place
where sport, pleasure, and politics were traditionally undertaken
and discussed (Derrida 1993). The awkward link of nature to
culture and private to public led Aristotle to downplay the value of
taste, for unlike more cerebral pleasures, it affiliated humans with
animals. In the nineteenth century, John Harvey Kellogg, whose
flakes we all know, believed that since original sin derived from
foodstuffs, so his product, an honourable foodstuff, would control
improper sexual urges. Contemporary science has bothered to clas-
sify the four distinct tastes – bitter, sweet, salty, and sour – but
psychology and physiology dedicate few resources to taste by comparison with proprioceptive senses. Basic laws of property, of private
ownership, derive from processes of cultivation: who owns the field,
crop, or stock owns the means of survival. Religion, on the other
hand, derives many festivals from harvest rhythms, and meals are
routinely consecrated: forms of transubstantiation and holiness
connect divine spirits to secular institutions via the gustatory, as
well as endowing the owners of animals with political power. The
irrationality doesn't end there: some of the worst apparently
'natural' famines around the world since the 1960s have taken place

close to oil riches and just jet-hours away from places that permit agricultural over-production and rotting as part of national and regional policy. In these places, the disposal of uneaten food as waste costs more than it would to transport the food to needy areas (Fine and Leopold 1993: 150; Mennell 1985: 20; Derrida 1993: 4; Clarke and Critcher 1985: 53; Aristotle 1962: 1176a; McQueen 1992: 16; Synnott 1993: 184; Beardsworth and Keil 1997: 20–21; Goody 1978: 135; Warde and Hetherington 1994: 767; Benthall 1995: 11, 31). Food is not given in a state of nature.

The binary decision-making we embark on with food: 'that is edible' versus 'that is not edible', or 'eat that as it is' versus 'eat that when you have transformed it' (by heating or peeling), are models for sanctioned and forbidden conduct more generally. This operation establishes the change that people wreak on nature, showing how cultures put order into chaos by explaining and controlling aberrations (like poisonous substances that appear edible) (Lévi-Strauss 1987; Douglas 1979). Food, then, *is* culture, with associated assumptions about the rest of our lives. At a less complex level, the bizarre spread Vegemite is commonly associated with Australia, and seen as a way for adults to remember through the palate the supposedly carefree period of their youth, not least through targeted TV commercials. (More on the history of Vegemite below.) Connections between food and subjectivity can be as extreme as they are common: research on public opinion in the US shows that vegetarians – who are thought to eat broccoli, quiche, brown rice, bean sprouts, and avocado sandwiches – are assumed to be anti-war, pro-drugs, and drivers of imported cars (the nineteenth-century belief was that vegetarianism quelled masturbation). Gourmets, by contrast, are expected to favour caviare, oysters, and French-roast coffee and are regarded as liberal, drug-taking sophisticates. Fast- or synthetic-food eaters are found to be religious, conservative, and liable to wear polyester. There are similarly wild and arbitrary national preferences in the appearance of food. Consider the colour of egg shells: white is popular in the US and the Middle East, and brown in the UK, while North America favours orange-coloured cheeses above others (Fine and Leopold 1993: 169, 187; Renne 1993; McQueen 1992: 16; Falk 1994: 68–70).

There is some interesting work that compares the 1991 contents of refrigerators from the mid-Atlantic US and County Cork, Ireland. Condiments, salad dressing, and sauces took up one quarter of US refrigerators but less than one-tenth in Ireland. Four in ten items were dairy in Ireland, double the amount in the US. Ketchup (described by President Ronald Reagan as a vegetable) was a major item in the US, but effectively non-existent in Ireland. Yoghurt marked a key difference: the regular variety was virtually the only category in Ireland, but the US favoured low-fat. Colas were found in 33 per cent of US fridges and 20 per cent of Irish, with the figures reversed for bottled water. Fruit was present in 11 per cent of US fridges, 2 per cent of Irish. Vegetables were around 10–11 per cent in both. Most US bread was brand-name, most Irish purchased from a local bakery (George and Smith 1993). We can explain some of these differences as resulting from fashions in medical and public policy, others by what is available from local farms, and the rest by custom and the work of marketing. All are to do with meanings.

And there are significant national differences in what happens when food migrates from cold storage. Elinor Ochs, Clotilde Pontecorvo, and Alessandra Fasulo (1996) analysed many hours of tape of Italian and European-American families at mealtimes. They found discussion generally broke food into four categories: pleasure, nutrition, reward, and material good. Whereas American families devoted most talk to the financial and dietary value of the food and their children's moral obligation to eat appropriately, the Italians focused on pleasures. US children were instructed to consume certain substances, with dessert contingent on obedience, and their needs were assumed to be ordained by their place in a developmentalist hierarchy. Italian children were thought to have individual preferences, like adults.

Preferences come from places: cookbooks, commercials, peers, health education, travel, empire, and so on (Italians 'got' pasta from China and the Japanese were given tofu by the Portuguese). People select foodstuffs in part by their social signification: steak produces strength (it helps you to lift this book), fish produces intelligence (it helps you to understand the argument). To Barthes, steak is 'the heart of meat'. It links strong bodies to vibrant animal life, with lurid blood residues signifying sanguine reminders of what once breathed within. The association with handing on power through the chewing teeth of the diner is strong. During the Second World War, the German and US governments gave their troops high-protein diets in search of strength. The legacy of these changes is an unbalanced world, where two-thirds of the global population is vegetarian, but where vegetarians are regarded (and frequently regard themselves) as aberrant in the First World. Pressure to provide healthy foods for the navy led to the development of frozen orange-juice concentrate and frozen dinners in 1944; these spread to consumers two years later. Similarly, the US military ensured during the war that Coca-Cola bottling plants were available near every front, across the Pacific and North Africa; this became central to the company's international expansion after hostilities had ceased, as government money had generated a local manufacturing and pro-motional presence for the product across the globe. And it was government that encouraged Coca-Cola to market its product as a drink in the first place, in response to the threat of its taxation as a medicine. Since that time, the firm has sought to 'localize' itself to keep in tune with cultural norms – so its 1990s TV commercials in Singapore carefully reference norms that the Singaporean govern-ment has identified as missing from 'Western' advertising (Ochs et al. 1996; Goody and Goody 1995; Barthes 1973: 62; Fiddes 1991: 11; Bernstein and Carstensen 1996: 168; Mintz 1993: 51, 1996: 26; McQueen 1992: 15; Lee 1997). A parallel to this is the history of the Australian vegetable-extract spread, Vegemite. This was launched on the domestic market in 1923. It was an instant and ongoing failure. But the Australian army issued battle troops with Vegemite as part of their ration kit during the Second World War. On their return home, the soldiers started a trend towards this bizarre substance (Ivory 1998: 84). In both cases (Coke and Vegemite), then, it seems as if governments can set up tastes as much as can companies or consumers.

Food is part of alternative myths as well as dominant ones. Julie Dash's film *Daughters of the Dust* (1991) offers a counter to conventional histories and ways of telling them. It is a folktale, with a full register of oral genres – individual, poetic, and rhetorical. One hot day in 1902, on the Sea Islands off the coast of South Carolina, an extended Gullah family and a photographer picnic together and say goodbye to their island origin and hello to the urban economy that awaits them on-shore. Poised at a classic dilemma/opportunity of modern life – the shift from agrarian to urban life – the film gives a particular spin on that great transformation of the last three centuries through the prism of an unwelcome diaspora. Now most residents of the Gullah communities in the Sea Islands of Georgia and South Carolina were (and are) descendants of Africans, brought there as slaves from the west of the continent between 1670 and 1800. They were sought for their expertise in cultivating rice in tropical conditions, knowledge that the plantation owners lacked. The new plantations were organized along the technical and labour-process methods of the enslaved West Africans. Cut off from many other forms of American life, and still engaged in old agricultural practices, these people have held on to their history and culture as well as refining it. In the 1990s they continue to have a distinctive subjectivity through the Gullah language and various birthing and naming systems, stories, craftwork, religious beliefs, and rice cultivation. The people refuse to employ rice cookers, so keen is their desire to keep up traditional forms of cultural knowledge, which by now in fact mix Native-American, European-American, and African-American methods from across the southern states of the US (Beoku-Betts 1995: 539–40, 546–47, 550–51).

Bambi Schieffelin has shown the ongoing subsistence significance of food for the Kaluli people of Papua New Guinea. Their valorization of *halaido* (hard) over *taiyo* (soft) connects to the notion of softness as an origin – the mud that birthed the world – and hardness as a human achievement. As children are new, they are soft, and must be kept away from other 'soft' foods, such as eggs, bird-meat (when the birds in question have high calls) which would inflect the child's acquisition of language, or yellow foodstuffs, which could impair health. Such substances are redolent of the softness of the other end of life, the decay that rejoins age to youth. Changes in the cycle of life see dietary shifts: when men marry and have young children, their new status is in part signified by a movement from fresh to smoked meat. Women do the same once they have begun to menstruate. Again, history plays a part: conversions to Christianity in the 1970s problematized these ritual markers as superstition. In the case of Australia's Pintupi people, following the advent of Christian missions sugar and flour became official foods; those who retained a gathering and hunting lifestyle also kept a gendered division of labour. Women worked with fruit, honey ants, grubs, plants, lizards, and feral cats and men sought wilder meat. The latter was a very symbolic practice, in that vegetables remained the staple source of food. In rural Ghana, men and women still eat separately as a marker of gender difference (Schieffelin 1993: 6, 65; Myers 1991: 74–75; Goody and Goody 1995).

When processed food and standardized, centralized food provision displace subsistence, the change is addressed via myth. Many myths have been promulgated by governments, especially after the Depression, when it became settled international policy that governments were responsible for the economic wellbeing of their citizenry, with the provision of food a central aspect. Here is Barthes on the topic:

> I read a big headline in *France-Soir*: THE FALL IN PRICES: FIRST INDICATIONS. VEGETABLES: PRICE DROP BEGINS. . . . The signified or concept is what must be called by a barbarous but unavoidable neologism: *governmentality*, the Government presented by the national press as the Essence of efficacy. The signification of the myth follows clearly from this: fruit and vegetable prices are falling *because* the government has so decided. (1973: 130)

Whereas Italian children may be encouraged to eat by being sold the myth of individual taste, and Americans by the force of economic persuasion, Newfoundland folklore includes the 'Crust Man', a brutish man who carries children off in their sleep for failing to eat bread crusts. Richard Hoggart records 1950s working-class English suspicions that the new object called tinned pineapple was actually 'flavoured turnip' (there are longstanding European beliefs that the turnip produces 'turnip blood' and spineless behaviour). Today, rumour in African-American culture includes beliefs that the Ku Klux Klan owns a national fast-food franchise, a malt-liquor company, and a soft-drink firm, which it uses to sterilize black men through additives to prevent reproduction and problematize virility. These myths encapsulate the long history of sexual mutilation of black men by whites (Hoggart 1971: 38; Beardsworth and Keil 1997: 55, 54; Turner 1993: 73, 2–3, 227, 149–50). Authenticity and deceit are at the heart of such rumours: how can you be sure of what you eat? In any strict sense, *no one* can, because to be sure would mean being able to calculate what is essentially contingent: human history, culture, and peristalsis.

As in tribal societies, responsibility for food purchase and preparation is powerfully gendered. In the US in the 1930s, women were bombarded by advertising that conflated diet with domestic power. As *Good Housekeeping* put it, 'your job is to be a manager of men as well as menus'. Controlling food and the home was essential. The other side to this, of course, is a narrow definition of life chances, and making the decision to commit political resources to the private sphere is hard to leave behind. Opinion polls from the northern UK in the early 1980s show that 'proper' meals are held to comprise freshly cooked meat, potatoes, and vegetables, which should be prepared by women and eaten in the family setting. Men prepare snacks and 'proper' dinners during times of crisis. Male tastes are allocated authority over female in such settings, and domestic violence is frequently explained as a reaction to dissatisfaction with cuisine. At the same time, these tendencies are historically specific rather than timeless: once women are in the full-time paid workforce, men *do* prepare more meals in Britain (Warde and Hetherington 1994: 764–65; Beardsworth and Keil 1997: 84–85).

But even then, various food forms remain gendered. Cakes are a litmus test of femininity, their height and shape representing a successful birth. Disaster in the kitchen speaks volumes. In Britain, university tests have shown, as they say, that whilst women are seven times more likely than men to have cooked the prior meal, they are ten times likelier to have baked the last cake. Sugary substances are feminized, unlike tobacco or alcohol. Chocolate has traditionally figured as luxury and fantasy, unlike onions or carrots (a recent attempt to sell chocolate-coated carrots in Australia failed). Most 'chocoholics' are women: excess in gender equals overeating, binge-ing, starving, and being self-critical. Chocolate is obscene but luscious, a temptation. In advertisements, female models frequently adopt prepubescent postures in sexualized modes that simulate fellatio ('For Girls who used to say No'). Gifts of chocolate are acts of patronage, whether from soldiers to children or suitors to their desired ones. Pictures of sweetmeats become what Rosalind Coward calls 'food pornography'. She argues that the pleasure women derive from looking at photographs of cakes, and the guilt they derive from reading about calorie values, reference a dialectical engagement with women's culture that is also an enslavement to heterosexist and misogynistic imaging, through devotion to commercial notions of beauty and domestic 'servitude'. Eating disorders have long been associated with sexuality. Clinical studies claim that anorexia (under-eating) and bulimia (binge eating) are contemporary urban middle-class conditions with distinct sexual connotations (the former associated with chastity, the latter not) (Barthel 1989; Coward 1987: 101–3; Wiedermann 1996).

We might consider here *Betty Crocker's Picture Cook Book*, first published in 1950 and instantly the gift of choice at bridal showers: it was the number one non-fiction book in the US that year and second in 1951. *Betty Crocker's Good and Easy Cook Book* was fourth in 1954. Second and third editions of the original were third in sales for 1957 and ninth in 1961 respectively. It is an all-time culinary bestseller after *Joy of Cooking* (Rombauer and Becker 1973) and the *I Hate to Cook Book* (Bracken 1960). Published by the flour company General Mills, *Betty's* is almost exclusively dedicated to breads, cakes, and pastries. 'Betty' was forty-eight women in the company's Home Service Department and a voice on a radio programme, until her redesign during the 1950s to be less functional and more the loving homemaker. From 1955, Norman Rockwell and other illustrators tried out images of her for a 1,600-member female jury (she initially had marcelled hair and a Cupid's-bow mouth). Betty still wears the red-and-white coverall uniform favoured by the female jurors. From the 1950s, parents bought 'Betty Crocker E-Z Bake Ovens' for their children, which actually worked (they could heat up the smallest Crocker cake-mix cake) (Lears 1994: 188; Beardsworth and Keil 1990: 139–40; Marling 1992; *People Weekly* 1996: 314–17; Willis 1991: 96).

At the same time as food is indubitably functional, it is also excessive. The very fact of food's necessity – for those suffering from famine, especially – draws attention to its associations with profligacy. The sin of gluttony is about transgressing good taste. Mikhail Bakhtin has written that social norms depend in part on nominating and evading grotesqueries, the abject, that which we had best get behind us. When the body eats and drinks, it reveals 'its open unfinished nature, its interaction with the world'. People labour in order to eat, and the completion of a meal is a sign of triumphing over that travail; or at least this happens in the joyous occasion of a Rabelaisian banquet, a feast of revelry that forgets ordinary work and mocks its social norms of polite exchange. Grotesque bodies are those forever embarked on 'the act of becoming'. The bowels process engorgement, spewing out what is not wanted and negating the work of the mouth, establishing exchange and sociability as norms rather than the solitary, restrained individual. So while food bespeaks ordinary, rhythmical periodizations of daily life, such as dividing twenty-four hours by mealtimes, it is also to do with self-management and self-restraint. Mind you,

Bakhtin's example of Rabelaisian excess may have described a form of life restricted to the upper echelons of medieval and Renaissance Europe. Some history is needed (Bakhtin 1994: 228–29, 233–34; Mennell 1985: 22).

HISTORY

Tyson Food Inc., the largest poultry processor in the world, has implemented a production system whereby it sources low-cost Midwest grain to feed chicken in Arkansas. The breast meat is then removed for use by the US fast food market. The remainder of the carcass is shipped to Mexico to be deboned by low-paid, female Mexican laborers. Finally, the 'yakatori stick', marinated chicken on a bamboo stick, is exported to Japan where there is a high demand for marinated dark-chicken meat. (Bonanno and Constance 1996: 5–6)

Everyday culinary meanings are partly to do with historical change. The global taste in sugar was consequent upon, and largely supportive of, the horror of Caribbean slavery from the mid-seventeenth century, where large plantations staffed by unpaid black labour generated wealth and taste for white money and mouths, which spread down the class structure as industrialization and urbanization dislodged European rural people from subsistence ways. The French taste for eating meat, so mocked by the British, was, ironically, introduced by the government because of a British blockade during the Napoleonic Wars! The United States' colonization/ invasion of the Philippines, Puerto Rico, Hawaii, Cuba, Nicaragua, and the Dominican Republic between the 1880s and 1930s was a search for plantation crops. (The new expansionist programme was announced at the Centennial Exhibition in Philadelphia, when the US introduced the banana as an international commodity available thanks to its new outward view. The 'new' fruit's conditions of exchange – imported by wealthy countries from poor ones – is metaphorized in international relations discourse by the derisory term 'banana republic'.) Today, Britain has related controversies over banana prices, with local retailers and the European Union calling for a free import market and Caribbean producers arguing that they are owed protectionism because of their Commonwealth connection. Locally, government action may change consumption across demographic groups. For example at the end of the nineteenth century, low-income diets were rich in fibre and carbohydrate but lacked energy, calcium, vitamins C and A, and protein. Middle- and high-income diets were characterized by more vitamins, calcium, and protein, especially. With the First World War, the government adopted a national policy that saw diets converge as a result of rationing and public-health advice, while financial pressures during the Depression encouraged US government scientists to freeze vegetables for commercial sale for the first time. Food reform within societies may, of course, take place not through economic change, but by the imitation of ruling-class consumption: medieval European foodstuffs were gruel, fish, game, and meat. Gruel was a pottage of vegetables; the aristocracy and gentry ate fish and game. A new merchant class consumed meat, using diet to signify its occupation and status. Personal demeanour in table manners – blowing the nose, adopting 'correct' posture, and so on – altered between the medieval period and the late eighteenth century. Individuals began to worry about what others thought of them: an anxiety commensurate with shifts in class mobility. This ability to see oneself with the eyes of another became important, as per Goffman from Chapter 1 and discussion earlier in this chapter of public–private shifts in the culture of consuming alcohol and tobacco. Older fashions also reflect industrial change; prior to industrialization, the Progressive Movement at the turn of the century, and Puritanism's 'Great Revival', 1830s America saw public drunkenness as quite acceptable, provided it did not affect work. Until this century, alcohol and other drugs were regarded in the US and UK as medicines, to be dispensed by mothers, doctors, and bartenders. With the new century came industrialized notions of everyday life (as we saw from Lefebvre in Chapter 1) that demarcated appropriate and inappropriate times and spaces of inebriation in accordance with the distinction between leisure and labour (E. Williams 1964: 23; Goody and Goody 1995; Mintz 1996: 19; Enloe 1990: 124, 127–28; Beardsworth and Keil 1997: 88–89; Arce and Marsden 1993: 299; Bernstein and Carstensen 1996: 166; Finkelstein 1989: 32, 33; Husch 1992: 295–96). At the same time, many people continue to eat in public with their mouths open, as cultural norms of food intake are at variance with etiquette!

It would be wrong to assume that *all* food shifts relate to economic change, gender, or class categorization. The fashionability of different regimes of medicine also played a part. It was very popular in the seventeenth and eighteenth centuries to treat melancholy with diet: obesity in men was connected to mental health and longevity. Sufferers were set on a regimen of milk, vegetables, exercise, and emotional tranquillity. Bodies were theorized at this time as hydraulic systems of pulleys, pipes, pumps, and holes in need of lubrication and sustenance via drink and food. Drugs and surgery were only secondary means of assisting in the orderly functioning of this machine. When international trade and imperialism brought new foods and drinks to Europe, they were interpreted as new hazards for the body, or ways of importing excess into the nation and its human forms. Workers were absent from this discourse. Their diet principally comprised cereals, not meat, and diet was not yet deployed as a means of disciplining them. With the spread of urban disease across Europe in the nineteenth century came a social-policy need to improve the health of working people. The consumption of meat also rose dramatically during the Industrial Revolution. By the turn of the century, North Americans were clearly on notice about obesity. What had been regarded as a sensible store against debility was now regarded as corpulence. Today, immigrant cuisines that were once stigmatized, such as the Italian and Greek, are valued, on health grounds. During the 1950s and 1960s, European countries settled into a pattern: 'heavy' food was associated with workers; rich cuisine gradually gave way to waist-conscious repasts for ruling-class executives and families; and middle-class professionals were captured by ascetic but experimental consumption. This changed with the growth of migration. In the Netherlands, the influx of Indonesians (200,000 since the Second World War) has altered the national diet significantly. Even Britain, an astonishingly homogeneous country in food terms for a First World nation, has gained variety in its national diet since 1980; the ethnic market grew from virtually nothing at that time to perhaps half a billion pounds in the 1990s, as a consequence of new settlers, additional commercial and tourist exchange, and increased world production (Turner 1982: 25–29; Fiddes 1991: 54; Lears 1994: 167; Bourdieu 1994: 185; van Otterloo 1987: 127–29; Paulson-Box and Williamson 1990: 10).

Such shifts are rarely to do with developments in consumer preference. Until a century ago, the US was a pork-eating nation. Then buffalo herds were destroyed, Native Americans confined to reservations, and southern slave culture put to an end. But when beef was found to offer additional by-products, corn displaced grass in feed-lots, and refrigeration lessened the need for salted preservation, pork became a choice rather than a staple. Today, Americans eat 38 billion hamburgers each year. Food has also altered its significance in the everyday spending patterns of Americans. In the 1950s it absorbed perhaps a third of household expenditure. Now the figure is a fifth. By 1900, US food production primarily took place in factories rather than homes or farms, with vitamin consumption a sign of the fact. Health education has resulted in a big increase in US fish and poultry consumption recently, with red meat down 2.5 per cent over the last twenty years. Dairy food provides only a small part of diets now because of the desire for low fat and an awareness of cholesterol's dangers. Fresh vegetables have at least doubled in use since 1965, with the canned variety displaced by frozen goods. In the late 1960s, Americans consumed 18 gallons of soft drinks per person a year; the numbers have gone up 60 per cent since then. Coffee is now behind soft drinks, with alcohol first: beer consumption increased by 44 per cent over the last twenty years, and the consumption of wine has doubled. Some patterns of consumption shift with changes in wages and salaries: alcohol, beef, fish, cheese, and butter are income-elastic. Many such changes have been to do with new ways of living: individuals living alone made up a quarter of US households in 1987. They spend less time eating at home, because it provides no economies of scale (and they may feel lonely). And between 1960 and 1987, the number of married women working doubled. Higher-quality food became affordable, even as there was less 'free' domestic time to prepare it. Immigration has increased supermarket diversity since the 1960s. But farming has only had two moments of innovation: over 70 per cent of US agricultural crops originated with Native Americans, while chemicals and biotechnology develop new forms as we write (Fine and Leopold 1993: 189; Eberts et al. 1995: 10; Beardsworth and Keil 1990: 145–47; Henneberry and Charlet 1992: 5, 8–9, 11, 13–14; Warde and Hetherington 1994: 767).

Of course, some of these historical changes come with struggle. Consider the introduction of margarine. It was granted a French patent in 1869, following a competition to displace butter held at the Paris World Exhibition. Margarine was first made in the US in 1875, but stoutly opposed by the dairy industry. Despite lack of evidence of any harm caused by it, the substance was outlawed in Missouri in 1881. The same thing happened in over half the States of the Union (others required that it be coloured pink to differentiate it from butter – though butter was also artificially coloured). When compulsory pinkification was declared unconstitutional, governments taxed the new invention at a higher rate when coloured yellow! Conversely, some very significant changes take place quite subtly. A quarter of a million tonnes of sugar was produced in 1800 – and 100 million tonnes in 1982 (the latter figure up by half from 1970). Sugar provides 10 per cent of global calories (Fine and Leopold 1993: 159–60, 173–77).

Geopolitical differences are critical to local changes in consumption. In 1954, the US Congress ushered in a new world eating order with the Food for Peace Bill. Subsidized sales of grain created Third World dependency, and support for extremist governments was assured if they were anti-Communist: many such nations legislated opposition parties and a free media out of existence. Signals about food did not operate nationally or regionally with any accuracy, and famine was the outcome. Countries on their way to independence from European colonizers became industrial sources of metals and ideological/political sources of reinforcement to the US, whilst apparently being assisted in the transition to freedom. The military side to this expansion – by 1952, the government had 131 overseas bases – was illustrated to people back home with photographs of soldiers handing out chewing gum, sweets, and fizzy drinks to children. The food side was that countries with very high levels of production suffered famines, whereas unfavoured but open societies did not (even when they had much greater and more sudden declines in food production) (Fine and Leopold 1993: 151–52; Sen 1996: 25; Lutz and Collins 1993: 35).

Today, partly as a consequence of US and other First World tastes and patterns of assistance/domination, less than 1 per cent of available crop types are used for food across the globe. The principal 'acceptable' crops are rice, maize, potato, barley, wheat, sorghum, and cassava. Other potentially cultivable flora have been dismissed, which increases the risk of crop failure in the Third World. This new set of restrictions demolishes traditional knowledge and derides other nutritional systems. At the same time as foodstuffs are massively standardized at the level of development and manufacture, their presentation is increasingly differentiated. More and more countries during the late 1980s and 1990s have imported cuisines from around the globe. On the one hand, customers are not told of the complex economics and politics behind their purchase, as the food is radically disaffiliated from its conditions of production and circulation. On the other, they are given a spice of difference to do with the geographical origin of items on the menu, an enchanting quality to what is on offer: tourism in a bowl, as per the Beefeater chain adding South Asian, Mexican, Cajun, and Thai food to its traditional fare under the slogan 'Discover the world and eat it' (Fine and Leopold 1993: 151–52; Cook and Crang 1996: 132, 144). So what happens at such places, when cosmopolitans gorge themselves on the globe? How do we eat?

EATING

It's not the food that's 'fast,' it's the service. So I refer to our kind of business as a Quick Service Restaurant, or QSR for short. . . . At McDonald's our credo is QSC&V: Quality food, with fast and friendly Service, sparkling Cleanliness, and a good Value. (Edward Rensi, President and CEO of McDonald's USA, 1995: xi)

We'll turn to fast-food eating for our case study. But first, some context. Books from the mid-1600s detail table settings, measuring distances between diners and explaining the need to use a tablecloth to hide people's lower bodies whilst eating. Personal control in public was a sign of prestige and social standing. What we now know as restaurants began as open kitchens in medieval villages that fed passing travellers, as abbeys and convents along the north European coastline, and as dens in Chinese cities. The modern form is commonly thought to have emerged after the French Revolution, when cooks left aristocratic households. Restaurants were named as such in France in 1825. They became sites for democratizing knowledge of different foodstuffs and preparations as well as spreading notions of correct conduct across societies, beyond the ruling classes (Finkelstein 1989: 34–36, 46).

And today? Most current conduct takes the former mode: lone male diners order loudly, wait impatiently, and eat and leave quickly; families show pleasure in the novelty of the food and surroundings; established couples have nothing to say to one another, and either observe the room or remember a better time; new couples flirt and imagine romance and/or sex (*The Joy of Sex* metaphorizes sex as eating); and regulars perform their special knowledge in an irritatingly public manner. Patriarchal interests easily take over from dining out during the enactment of hetero-sexual conventions. The amount a woman eats, and how she eats it, are frequently determined by the man's pleasures: staying on for port, rushing off to work, or making out. The venerable 'Girls' Night Out' offers alternative pleasures. But such pleasures are often contested by men 'sharing' public space. There are also much more formalized, collective experiences of eating together: Jack Goody instances army messes, school canteens, and mealtime at St John's College, Cambridge. In each case, the menu is supplemented by another list, of diners' names. This amounts to a roll call for the military and the school, with sanctions liable to fall on those who fail to turn up. At St John's, the list is a ritualistic instantiation of hierarchy: the Master and the President are at the top (unnamed), followed by other Fellows in order of seniority. This provides a much-scrutinized marker of social standing, not unlike the Top Forty (Finkelstein 1989: 39–40, 45, 49–51; Comfort 1978; Goody 1978: 130, 132).

Dining out is subject to the contingencies of time and place. Robert Hanke has looked at shifts in the discourse on food in the *Philadelphia Inquirer* and *Philadelphia Magazine*. He assumed he would find what a marketing consultant had suggested: 'Food has changed from just being fuel. Now it's news, fun, sex, entertainment, self-expression and art. . . . Food has replaced sex'. In the early 1960s, the *Inquirer* ran recipe columns and advertisements related to home dining, with women as the exclusive targets. Functional aesthetics was connected to home economics: simplicity and thrift were called for, other than on special occasions (as per Betty Crocker). In the 1970s, a special section appeared in the Sunday *Magazine* on places to go, dramatically displacing 'Food and Family'. Syndicated gourmet guides were male-authored. The restaurant was now described as a public, commercial, and cultural site of urban sophistication, even attracting the ultimate 1970s fetish: invest-igative reporting. By the 1980s, the Sunday food section included a wine guide, and food writers were known as critics, offering instruc-tion on enjoyment rather than production (knowledge about, not knowledge of how). Taste was not taken for granted, but schooled.

Equivalent networks of gossip emerged, along with guides on obtaining the best service in a restaurant. The *Inquirer* was not Robinson Crusoe: around 25 per cent of US newspapers added 'Style' pages between 1979 and 1983, 38 per cent of those with circulations of more than 100,000. In the decade to 1985, the Netherlands saw an increase in the number of restaurants to 6,000, up 130 per cent. Today, fairly rigorous distinctions are drawn between *dining* out (costly, occasioned, planned, and dressed for) and *eating* out (easy, standardized, and requiring minimal presentational effort): both are to do with styles of life as much as food consumption (Hanke 1989: 221–33; Finkelstein 1989: 38; Fine and Leopold 1993: 167; van Otterloo 1987: 136). We went looking for one of these styles.

Our concern from now on will not be with high-culture dining. Its strange terpsichories and fetishes are fascinating, but so is the standardized, popular version of public eating – and there is even now some cross-over. Fast-food chains specialize in lobster, steak, and gourmet burgers, while United Airlines colours its flight menus with quotations from Virginia Woolf and claims that its food comes from 'a lifetime of discipline', as per 'the collected works of say, O'Keeffe, Bach or Dickinson'. Once more, aesthetic and anthropological accounts of culture are blended; though whilst feminist expectations are met, it's a very Eurocentric menu of great artists.

Fast-food franchises began in the US in the 1950s, in response to rising labour costs. The industry decided that reducing the workforce to a strict roster of required hours, transferring labour to the customer, introducing plastic and paper products, and dismissing supermarket purchasing in favour of institutionalized pre-preparation (processed, sliced cheese and individual packages of ketchup) were surefire means of reducing expenditure (Reiter 1996: 43). In short, the industry was born from, and is sustained by, casual labour and environmental degradation. It is a service-industry model of exploited workers and despoliated space.

In the UK of the 1990s, at least one snack food is consumed each day by 75 per cent of adults and 91 per cent of children, often in place of a meal. The industry refers to this as 'grazing', when brief moments displace the nominal three set occasions each day, supposedly at least two of them at home and all three on weekends and holidays. It is backed up by low wages. One in fifteen Americans get their first job with McDonald's, and 1994 saw fast-food outlets outselling full-service restaurants in the US for the first time. A poll taken in 1986 found 96 per cent of US schoolchildren could identify Ronald McDonald – second only to Santa Claus. That year, each American ate out 192 times. Half the population of the US lives within three minutes of a McDonald's and there are over 110,000 fast-food restaurant chain outlets. In the mid-1990s, fast-food franchises accounted for over a third of the country's restaurant trade. McDonald's controls 17 per cent of the country's eat-out market, and has over 12,000 outlets in more than seventy countries, relying on global sales for most of its profits. Its overall receipts outstrip the GNP of many nations. KFC has 6,000 outlets across fifty countries (Fine and Leopold 1993: 165–66; Ritzer 1993: xiii, 2–3, 5; Eberts et al. 1995: 1, 17; Rensi 1995: xii; Reiter 1996: 48).

As US food culture becomes more homogeneous, it promotes homogeneity around the world. Three-quarters of UK families miss at least one of the supposedly conventional meals a day (62.5 per cent go without breakfast). There are clear connections to the decision not to prepare food, which in turn leads to accusations of laziness, health risks, inadequate femininity, and a host of other alleged failings. Some of this calumny is directly associated with mass production. Frozen dinners were first marketed in the US in 1953 as a meal to be had in front of the TV or in an emergency: there has been some carry-over from these origins into notions of low quality. More seriously, the long-term implications of global dietary norms shifting from grains to meat are very serious indeed (Fantasia 1995: 202; Henneberry and Charlet 1992: 16; Beardsworth and Keil 1990: 142; Mintz 1993: 51).

There is a correlation between the spread of fast-food franchises around the world and various social developments: increased youth discretionary spending, growing numbers of women in the workforce, diminished emphasis on familial eating, additional traffic congestion, and eating on the job. Not surprisingly, then, the fast-food restaurant is associated with entertainment, emotional politics, professional convenience, and class access. McDonald's sells a nonconflictual family occasion of eating as much as it vends food; or so it seems. But by and large, the clientele consists of white-collar workers eating individually and adolescents hanging out together. The chain even advertises itself to the latter in some countries as a place where table manners are not required. Sensational expectations were engendered amongst Russian and Chinese shoppers in the

1990s when the first McDonald's opened there: Moscow teenagers offered to break through the lines/jump the queues to buy hamburgers within a quarter of an hour, and opening day in Beijing saw 40,000 customers served. A little sad, when you consider the hamburger was invented in the Baltic states, taken up by German sailors on return to Hamburg, and then popularized in the US by Midwestern migrants as a European delicacy. Today, its international popularity is a symbolic connection to the US, modernity, and efficiency as much as it is to do with global domination, especially for those used to state socialism: the company used to have a game where players had a multiple-choice test about the composition and size of, for example, the Berlin Wall that they could play in the new restaurants (Ritzer 1993: 2–3; Fantasia 1995: 230; Rensi 1995: xii; Stephenson 1989: 230).

For critics imbued with a less commodified model of inter-subjectivity, this is disturbing. It raises the prospect of 'huge groups of people drinking Coke together, and eating french fries' becoming 'the definition of friendship' (Dessaix 1990). Meanwhile, new managerial and promotional systems are being developed at such institutions as Burger King University (formerly Whopper College), KFC's College of Chicken Knowledge, and Hamburger University, where McDonald's offers a Bachelor of Hamburgerology that can be counted towards a degree at less focused liberal-arts institutions. Burger King University faculty specialize in what is called 'The People Game', training franchisees to control their employees via a weird combination of social psychologist Abraham Maslow's hierarchy of needs and industrial engineer F.W. Taylor's principles of production-line measurement: at some institutions, tomato ends and cores are weighed to measure waste, and workers are checked individually to see whether they fill bags of fries beyond the planned yield of portions per fry. The food colleges include classes on keeping unions out of each operation. The key to this is cajoling employees into believing they will be better off without political representation – rewarded on their merits and supervised in line with their personal needs, via sound relationships with local managers. The faculty mantra is 'Don't SPIT' when unionization moves are afoot ('SPIT' is an acronym for 'spy, promise, interrogate, or threaten'). And as young people drop out of the fast-food labour force in search of better jobs, the corporations change their public-relations image of youthfulness to attract employees who will work for the minimum wage. Latest techniques include hiring retirees and the mentally disabled to take slots young people won't accept (there is a McMasters programme for seniors) and offering higher wages in suburban, white-dominated North America compared to the inner cities, plus emphasizing families in advertising (Dessaix 1990: 276; Reiter 1996: 68–70, 89, 101, 133, 146; Stephenson 1989: 239–40).

In France, where fast food is still new (about 5 per cent of the restaurant business, but growing rapidly since the late 1980s), McDonald's has gone through a series of transformations. In the 1970s, it was chic: the intelligentsia frequented the few outlets, and fashion shows associated themselves with hamburger stands. But by 1989 this otherness had become ordinary fare. French fast-food chains had started, naming themselves France-Quick, FreeTime, Magic Burger, B'burger, Manhattan Burger, Katy's Burger, Love Burger, and Kiss Burger. Half the industry 'sounded' American, and the national language itself seemed under threat. The government created a National Council of Culinary Art within the Ministry of Culture, dedicated to 'protecting the culinary patrimony' from fast food and other stresses (Fantasia 1995: 202–3, 213, 224, 205–7). At the same time, this also indicates the ambiguous place of the US in global popular culture – it offers what people want, but sometimes seems to do so at the cost of what 'makes' them a people.

This information is very helpful; but does the political economy of fast food capture what *happens* when we eat out? In order to identify the orientationals for everyday eating that operationalize much of this background machinery, we did something very simple: visited a food mall to observe a variety of events where people approached food counters, made selections from menus, ordered, and came away with their choice of available foodstuffs. There was a specific reason for this interest in, by and large, fast-food delivery and receipt: it has a highly minimalized format that is not like eating at home, for example, where there may be a long process involving shopping lists, decisions, food preparation, last-minute additions of side-dishes, and so on. And it is unlike the complexity of sit-down restaurants where many other social events go on alongside eating itself: restaurant statuses, problems of social status between waiters and clients, complex differences between *à la carte* and special dishes, etc.

The fast-food situation appealed to us, in the same way that two-party conversation attracted Sacks in his early work on conversational sequencing (1995a: 95–103). Sacks suspected that the routine grounds of conversational sequencing could be built up from the regularities or orientationals observable in two-party talk. Two-party talk has reasonably definite sequential features that cannot be found when more than two persons are talking. If party A speaks first, then party B speaks next – and so on, thus structuring the entire conversation as an 'A-B Reduplicated' chain, to use Sacks' term – even if that chain is only minimally reduplicated. Clearly, that basic orientational is not available for talk with two-plus parties. Much more complex orientationals have to be considered (Sacks et al. 1974).

So, in a similar way to Sacks, we wondered if it might be possible to describe basic orientationals used in getting fast food. For example: are there routine sequences? How do eaters and servers know the sequence of units involved? How do they know that a unit of the sequence has been completed and the other should then speak or act in a particular way? How can participants know entire sequences have been completed and the transaction is over? These are the sorts of matters we went looking for at a food mall, which we'll simply refer to as 'Food Fair'. Our results were distinctly different from those found in the Netherlands and France, where the propensity to line up in queues is markedly less than in Anglo-dominated countries; and in Britain, where employees resist the mantra of 'Have a nice day' (Stephenson 1989: 232; Fantasia 1995: 221; Reiter 1996: 59).

The first thing to notice about Food Fair is that, as a device for getting food, it contains no instructions. Its designers and managers assume that users arrive pre-equipped for its use. In that sense, Food Fair is a cultural site: designed for routine users, with the techniques of use assumed to be transparent. As one enters what is effectively a horseshoe arrangement of ten stalls and outlets – McDonald's, Red Rooster, The Kebab Co., Mozzarella's (pizza/pasta/foccacia), The Seafood Bar, Avocados (sandwiches and rolls), Sing Yin Oriental Emporium, Muffin Break, NZ Natural (ice cream and fruit juices), and Gravy Stain (roasts) – a number of features become evident.

At the small 'independent' businesses like 'Avocados', people form a single line across the serving space. The arrangement of things is like a public bar. The servers are, to this extent, expected to notice the order of arrival at the counter and, in cases of doubt, to ask 'Who's next?' From time to time, customers are selected out of turn and may then offer such correctives as 'I think this person's before me'. There does not appear to be an equivalent utterance – at least in this place – for clients who believe they have missed their turn.

By contrast, at the franchises (like McDonald's and Red Rooster), the clients sort themselves into rows and columns, with one person serving at each register generating that formation. This is in keeping with the scientific management characteristic of McDonald's; the corporation has defeated 400 union-organizing efforts in the US and tries to impose this policy on international franchises. It takes fifteen minutes to train new employees, who are estimated to attain maximal efficiency within half an hour on the job, thanks to food preparation organized by timers, beeps, pre-allocated amounts, computer measurements of deep-frying fat, and cash registers labelled with food genres – rather than monetary ones – that are programmed to highlight additional, complementary items to be offered to customers during a sale (Fantasia 1995: 210–11). So the franchises have (a) more points of service and registers along the counter, and (b) a more definite routine for the accomplishment of the event. The latter began to fascinate us. But, for now at least, a first orientational at Food Fair appears to be that users make a primary distinction between independents and franchises, expecting the former to be locally negotiated, and the latter to follow pre-allocated routines. Independents can be used, as it were, conversationally, such that the movement from initial interest to final purchase cannot be known in advance – at least while there is reasonable attendance at the counter by customers. Franchises, by contrast, appear to be more like debates than conversations – in the sense that, in a debate, who is going to talk (and act), when, for roughly how long, and what they are going to perform via talk and action, can be fairly well known in advance.

This division between independents and franchises carries different significations. If the name and display of fresh foods at Avocados signifies seriousness, vegetables, and small business, then the name and invisibility of the food at McDonald's carries opposed meanings: fun rather than seriousness, meat rather than vegetables, large rather than small business. Hence an interesting cultural paradox which may need some further investigation: health and smallness go with conviviality, while fun and big-time go with the routinization and the predictability of pleasure. While Avocados is a group of adults on both sides of the counter chatting about sandwich composition, McDonald's has mostly teenagers serving adults and children in repeated, stock ways. We shall look at some of those stock ways and follow a single customer through the service delivery at McDonald's.

A white man in his forties heads left, away from the central eating tables, to a point at the counter where there are fewer people in the line. He stops several paces back from the counter and looks up at the lights (the backboard menu). His chin is up, expectant, and he takes a step towards the counter, dropping his head. A young woman comes in response to this. He makes a little dance-shift to allow a previous customer past with her meal, then leans on the counter, legs crossed, and tells his server what he wants to order. He asks for a medium quarter-pounder meal. She pushes the appropriate button on the computer-register. He adds 'with Fanta', presumably to avoid the default of Coke. She revises the ordering notation on the computer. Immediately he has ordered, she asks whether he wants dessert(s): 'Do you want desserts with that?' Then, quite quickly, his server moves around, collecting items from the slides, bins, and dispensers behind her, carefully avoiding co-workers performing similar operations. She returns and hands him the bag of food on a tray. Money is exchanged; she smiles. Her badge shows her name to be Sarah, and she is wearing a McDonald's Team Spirit Badge and a bigger badge reading: 'Try a Passionfruit Sundae 95 cents'. This process encapsulates what the industry refers to as 'the food triangle'. Comparatively nutritious food – the burger – is not particularly profitable. The real money is made on drinks and fries, where huge mark-ups are feasible (say, 400 per cent over the cost of preparation and service). If these items are not ordered, staff are expected to suggest them, along with a dessert (Reiter 1996: 83–84).

From this rather brief and basic description, we can notice a number of orientationals immediately. First, the customer does not approach the counter immediately, but stands back a few paces. The majority of McDonald's and Red Rooster customers appear to do this. A few others know what they want in advance and step into the first available slot at the counter. For the rest, there is an invisible decision line. Behind that line, the illuminated menus can be inspected. In fact they appear to have been angled specifically for best viewing from that position, two or three paces back. Again, behind the line, there is no necessary commitment from the prospective customer. He is not yet in eye contact (hence interaction space) with the server and could retreat from any actual purchase. Breaking the line by moving forward and dropping his head into alignment with the server commits him, and he takes a single turn by repeating one of the items from the menu. This is the main business of the transaction. This unit is in progress once the customer's body has moved across the decision line. However, the line itself can move, depending on the density of the traffic. At busy times, it appears to be five or six paces back from the counter. At slower times, it is just two or three paces back. Buyers and servers, then, orient themselves to shifting and negotiable ways of constructing the main purchase unit (ordering the meal). What a person is (deciding, undecided, committed) is visible from their bodily location *vis-à-vis* an invisible, shifting barrier.

Customers appear to monitor their positions with regard to this barrier. We observed certain people who wished to remain uncommitted for a fairly long period (two or three minutes in some cases) moving back and forth with shifts in the barrier line. At the same time, servers also appear to monitor customers' positions with regard to this threshold, thus precision-timing their requests for orders ('May I help you?', 'What would you like today?', and so on).

The arrangement of things at the McDonald's counter shows a further complication of the two-party arrangement. For servers, there is the issue of colleagues on one side of the counter, and for clients there are fellow-customers on the other side. To get through their first talk unit (the order) successfully, clients sometimes have to allow persons just served to pass by, perhaps at the same time as they are talking to the server. Time after time, we saw exactly the same 'dance' from customers doing this: a localized version of the do-si-do move. At point-of-service, a committed customer starts the ordering unit from the first point of eye alignment with the server. As he or she proceeds even closer to the counter, another customer, who has just been served, turns with their tray slightly to one side. They go around each other's backs and the ordering unit proceeds. At this point, there is room for final corrections should any be needed by either party (in this case Fanta for Coke by the customer, and the option of desserts by the server). Next, the payment required is mentioned by the server, though money does not yet change hands. The amount is rung up on the register and stays there for a while as the server performs a more complex dance around her (or in this instance more rarely his) co-workers. This appears to be a more trained procedure involving apparently friendly competition for single burgers, being first to the fries, and so on – and a good deal of smiling accompanies the complex weavings. The main point of the dance appears to be to return to the customer as quickly as possible to avoid a wait on the server's side (parallel, perhaps, to the decision-line delay on the part of the customer). Once the meal is assembled and in its bag, the cash is taken and entered into the register (this particular McDonald's did not have the 'Dine in' or 'Take away' option: all meals were served as 'Take away' or 'To go'). Then there's only the obligatory 'Have a nice day' or 'Enjoy your meal' (to which the reply is either nil or a simple 'Thanks'). Then, with bag and/or tray in hand, the incoming customer becomes an outgoing customer and may have to return-dance with the next one.

This allows us to draw up a minimal set of actions involved in getting fast food. It might, in the case of Food Fair, run as follows:

1 Customer: Primary decision – choose independent or franchise
1.1 If independent, anticipate local negotiation
1.2 If franchise, expect the following steps:
2 Customer: Stand behind decision line and either exit or step forward (point of commitment)
3 Customer & Server: Eyes meet
4 Server: Greeting unit ('May I help you?')
5 Customer: Dance with outgoing customer if necessary + Ordering unit
6 Customer & Server: Corrections to order if necessary
7 Server: Request for payment + Register work + Dance with co-servers if necessary + Assemblage of meal + Take payment + Register work + Departing unit ['Enjoy your meal']
8 Customer: Response ['Thanks' or nil] + Dance with new incoming customer if necessary + Obtain seat in the mall.

This sequence is interesting in a number of ways. First, it is highly economical. In its minimal realization (with no customer decision-making, no corrections, and so on) it would allow for very few moves.[1] Moreover it appears to be able to expand and contract in accord with the amount of traffic at the food stand. Secondly, some of the routine contents of the sequence slots contain their own micro-economies. A case in point is the server's greeting slot: 'May I help you?' does not require (though it sometimes receives) a return greeting; it routinely generates the customer's order. Contrast such possible greetings as 'How are you today?' and so on. The same goes for the server's departing unit. If it contains 'Enjoy your meal' or 'Have a nice day', a response such as 'I will' or 'I'll try' is possible but by no means necessary. 'Thanks' is probably sufficient. Thirdly, while the sequence can be stripped down to very few moves, it contains, as it were, expansion slots which anticipate routine organ-izational variations. These particulars may have to do with the micro-architectural organization of the food outlet: hence the slots in the sequence which allow means for dealing with clients moving both ways in a line of bodies or with servers moving in competition for goals. Or they might have to do with the fact that franchises must allow some consumer choice within standard packages: hence the carefully slotted zone for corrections which, if not taken up by customer or server, will result in a default version of a meal. Indeed, in some of the cases we observed during a couple of hours at McDonald's, these expansion slots were taken up at some length. Cases in point were people trying to order vegetarian versions of packages, trading in discount coupons, being assured that meals were nearly ready (in cases of large or complex orders), rejoining friends or family in queues/lines after leaving them temporarily without being assumed to be separate purchasers, and so on. The expansion slots appeared to be able to cope with most of these fairly predictable ways of making a very routine process slightly more complex.

One thing the sequencing resources did not appear to cope with well was continued surveillance from two outsiders with clipboards. When it came to this matter, new procedures had to be improvised on both sides. The manager asked us over to inquire where Toby was from. He replied, 'New York.' He asked whether Toby had been sent by 'central office, to check up on us'. Then he asked if Toby was with 'the competition'. When we said why we were there – in a sense, to observe our own purchasing practices – honour was served. But a combination, presumably, of the time we spent in the vicinity looking at proceedings, walking around with a clipboard, and perhaps the way we 'looked', made us resemble time-and-motion men. Ester Reiter, who did many months of unpaid fieldwork as a Burger King worker towards her dissertation research, had initially approached McDonald's of Canada for permission to work there and attend Hamburger University. The response was a letter to her departmental chair insisting she 'cease and desist from all efforts to enter McDonald's'. Burger King was happy to use her free labour, but barred her entry to Burger King U (Reiter 1996: 77–79). Of course, it would not do, in an interconnected financial world, to be too reflexively moralistic about this: as one critical ethnographer discovered towards the end of his research into McDonald's, his faculty pension plan included some company stock (Stephenson 1989: 238)!

There can be no better instances than these little tales of how the micro-politics of meaning and the macro-politics of international political economy are intricated. When Humphrey Bogart meta-phorizes his mimetic desire for Ingrid Bergman in *Casablanca* (Michael Curtiz, 1942), he juxtaposes that impossible passion with the war, saying their problems 'don't amount to a hill of beans in this crazy world'. But each matters, and each needs its own history and analysis. That necessitates blending knowledge derived from a wealth of comparative theory and public discourse with site-specific applications – or else, by combining background analysis of a cultural problem with discussions of local circumstances.

NOTE

1. Note one apparently uneconomical feature: the amount is rung up on the register *before* the meal is served and the money is taken *after* it has been served. In most sales situations, goods are exchanged for cash and then rung up. McDonald's appears to be an interesting exception. New customers might wonder why, having been told the amount payable, they have to wait to hand over payment. No doubt, though, there are interesting economies to this feature: it clearly identifies customers, servings and amounts of cash, and it saves the server from waiting for the cash to be found and counted.

3

Sport

Look, do it slower and cut down your reps – you'll never get big this way. You should be able to handle more weight than this; why don't you let me spot you? (Male bodybuilders to Alan Aycock, 1992: 351)

We are a band of baseball players
From Cincinnati City;
We come to toss the ball around
And sing to you our ditty;
. . . The ladies want to know
Who are those gallant men in
Stockings red, they'd like to know. (Cincinnati Red Stockings Team
Song, 1869, quoted in Schreier 1989: 104)

Christopher Lasch, a prominent 1970s critic of popular culture, thought American sport was a degraded version of 'release from everyday life'. What once produced heightened awareness through intense concentration and a replication of childhood's singular obsessions offended twentieth-century social reformers. They sought to harness this loose energy to nation-building and economic productivity. At the same moment, capitalism transformed sport into a practice of spectatorship. Lasch's critique typifies the view of sport from a Romantic desire, common to both left and right, for what is always-already lost, with the body shifting from free play to lax consumption (Lasch 1979: 181–82, 185). There are alternative views. In *Live Alone and Like It: A Guide for the Extra Woman* (1936), Marjorie Hillis recommends that single women occupy themselves watching boxing bouts and art exhibitions. No wonder: the histories of sport and art both describe a movement indoors, blending discipline and spectacle in enclosed spaces. This is an increasingly media-based activity, crossing genders in just the way

Hillis imagined: in 1995, more women than men in Britain watched Wimbledon tennis on television. The numbers were nearly equal for boxing, whilst NBC targeted women and families in its 1996 Olympic coverage by narrativizing the life-stories of contestants rather than their statistics, to such effect that 50 per cent of the audience was adult women and 35 per cent men ('Sport' 1995; Remnick 1996: 27).

Sport is a complicated site of commerce and discipline. It captures the duality of the title to this book: part of popular culture via entertainment networks of media and stadia spectatorship, and part of routine leisure activities.

A LITTLE HISTORY

Most histories of sport argue for a break that occurs with European industrialization; prior to that point, it is thought, distinctions between work and leisure are irrelevant: capitalism transformed carnival, ceremony, and play into precisely delineated changes in production. That position is under challenge. It reduces precapitalist ideas about sport to the utopia of festival, whereas the ball games of fourteenth-century Japan or seventeenth-century Florence symbolized courtier diplomacy, and warfare was defined in the Renaissance as a sporting art. Many linguistic antonyms to the concept of work were in use prior to capitalism: Latin opposes active and contemplative lives, while sixteenth-century Italian and French and fifteenth-century English include elaborate ideas about recreation. There are discourses everywhere about boredom and the need for distraction amongst élites. Rather than a brutal division of labour subjecting working-class leisure pastimes to standardization and commodification, sports descend through social structures, often to positive effect: British ruling-class dismay at the supposed drudgery of professional cricket (a regular incantation since the turn of the century) venerates heritage by faulting the here-and-now as cheapened by money, but that economic transformation equally made for new labour markets (Burke 1995: 138–40, 142; Marqusee 1994: 28). Today, the very notion of leisure as distinct from sport is problematized by the digitalization of middle-class life, with computer games an office staple and major business deals done from (if not in) the bedroom. When Garfinkel refers to a game as 'an encapsulated episode', he offers the right flexibility to deal with such historical variations (1963: 27–28).

The sport sociologist and historian Norbert Elias analyses social structure synchronically and diachronically, coining 'figuration' to designate how people inhabit social positions. The figural keys to sport are exertion, contest, codification, and collective meaningfulness. They guarantee its magic attractions – tension and catharsis. Elias asks why there is such fascination with rule-governed contests between individuals and teams, an excitement and passion equal to war but with a fraction of the devastation. He answers by tracing a trend that has fanned out vertically and horizontally from the European ruling classes since the sixteenth century. It codifies sentiment and behaviour, supplanting excess and self-laceration with temperance and auto-critique. This displacement of tension and the search for ordered leisure has allocated to organized sport the task of controlling and training gentry, workers, and colonists alike. High tension combined with low risk, binding popular appeal to public safety in a utilitarian calculus of time and joy (Elias 1986b: 19–21, 38–39; 1986a: 165, 173–74, 150–51, 155, 159). Henning Eichberg (1986) points to contradictory shifts in European sport between the thirteenth and nineteenth centuries, bringing enclosure and the open air into an ambiguous relationship. Sometimes, sealed-off spaces are deemed appropriate for ruling-class privacy (squash), with field-like surroundings suitable for school exercise (rugby union). But the spatial separation of sport from nature in late nineteenth-century industrialization marks a trend. Bodies in motion are progressively contained, enraging hygiene movements but permitting surveillance, spectacle, and profit.

The history of global sport sees most nations importing games from visitors or colonists; these games are taken up by ruling classes and progressively diffused through society. There are few institutionalized home-grown pastimes. In Latin America, most of today's games were introduced by British sailors to port towns or capital cities in the nineteenth century. Where there was a substantial resident British presence, expatriates began their own competitions, which devolved down the social strata. Sometimes, middle- and ruling-class locals returned from travelling in Europe with sporting ideas and drives that were gradually democratized and professionalized. This is not to deny the continuing importance of indigenous games, such as Bolivian *tinku* or Australian Rules. But they generally thrive amongst isolated peoples or Romantic élites in search of a renewed bucolic idyll, like the ruling-class Argentinians who have revived *pato* (a gaucho sport) as an alternative to polo for showing off equestrian skill and social superiority. Such trade in culture is never entirely welcome: once the international division of sporting labour began in earnest in the 1980s, the Dominican Republic, where baseball had become a popular domestic game, found its local leagues ripped apart by the attentions of US scouts. On the other hand, local newspaper stories about Major League games repatriate stars by focusing on the fortunes of expatriate Dominican players, to the virtual exclusion of their clubs. And in the mid-1970s, business interests decimated Canadian ice hockey to revive the US league. Radical critics called for community activism to reclaim hockey's supposed connection to the social world. This position saw sport as designed to reflect a population back to itself, an authentic self-expression akin to nineteenth-century novelist Herman Melville's idea of American realism but endangered by commodification from below (in a geographical sense). This demonstrates a Romantic organicism that denies the partial view of nation and community provided by men's sport. It also forgets the financial base of Canadian hockey, concentrating on new sources of funding and neglecting local history (Mason 1995: 13; Arbena 1993: 106–9; Klein 1991: 81; Gruneau and Whitson 1993: 24–27).

How should we make sense of sporting capitalism, given that expenditure on sport in the US fluctuates with macro-historical events – in the US, the Korean and Second World Wars reduced consumption – but not in terms of conventional business cycles? Attendance at the four major North American codes (hockey, football, basketball and baseball) has shown steady growth through most recessions, and the gross national sport product is expected to be US $121.1 billion by the turn of the century. There are two key aspects of this success. First, sports themselves have corporate rules, governance, and legal personalities, in addition to company ownership of teams. Secondly, they offer advertising and goodwill (in the accounting sense) to sponsors, which have been involved since the 1860s. In the really big sponsorship areas, such as motor-racing, there is a direct tie-in between building an image and targeting customers with products related to the sport. The process began when Gillette paid US $100,000 for radio rights to the 1939 World Series and marketed a tie-in that sent sales figures up 350 per cent.

Today, the company provides airline travellers with an in-flight TV-highlights magazine to the same end. In the 1980s, Macintosh sold US $3.5 million of computers the day after a Super Bowl commercial, and US $155 million over the next three months. Fox (the TV station) and Frito Lay (potato chip manufacturers) coordinated the 1995 football season to such a degree that TV highlights programmes cut from commentators on a play to commercials of the same people eating Wavy Lay chips, while each packet of the product came with a Fox National Football League schedule. This second aspect is a key to the unique nature of the first: because the life-world of sport is said to transcend commerce, it confers prestige on commercial associates (Vogel 1995: 244–45; Sabo and Jansen 1992: 170; Cashmore 1994: 143; Montemayor 1995; Marshall and Cook 1992: 308, 311, 319–20).

The most dramatic recent commodification concerns the Olympics. When the International Olympic Committee (IOC) President saw an athlete's bag covered with an airline logo in 1972, he had it removed from the Munich Village. But whereas the 1976 Summer Olympiad in Montreal gained 81 per cent of its funds from government sources, the equivalent figure for the Los Angeles Games of 1984 was 5 per cent. That year, the decision to sell the privilege of carrying the Olympic torch for US $3,000 per kilometre drew a Greek protest delegation. But by 1988 in Seoul, even the Soviet Union had shifted its interest in sporting success away from national and socialist prestige and towards new markets. Sports had been corporatized, and expansion now relied on television. US rights to the 1996 Atlanta Games cost US $715 million, compared to US $401 million for 1992 in Barcelona. This is part of a major reconfiguration away from the idea of amateur sport as a public good *provided by* the state, to the state as an indirect servicer of private investment that then has a multiplier effect (Houlihan 1994: 156; Real 1996: 14; MacAloon 1987: 130; Pettavino and Pye 1994: 213).

Another way of understanding this is to say that sports are expansionary. As commercial interests lobby for golf's inclusion in the Olympics, and First World wealth seeks new places to play, pressure on governments to turn over land for links development intensifies from multinational airlines, construction companies, property developers, and equipment manufacturers. The Global Anti-Golf Movement began with the 1993 Malaysian Conference on

Golf Course and Resort Development. Throughout Asia and the Pacific, local communities have protested against the expansion of golf, which is environmentally rapacious. Opposition in Indonesia has led to imprisonment, as farmers and others protest against siltation, erosion, pollution, and the loss of heritage caused by new resorts. In the US, successful opposition from environmentalists has seen a massive public-relations campaign in retaliation (Serrano 1994: 273–74; Schoenfeld 1996).

Not all sporting commodification has negative consequences. Certain companies have seen potential in supporting fringe actors and practices in sport, ameliorating the chauvinism of traditional amateur games bodies. Adidas began courting emerging sovereign states long before the IOC. The company dedicated resources in the 1970s to forwarding the claims of African and central European sports federations; when sporting attire was selected to outfit teams, they drew the obvious reward, plus free advertising. Since the first attempts by women to gain access to marathons, in the 1960s, Avon cosmetics has funded races, employed lobbyists, and connected the sport to beauty and makeup. Many businesses broke down gender segregation in sport by supporting employee athletics. This doubled as a drive towards productivity gains: Canada had a 1970s campaign called 'The Human Body as Machine', and has since developed a neocorporatist sport system of government, business, and amateur associations. Corporate support is contingent, of course. Avon cut sponsorship of women's tennis after the 1981 lesbian palimony suit against Billie Jean King (Houlihan 1994: 164; Cooper 1995: 72–74; Brodeur 1988: 233; Harvey et al. 1995; Lurie 1994: 123–24; Savan 1994: 225; M.A. Hall 1993: 56). Which brings us inevitably to the body.

THE BODY

Joseph Maguire sees four types of sporting body, that respectively discipline, mirror, dominate, and communicate. The disciplined body is controlled by both coaches and the athlete him- or herself, remodelled through dietetics and training to police performance. The mirroring body is a machine of desire that encourages mimetic conduct via presentation as a desired other, and synecdochically, through the purchase of commodities associated with this other (as bodybuilders put it, 'Let the mirror be your guide'). The dominating body uses physical force, both on the field and – potentially – off it, frequently in a gendered way. And the communicative body is aestheticized as balletic and beautiful. As Maguire points out, these categories blend with one another, and can be internally conflictual or straightforwardly functional. They are the outcome of history, publicity, and privateness: human, commercial, and governmental practices that involve implicit negotiations to maintain boundaries (Maguire 1993a; bodybuilders quoted in Bolin 1992: 384). How has this status come about?

In Ancient Greece and Rome, the body was the *locus* for an ethics of the self, a combat with pleasure and pain that enabled people to find the truth, to master themselves (Foucault 1986: 66–69). This combination of austerity and hedonism was achievable through training:

> The metaphor of the match, of athletic competition and battle, did not serve merely to designate the nature of the relationship one had with desires and pleasures, with their force that was always liable to turn seditious or rebellious; it also related to the preparation that enabled one to withstand such a confrontation. (Foucault 1986: 72)

To Xenophon, Socrates, and Diogenes, the body is always in need of exercise. Sexual excess and decadence are the equivalent of sporting success. Like that success, they can lead to failure unless there is also an examination of the conscience and physical training. This temperance – not abstinence, but desire moderated with service – becomes a sign of fitness to govern others. (Of course, in many contemporary sports, we see managers and coaches who specialize in a comprehensive lack of self-control!) The desires implanted by nature can be held in check, their conquest analogous to the victories over adversity that the city-state needs. This training cannot end, because fitness is both contingent and necessary. Aristotle and Plato favour regular flirtations with excess as part of this 'circularity of ethical apprenticeship'. Ethical athletes learn to engage in exercises directed at their own development, enabling them to rule others. This is distinctly gendered. The capacity of young men to move into positions of responsibility is judged by charioteering and man-management. Their ability to win 'the little sports drama' is akin to dealing with sexually predatory older males (Foucault 1986: 72–77, 104, 120, 197–98, 212).

The sexual ethics of Ancient Rome attaches anxieties to the body and sport. Spirituality has emerged to complicate exercises of the self as training for governance:

> The increased medical involvement in the cultivation of the self appears to have been expressed through a particular and intense form of attention to the body. This attention is very different from that manifested by the positive valuation of physical vigor during an epoch when gymnastics and athletic and military training were an integral part of the education of a free man. Moreover, it has something paradoxical about it since it is inscribed, at least in part, within an ethics that posits that death, disease, or even physical suffering do not constitute true ills and that it is better to take pains over one's soul than to devote one's care to the maintenance of the body. But in fact the focus of attention in these practices of the self is the point where the ills of the body and those of the soul can communicate with one another and exchange their distresses; where the bad habits of the soul can entail physical miseries, while the excesses of the body manifest and maintain the failings of the soul. . . . The body the adult has to care for, when he is concerned about himself, is no longer the young body that needed shaping by gymnastics; it is a fragile, threatened body, undermined by petty miseries. (Foucault 1988a: 56–57)

But it remains a body in need of vigilance, in fact more so than before. In place of the excesses that preoccupied fourth-century BC Athens, first-century AD Rome is principally concerned with frailty; the finitude of life and fitness. The key to life is moral arguments that are imbued with 'nature and reason'. Exercises of the self are joined to this more elevated search for truth. Man has fallen from Eden, and he knows why. The repeated renunciation of desire increasingly characterizes his response to this descent (Foucault 1988a: 238–39).

These assumptions have spread across the globe with the rise of public education. Today, most young men living within industrialized societies receive their initial training in masculinity – their first self-conscious address as a gendered subject – through bodily and ethical regimes that equate body and mind: a 'visual economy' of public and private sites. It shows boys how to be boys and men. This economy came into being at the uneasy meeting of nineteenth-century rites of industrial modernity and auto/homo-eroticism/

sociality, of Muscular Christianity and nature cults. Muscular Christianity was a nineteenth-century ruling-class British education that combined the physique with the spirit, binding mind and body under the sign of health as a way to indoctrinate future leaders of the nation with discipline, service, and authority, through the orderly conduct and competitive but neighbourly ethos of games. Muscular Christianity had complete faith in the transformation of individuals through continuous exercise. The body became subject to a moral-scientific gaze, and pastimes were codified, in a doubling move of internalized self-monitoring and externalized intersubjective government (Hatt 1993: 62; Lewis 1985: 22; Hargreaves 1986: 13; Elias 1986a: 151).

Maguire's four types of sports body reflect a century of science applied to masculinity/femininity, with early Darwinism very influential. In the nineteenth century it was thought that women could only bear healthy children if they exercised in moderation (picking up an anxiety dating back to sixteenth-century Europe that excessive exercise would literally transform women into men). Today, three discourses articulate science with gender through sport. Categorization labels certain physical and behavioural norms as male or female, explained with reference to nature or society. Activities coded as male are evaluated to see whether they 'contaminate' women participants by problematizing their femininity. Sex-role analysis accounts for differences in the uptake of sport by girls and boys through socialization. And androgyny studies 'permit' intermingled behaviours across genders. In each case, conduct attributed to social groups is rearticulated on to individuals as norms that should guide each person. Against these social-psychology approaches, distributive critics emphasize inequalities of opportunity and power. A sociological model displaces a psychological one, but it remains a liberal position: as long as conditions are in place for equilibrium ('the level playing field'), whatever happens from that point is meant to be. Sport is in need of equalization, not transformation. By contrast, the left problematizes the overall historical, social, economic, and cultural place of sport, arguing that it mystifies labour oppression by diverting attention from 'real' politics: football on Saturday + church on Sunday = no revolution. An alternative approach to all of these is suggested by Aaron Cicourel: games are autonomous from what comes before and after them in social time. But Cicourel's position, as we shall see, in effect returns us to Lasch (that is, where we started this chapter): sport as a 'release' from the everyday (Fiddes 1991: 176–77; Park 1994: 70; Hargreaves 1986: 48, 30–31; Dewar 1993: 151–57; M.A. Hall 1993; Mitchell and Dyer 1985: 96–97; Cicourel 1964: 208).

Making bodies responsible and responsive to a calculating logic of profit and loss, of opportunities taken up and forsworn, helps to increase productivity. And yet, this control of the body cannot simply be read off against a prevailing mode of production. Standardized systems of production characterize all modern industrial entities, regardless of their economic politics. The management of time and motion is common to all. And the human sciences that define subjectivity, efficiency, sanity, criminality, wellness, and so on are relatively autonomous from the economy as discourses and institutions. Although sport is increasingly run on businesslike lines, and comprises castes that differentiate categories of person in violent ways, knowing this does not tell us about the systems of power that control the sporting body, the quotidian effect on it of power-through-knowledge. Here we need some additional history.

Sixteenth- to nineteenth-century Europe saw the population progressively subjected to penology, medicine, psychology, and sexology. As well as being made subject to these *knowledges*, bodies fell subject to *physical* discipline in prisons, hospitals, asylums, and sexualities. The distinctively modern component of this institutional and discursive power was a double movement that exerted control over both the inside and the outside of the body, rendering it efficient, aesthetic, and self-monitoring. Exercises were undertaken by both the controllers of institutions *and* those under their control, who were taught to internalize surveillance by identifying their own interests with corporate ones (Foucault 1979a).

This governmentalization views sport disciplining the body as, by turns, orderly and extraordinary, competent and excellent, fit and capable. Here, then:

> the body is also directly involved in a political field; power relations have an immediate hold upon it; they invest it, mark it, train it, torture it, force it to carry out tasks, to perform ceremonies, to emit signs. This political investment of the body is bound up, in accordance with complex reciprocal relations, with its economic use; it is largely as a force of production that the body is invested with relations of power and domination; but, on the other hand, its constitution as labour power is

possible only if it is caught up in a system of subjection (in which need is also a political instrument meticulously prepared, calculated and used); the body becomes a useful force only if it is both a productive body and a subjected body. (Foucault 1979a: 25–26)

This is the condition of modernity. It is insufficient simply to extract labour. The body must not be *forced* to work if it can be *willed* to do so. And the grand feature of modernity is that the will – an *individual* site of power – is elevated, even as the population – a *collective* site of instrumentality – increases. For Elias, the sporting subject embodies Europe's insistence that its citizens combine 'regularity and differentiation' in their daily conduct. The governmentalization of everyday life in Britain during the eighteenth century pacifies sport via the imposition of organizational and behavioural rules (Elias 1986a: 151, 173).

Michel Foucault discerns twin registers within the seventeenth- and eighteenth-centuries' 'great book of Man-the-Machine'. The 'anatomico-metaphysical register' details the relationship between body and self. This gains additional meaning with its uptake by a philosophy founded on the notion that thought brings the subject into play and is therefore critical to its formation, and by an academic medicine founded on the notion that this body can be comprehended by finding out how it operates. A second register, 'the technicopolitical', details the relationship between the body and social management via the overall population's wellbeing using 'a whole set of regulations and by empirical and calculated methods relating to the army, the school and the hospital, for controlling or correcting the operations of the body'. The registers merge in the eighteenth century in the concept of docility, which 'joins the analysable body to the manipulable body' so that it can be 'subjected, used, transformed and improved' (1979a: 136).

Consider how modern sport matches Foucault's list of systems for marshalling bodily activity. Timetables were adapted from monasteries to 'establish rhythms, impose particular occupations, regulate the cycles of repetition' in educational institutions, factories, and hospitals. In the twentieth century, they characterize the modern Olympics and the rise of sport's political arithmetic, the statistics of individual and team achievements. Timetables were historically connected to *'temporal elaboration'*, matching the passage of time with the execution of physical acts. A contemporary elaboration might be the motion between hurdles or the final step prior to reaching the long-jump board. The gait of a runner is carefully analysed and corrected in accordance with sport-science fashion, much as the gait of a soldier was managed in the seventeenth century. A programmed rhythm is set up from without, by experts, and enacted and monitored within, by the body itself. This elaboration of time via an articulation in the body is developed through *'the correlation of the body and the gesture'* (the famous Australian cricketer Don Bradman attributed his batting success to ballroom dancing). Each movement is supposed to be maximally efficient and indicative of the rationality at work in all other parts. This 'instrumental coding of the body' breaks down activities by time, gesture, and object into a syntax, known by the eighteenth century as the military manoeuvre. It determines when and how body-part and object come together. Today, we might think of the movements of a discus-thrower, a complex amalgam of signification, labour, and material. Power synthesizes the body and its task into an 'apparatus of production'. This disciplinary regime is predicated on a much more positive sense of time than its monastic antecedents. Time is potentially limitless. New efficiencies can always be introduced by splitting tasks into miniature components, deriving formulae for the quickest means of performing them, and observing the outcome. Once it has become a mechanical entity, the body can be renaturalized. In place of a prescriptive training that lays down movements in terms of a non-human physics, the biological starting-point of the person becomes central. The body as a 'natural' condition becomes the object of study, in order that it can form the basis for rationalization – that it can become 'unnatural' (Foucault 1979a: 149, 151–56).

The function of training is to 'organize profitable durations', regulating bodies to attain their full potential for production. Time and activity are accumulated inside people as capacities for rational and useful work, via exercise, 'that technique by which one imposes on the body tasks that are both repetitive and different, but always graduated'. Exercise enables individual subjects to be assessed against abstract ideals, other participants, and their own records. It provides 'a subjection that has never reached its limit . . . [a] political technology of the body and of duration'. The professional élite of athletics amasses 'profitable durations'. In other words, time and space are miniaturized in the cause of maximal output from minimal input; hence the pressure to use steroids and other performance-enhancing drugs in sport. The 'ultimate capacity of an individual' becomes 'the possibility of accumulating time and activity'. The labour process is divided, scrutinized, and regulated according to individual bodies and practices. Labour is split into small units, at the same moment as large industries and zones of knowledge determine its conditions of existence (Foucault 1979a: 157–62).

This increasingly came to be a national question in eighteenth-century Europe – a problem of how to make populations healthy and productive. '[B]iological existence was reflected in political existence' through '*bio-power*'. Bio-power 'brought life and its mechanisms into the realm of explicit calculations and made knowledge-power an agent of transformation of human life'. Managing bodies meant running a country. The very existence of the body came up for negotiation; it was transformed into a pliable organism rather than a living human, and an organism that was routinely problematized (Foucault 1984: 143).

Foucault sees this tension between power enacted *over* the body and power enacted *by* it as beyond resolution:

> Mastery and awareness of one's own body can be acquired only through the effect of an investment of power in the body: gymnastics, exercises, muscle-building, nudism, glorification of the body beautiful. All of this belongs to the pathway leading to the desire of one's own body, by way of the insistent, persistent, meticulous work of power on the bodies of children or soldiers, the healthy bodies. But once power produces this effect, there inevitably emerge the responding claims and affirmations, those of one's own body against power, of health against the economic system, of pleasure against the moral norms of sexuality, marriage, decency. Suddenly, what had made power strong becomes used to attack it. Power, after investing itself in the body, finds itself exposed to a counter-attack in that same body. (1980: 56)

This should act as a corrective to such celebrations as *Ms* magazine's 1988 valorization of the heptathlete and long-jumper Jackie Joyner-Kersee for being 'just what women of the 80s have been waiting for . . . as an athlete she is in total control of her body. And as a businesswoman she plans to maximise her potential'. Joyner-Kersee symbolizes the discipline and control of the body, its subjugation to discriminatory social relations. Knowledges and modes of produc-tion organize such a body – in fact they define it – far more than the virtuous meritocrat who 'owns' it. It is not incidental that she was said to have as 'her dream: to go to Seoul, Korea, where she would compete against other human machines' (Kort 1988: 31). This statement exemplifies the contradictory nature of the expressive and disciplinary sides of dominant sporting discourse. There should be no fit between 'dream' and 'machine': machines cannot dream because imagination is inviolably 'living'. But sport is a world in which dialectical play between the Romantic humanism of elaborated fantasy and the steely wheels of engineering is simply not permitted.

The methods of exacting this power may be used against the wielding of power; but that power then regroups. Foucault instances battles over masturbation and its prohibition across family, capital, health, morality, and education:

> The body thus became the issue of a conflict between parents and children, the child and the instances of control. The revolt of the sexual body is the reverse effect of this encroachment. What is the response on the side of power? An economic (and perhaps also ideological) exploitation of eroticization, from sun-tan products to pornographic films. Responding precisely to the revolt of the body, we find a new mode of investment which presents itself no longer in the form of control by repression but that of control by stimulation. 'Get undressed – but be slim, good-looking, tanned!' For each move by one adversary, there is an answering one by the other. (1980: 57)

Foucault's hope somewhere in all this is to avoid prescribing morality for others; instead one should make one's life an aesthetic event beholden not to law or religion, but to 'the pleasure of the other' in relation to the pleasure of the self (1983: 62–63).

If we start with the body, then sport – currently so competitive and commercial, and conventionally experienced as a pedagogic imposition – is a good site for such an ethics to emerge, as per the parodically competitive world described in the ethnographic film *Trobriand Cricket: An Ingenious Response to Colonialism* (Jerry Leach, 1976), where previously colonized peoples mock their imperial past by adopting, adapting, and subverting Englishness on the field of play as they rewrite the rules of cricket. Nor need we be tied to the androcentrism of Foucault's history. This older tradition of making the body testable and visible may offer ways of knowing the commodified, macho body of sporting modernity.

SPORTSEX

Organizers promoted the fourth Gay Games in a 1993 issue of *Advertising Age* as 'THE WAY TO REACH THE AFFLUENT GAY MARKET'. Fundraising methods included inviting lesbians to pay US $30,000 for a tennis lesson with Martina Navratilova. As the scientific management of sports training becomes more finely tuned following the appearance of biotechnology and sports science, the material stakes of medals, sponsors, and media textuality get higher. With surveillance both at the site of performance and far from it, the body is constantly made vigilant of itself. The writing of the ascetics of the Ancient world resonates today (Synnott 1993: 22). And the mix of commodification and self-aestheticization has powerful implications for everyday norms of being a person.

Consider women's bodybuilding. It has gone through major shifts over the past decade that show all these discourses at work: this is evident in the watershed film *Pumping Iron II: The Women* (1984), which records the Women's World Cup at Caesar's Palace. The competition is thrown into confusion by powerlifter Bev Francis, who juxtaposes her own refusal to 'go out there trying to cocktease' with accusations she is 'an overmuscular woman'. At a judges' meeting prior to the event, convened to deal with this new body shape, the chair explains their task to his colleagues:

> We hope that this evening we can clear up the definite meaning, the analysis of the word 'femininity' and what you have to look for . . . we're looking for something that's right down the middle. A woman that has a certain amount of aesthetic femininity but yet has that muscle tone to show that she's an athlete. . . . Women are women and men are men and there's a difference, and thank God for that difference. . . . We don't want to turn people on . . . uh, off . . . we want to turn them on.

Bodybuilding has developed since then to the point where men and women in competition enter what ethnographer, judge, and participant Anne Bolin sees as a state of 'liminality and antistructure' that problematizes gender binaries even as it heightens tension over the relationship of muscularity and sex (1992: 381–82).

Of course, the sporting body has always been bracketed with sex – Athenian philosophers expressed concern for the wellbeing of ancient men panting after younger ones in gyms. The connection has become more complex with time, as a few examples will show. In the 1890s, Oskar Zoth ingested liquid extracts from a bull's testicles to improve his cycling and swimming, and the last English FA Cup Final before the Second World War was allegedly decided by which team took monkey-gland tablets in training (the losers). Controversy surrounded Mississippi State University in 1992 when the football team castrated a bull 'to prepare mentally' for an upcoming game. Indian wrestling ascetics have long constrained the flow of semen to exercise power and authority: celibacy and the mat. Today, anabolic-androgenic steroids that provide testosterone are central to sport. Pressures on performance and the requirement to overcome chronic injuries have led to their widespread use. Weightlifting has become notorious since the spread of synthesized proteins in the mid-1950s. Steroids are officially proscribed by all international sporting authorities. They are dangerous to the liver and may cause cardiac damage and sexual problems. (The mad-weightlifter disease that reportedly sends users into 'roid rage' is unconfirmed.) The US Department of Health reported in 1991 that a quarter of a million schoolboys were taking steroids, mostly in athletic programmes (Alter 1995; Klein 1995; Marshall and Cook 1992: 308; Moss et al. 1993; Sabo 1993: 7; Lueschen 1993: 97). More on this later.

The male body is sport's principal currency. The boxer's or cyclist's photograph that is analysed to cut the body into tiny bits is more public and explicit in its evaluation than any comparable site of display. As sports move away from violence and towards inclusive audience strategies, the boxer is transformed or supplanted by the centrefold. The lengthy process of ocular invigilation that Elias has demonstrated, a progressive displacement of speech by sight as the critical hermeneutic method in early-modern Europe, at last moves on to men in the sexual way that colonized women much earlier. Male pin-ups are common today in teen magazines and even British tabloid newspapers. The 1993 Miss Wintersun contest at Surfers Paradise, the first step towards election as Miss Australia, was won by a man called Damian Taylor (Dyer 1992: 104; Harari 1993). The following year, *Sports Illustrated*'s notorious swimsuit issue featured men for the first time.

Sam Fussell claims muscles are 'the latest props of the dandy' (1993: 577). Sport allows men to watch and dissect other men's bodies in fetishistic detail; and so provides a space for staring without homosexuality necessarily being alleged or feared. The fetish of admiring body-parts ('look at those triceps') gives a scientistic pleasure and excuse. A man weightlifting at close proximity gives off signs of pleasure-pain akin to facial correlatives of the male orgasm, a sight otherwise denied to men who define themselves as straight. One lifter has said a good pump is 'better than coming'; no wonder male prostitution is as common in such gyms as the disavowal of homosexuality (Morse 1983: 45; weightlifter quoted in Shilling 1994: 144; Klein 1995).

The overtly gay sporting body is a complex signifier in a sphere where homophobia and hypocrisy are rife. Women's college teams in the US are regularly vilified in the media in sexualized language, and despite the significant number of lesbians in the former Women's Professional Basketball League, 'out' players have been harassed and fired. College coaches are known to begin the first practice of the year with the requirement players not be 'lesbian during the season'. Like Billie Jean King, Martina Navratilova lost major endorsements when her sexual practices became public, litigated knowledge. Out sports stars include former NFL (National Football League) running back David Kopay and offensive tackle Roy Simmons, major-league outfielder Glenn Burke, Olympic gold-medal swimmer Bruce Hayes, English football striker Justin Fashanu, diver Greg Louganis, Australian rugby league forward Ian Roberts, bodybuilding world champion Bob Jackson-Paris, golfer Muffin Spencer-Devlin, skaters Matthew Hall, Rudy Galindo, and Doug Mattis, and Olympic decathlete Tom Waddell. The names are few: intense but denied connections between sex and sport make the terrain risky, as Louganis' rejection by NBC showed when he offered his services as a commentator for the Atlanta Olympics. A member of the Canadian women's hockey team coaching the triumphant Mighty Dykes at the New York Gay Games was said to have dodged Canadian cable crews during the event. That's hardly surprising when films like *Personal Best* (Robert Towne 1982) suggest that 'lesbianism is just something you catch in the locker room, like athlete's foot', to quote press critic Rex Reed. The moral panic about girls becoming lesbians through sport extends beyond education and into allegations of compulsory homosexuality. In 1993 cricketer Denise Annetts complained to the New South Wales Anti-Discrimination Board that she had been dropped from the Australian national side for being straight; a rare opportunity for the women's game to gain publicity in the mainstream press. New team captain Belinda Clark retorted: 'I'd actually like to slap her around a bit.' Homophobia was at least helping to dispel the image of compulsory pacifism for women; but the incident led to a complicated nexus of public policy, private sex, and sport (Cahn 1994: 246, 266; Lenskyj 1991; Pronger 1990: xi; Reed 1994: 24; Pener 1994: 28; Rex Reed quoted in Russo 1987: 278; Blinde and Taub 1992; Clark quoted in Wilson 1994; Burroughs et al. 1995).

SPORT AND SOCIAL POLITICS

Since the 1920s *Middletown* study of middle-American life found that high-school loyalties developed and class differences slackened in Muncie, Indiana with the arrival of basketball, sport has been heralded for its integrative capacities. Sociologists have correlated suicide rates at Thanksgiving, the Super Bowl, the World Series, and the Fourth of July, and found lower levels than at other times of the year. But when researchers went back to Indiana in the 1930s, school-stadium debts had made it a Depression liability of horrendous proportions. And while self-mutilation may diminish during TV sport, reports of domestic violence by men against women are said to increase dramatically during the Super Bowl. More positively, the 1920s and 1930s found many on the American left using sport as a vehicle of local political identification and organization against the status quo. Battles were fought on US campuses between footballers and anti-war demonstrators over perceived structural homologies between Vietnam recruitment and college sport, while the Oakland Athletics were the anti-war baseball team of that era (Lynd and Lynd 1956: 212–13, 485; 1965: 291–92; Jarvie and Maguire 1994: 19; Cobb 1993).

There are clear connections between training soldiers and athletes, and between the strategies of generals and coaches. The classical military strategist Karl von Clausewitz described a trinitarian form to war and the state: material enmity, military presence, and political

leadership. Sport's version would be a national divide, team competition, and management. Consider some history. Pierre de
Coubertin founded the modern Olympics in 1896 to redeem French
masculinity after the shocks of the Franco-Prussian War; the
Mexican Revolution moved quickly to institutionalize sport in
the 1910s as a sign and source of national unity; and when the
Argentine Olympic Committee was founded in 1922, it promised to
work for 'the perfection of the race and the glory of conquering
what is noble, worthy, and beautiful'. John F. Kennedy established
his President's Council on Youth Fitness to counter a 'growing
softness, our increasing lack of physical fitness', which constituted 'a
threat to our security'. The Peace Corps argued in 1963 that sports
were a more productive terrain for its mission than teaching because
they were 'least vulnerable to charges of "neo-colonialism" and
"cultural imperialism" '. Perhaps, but sport can be serious business.
The 1969 Central American Soccer War broke out when the
Honduran government expelled Salvadoreans following a match
between the two countries. Some later revolutionary movements,
such as the Sandinistas in Nicaragua, abolished professional sport,
focusing instead on nation-building through a policy of sport for all
(Allison 1994: 92; Arbena 1993: 110–12; Shapiro 1989: 71, 74;
Kennedy quoted in Lasch 1979: 183; Corps quoted in Kang 1988:
431).

These anecdotes illustrate the utilitarian as well as the symbolic
side to nations and sport. A healthy, fit population reduces the cost
of public health, guarantees a functioning workforce, and helps
tourism. A recent Aoteoroa/New Zealand Minister of Recreation
and Sport referred to his portfolio as a route to 'social and economic
prosperity' through the promotion of 'active, physical lifestyles'.
He identified an additional benefit: 'being *into* sport' ensured being
'*out of* court'. This longstanding criminological obsession deems
familially based and formal sporting activities to be worthy,
integrative norms, whilst informal leisure is demonized. Even the
former Jamaican Socialist Prime Minister, Michael Manley (also a
distinguished historian of cricket) pushed this line. Here, male
violence is seen as a danger that can be pacified and redirected into
an appropriate sphere: literally, national fitness. (Miss E. Callinan in
Look Up! Plain Talks with Working Boys (1906) reminds her young
readers that 'the very word "recreation" teaches us that our play
should *re-create* us, or make us anew – fit for the duties of life'. At

the same time, she warns that playing soccer may lead to 'bad language', 'bad company', and 'public-houses'. The young man must ask himself a question: 'Which is of the most value – your soul or a football match?' The answer lies in what must logically follow: fitness 'for Monday's work or for God's house on the next Sunday'.) Just as schools have often used the gymnasium for discipline, so too has the nation. But more than that, sport becomes inflected with an ethnocentric, sociobiological notion of correct behaviour, whereby delinquency is associated with racial minorities and youthful muscularity. With diminished employment prospects in the latter half of this century, such moral panics are as much to do with governments preparing people for a leisure-defined poverty as with training them to work (Minister quoted in Volkerling 1994: 8; Agnew and Petersen 1989; McMurtry 1993: 422; Callinan 1906: 77, 81–82; Griffin 1993: 119; Scraton 1987: 169–71, 174).

The message is clear: good cultural politicians know the importance of sporting terrain. Take St Paul, who gave sport a key role in self-denial:

> Know ye not that they which run in a race run all, but one receiveth the prize? So run, that ye may obtain.
>
> And every man that striveth for the mastery is temperate in all things. Now they *do it* to obtain a corruptible crown; but we an incorruptible.
>
> I therefore so run, not as uncertainly; so fight I, not as one that beateth the air:
>
> But I keep under my body, and bring *it* into subjection: lest that by any means, when I have preached to others, I myself should be a castaway. (Corinthians I, 9: 24–27)

The first Olympic Games had been professional: in fifth-century BC Athens, victory in a sprint brought enough money to live comfortably for three years (Skillen 1993: 349). For St Paul, a business matter – winning the prize – was also a sign of self-mastery, especially for those wont to breach what they preach. This combination of finance with ethics is crucial: the body becomes simultaneously a source of success, a site of reward, and a subject of rule.

A *moral entrepreneurship* in sport matches its commercial side. Amateurism and educational policy run alongside commodification. They have frequently been in dialogue, but the outcome generally follows the money. Business borrows the language of ethical improvement and bodily perfection. These cultural rather than commercial technologies may be bound up with notions of fairness and intersubjectivity, but they are easily redisposed. Consider the official narrative of baseball. In 1905, Albert Spalding, an American sporting goods manufacturer, was worried by the (correct) popular belief that baseball derived from British children's pastimes. Anxious that this diminished its ability to be *the* national game, he charged a six-person commission with identifying an individual who could be promoted as its inventor. Abner Doubleday was named, because the witness to the commission who had the earliest memory of baseball saw Doubleday playing it in Cooperstown, New York, in the 1830s. Spalding publicized this as indicative of American exceptionalism: baseball was unlike the worn-out sports of the rest of the world. In the process, he no doubt expected to sell a good deal of equipment. Meanwhile, the so-called 'Progressive Era' saw the promoters of segregation, religion, and temperance policing (and where possible prohibiting) the boxing film, especially when it featured African-American men displaying skill and power superior to that of their white opponents (Gruneau 1993: 91–92; Arnold 1994; Guttmann 1994: 71–72; Streibel 1989).

We have noted that nineteenth-century Europe and North America saw a rapid codification of sports. Team activities were transformed into public sites for collective competitive masculinity. Men were trained to be loyal labourers or colonial/imperial masters, as Muscular Christians migrated to empires and businesses, spreading sports across the world, reincarnating the Olympics. The contemporary corollary is the process folding back on itself: much was made in the British press in the early 1990s of the fact that the English rugby union side listened to a recording of the Agincourt speech from *Henry V* before playing the French. The other side to this is the famous 'Scandinavia beats the Dead White Males' remark by TV commentator Bjoerge Lillelien after Norway had defeated the English soccer team in 1981. Unable to contain himself, he started screaming the names of the vanquished: 'William Shakespeare, Francis Drake, Winston Churchill . . . we've beaten you all' (Hearn 1992: 215; Maguire 1993b: 296; Lillelien quoted in Hoberman 1993: 22).

National mythmaking through sport is common across continents, providing ethical norms that argue for, train, and generate new habits amongst the citizenry. But fissures appear. In 1990, the

LA Times ran what has become an infamous interview with British Tory politician Norman Tebbitt, who charged migration with endangering the 'special relationship' between the UK and the US. He also suggested Britain impose a 'cricket test' on migrants: 'Which side do they cheer for?' would sort out whether South Asians in England watching the local side play Pakistan or India had adequately assimilated. In the House of Commons itself, Tebbitt related this question to death threats against Salman Rushdie, before warming to his real intention: keeping Hong Kong Chinese (British subjects) from migrating before 1997. After Hassiba Boulmerka won the women's 1500 metres at the 1991 World Athletic Championships, she was fêted by President Chadli Benjedid on return to Algeria. Boulmerka was denounced by segments of Islam, however, for displaying her legs on television, and subsequently moved to France, winning Olympic Gold in Barcelona under the pall of death threats. Indeed, many countries have refused to include women in their Olympic teams at all, for religious reasons (Tebbitt quoted in Marqusee 1994: 137–38; Jarvie and Maguire 1994: 175; Guttmann 1994: 129; Vines 1988: 49). During the midsummer 1994 World Cup, Iranian TV viewers were reportedly given a special montage: whenever US cameras cut to shots of the crowd, programmers in Iran edited in footage of people in winter garb from other matches, hiding decadent Western attire from their fragile audience.

The uneasy meeting-ground of nation, sport, and media can put significant political issues on the international public agenda, especially via the Olympics. Leni Riefenstahl's film *Olympia* (1936–38), for example, sparked debate about Nazism. The entry of the Soviet Union into the Olympics in 1952 produced medal-table rivalries along Cold War lines, nourished and analysed by the press. The black scarves, socks, and saluting gloves worn by Tommie Smith and John Carlos after the 200-metre sprint in the 1968 Mexico Games captured the world spotlight for African-American politics (if not the attention of the *New York Times*, which found room to report the event only on page 59). Later, minute-by-minute coverage of the 1972 Munich murders and political boycotts of sporting competitions by African nations, the US, and the USSR emphasized the deeply conflictual intersection of cultural politics and international affairs (Given 1995: 47; Goldlust 1987: 118).

Sport opens up major ideological differences to global public view, frequently via transnational protocols that go beyond chauvinistic individual interests. Our contemporary moment sees intra- and trans-nationalism (the Olympic, Pan-American, World Student, European, and Commonwealth Games, and the World Cups of soccer, track and field, and so on), while diasporic movements and First People dispositions gather momentum as sources of political and/or sporting power through protests at international sporting events and the global trade in players. The most concentrated and powerful intersections of nation and sport take place at these media-saturated, time- and space-compressed, international competitions. The nation and TV have been crucial sites for both solidarity and exclusion: here sport expresses, directly and indirectly, material conflicts, as in the long-term sporting ban on South Africa during the 1970s and 1980s (Nafziger 1992; Shapiro 1989: 78).

ON DOING 'WE'S': WHERE SPORT LEAKS INTO EVERYDAY LIFE

'Does it hurt?'
– Laurie Lawrence, swimming coach
'Yeah, it bloody hurts'
– Swimmers
'Does it hurt as much as this?'
– Lawrence, running his knuckles across a brick wall until they bleed

This brings us to a site that embodies the tensions between regimentation and excess which characterize the outer limits of the contemporary sporting body (previously analysed by Miller 1990). The 1988 Summer Olympics on Australian television was dominated by images and sounds of Laurie Lawrence, coach of Australia's only male gold medal winner, 200-metre swimmer Duncan Armstrong. Lawrence's body and brain were depicted, cut up, slowed down, analysed and repeated more than his charge's, a reaction to the fact that he screamed, cried, and dived into the pool during the medal ceremony. Lawrence's vicarious pleasure at what he called 'the animal' or 'the bastard' became metonymic for identifications of male sporting commentators and followers: this individual swimmer succeeds as an Australian, and I am an Australian, so I have succeeded. The commentary on the coach evoked the lovably larrikin male, admirable for his histrionic fallibility and spontaneity. 'He wanted to swear, but he didn't,' as one voice-over put it over a slow-motion close-up shown again and again in news bulletins.

Lawrence is a deceptively competent player in a complex system of signification and struggle. He is mystified here as a harmless, gormless, simple man. Most larrikins can be cultivated in this way, as carnivalesque puncturers of bureaucratic anality. But such an account is far distant from the entrepreneurial power and selectivity they exercise: Lawrence's tactic of keeping Armstrong on the shoulder of the race leader permitted a last-second victory through 'surfing' (Budd 1989). So once more, we see an awkward negotiation of Foucault's binaries of hedonism and control, with denial valued less than calculated risk and the capacity to ride boundaries. Profiles of Lawrence routinely work through this dualism, stressing mania and asceticism in equal measure. Australian newspapers sought out consultant psychologists to establish the state of Lawrence's sanity after the Games, citing his Oedipal references to Armstrong ('he did it', 'we did it', 'my boy') and aberrant behaviour, such as running around the pool, evading security guards, diving into the water, and interrupting the medal ceremony in search of recognition ('Dunc, Dunc, turn around. I know you, Dunc'). This interrogation anointed him as the king of instinct, disavowing the scientific management that is his professional day in favour of a convenient, if unstable, individualism. Armstrong, too, performed a self submerged in the waters of managerial charisma: 'We swam such and such a time. . . . Oh, I mean Laurie and I.' Coaches are key figures in health, vitamins, schedules, book learning, promotion, and intrasport politics. The history of coaching and sports administration coincides with the advent of time-and-motion experts. And the relationship of coach to subject is characterized as 'paternalistic authoritarianism' (Goldlust 1987). Coaches enunciate the world in which athletes live, presenting authoritative accounts or justifications of existing sporting practice. These pronouncements are connected to issues wider than sport itself, notably law and order and the motivation to work.

The duality of Lawrence's persona brings out the Janus nature of sport: its transcendent spontaneity and pleasure back on to an ordinary world of training and discipline. Structural homologies with industrialism are obvious to proponents and critics alike. Critiques come from groups traditionally excluded from public sporting space: women, First Peoples, minorities, and the disabled.

In his provocative comparison of rock music's progressive cultural capital *vis-à-vis* sport, David Rowe suggests the latter has been 'severely compromised by its fraternization with "straight" society'. Associations with the disciplinary complexes of school and nation have hampered sport's capacity to engage with resistive politics (Rowe 1995: 10); its acquisitiveness and self-denial represent religion and the work ethic. But contemporary sport is dedicated to 'Merit, Justice, Desire, Will'. For justice has a dialectical relationship with merit, and will with desire. These are central precepts of modernity: not merely its individualistic, accumulationist side, where the state adjudicates between citizens competing for the material benefits of life, but also the more collective side of the modern, with the desiring subject's wishes considered alongside the needs of others: the 'nice' part of teamwork and discipline (Early in Early et al. 1996: 5, 7). No wonder we find both leisure and transcendence in our paradoxically everyday involvements in sport.

Let us return to Armstrong and Lawrence of Australia. Armstrong wins the gold medal. We watch him on TV. The camera pans to the coach, who leaps to his feet and shouts, 'We won! We won!' At once, this is spectacular – at least for the moment – and also a very ordinary (perhaps even forgettable) event. But is there something in its ordinariness that turns out to be very important for understanding sport and culture? If so, an ethnomethodological treatment might bring this out.

But if we consider the general question of ethnomethodology and its historical relation to games and sports, we find that in the early history of ethnomethodology at least, games with rules appear as something of an *exception* to the everyday, where 'play' occurs according to the contingencies of the event rather than fixed rules. Games may even have been the paradigmatic instance of the non-everyday – the foil – against and from which ethnomethodology got its initial sights on the problem of the quotidian as informally reflexive rather than formally ruled.

In an early paper on trust, Garfinkel (1963) distinguishes between the basic and preferential rules of a simple game like tick-tack-toe (noughts and crosses). The upshot of this distinction is far from clear or fixed. Garfinkel mostly uses the distinction in order to mount a 'breach experiment', where preferential rules are embroidered to get people's reactions on the social-psychological level of trust. For example, he reports that it is not against the basic rules of chess to swap two black bishops with each other prior to a move – just a bit odd. Cicourel used Garfinkel's demonstration to distinguish between formal games and everyday events. Embellishing Garfinkel's account, he wrote as follows:

> The differences between games and everyday life point to the difficulties which the sociologist may expect to encounter when he seeks to measure behavioral states which reflect norms and to study the process of role-taking. One critical difference lies in the fact that in games timing provides a delimited context in which success and failure is to be decided, for accomplished play is what Garfinkel calls 'an encapsulated episode.' The outcomes of games, then, are not at all dependent on the development of later situations '*outside*' the conditions of play. In everyday life matters may not be decided for an indefinite time period. Or they may be re-decided time and time again. Another point is that it is misleading to speak of 'rules' and 'norms' in the same way that one can speak about basic and preferential rules in a game. The term 'rule' when used in everyday life does not carry the same precision and meaning that it does in a game. This is because events in everyday life do not have the absolute bounded conditions which can be found in games. (1964: 207–8)

The effect of this argument was to leave games on one side of the coin and everyday life on the other, though this was no doubt far from Garfinkel's intention. It brought ethnomethodology, wrongly we think, into line with the idea that game events are time-outs from the everyday. It made games look as if they were determined by fixed rules, with everyday life a site for the continual local construction and renewal of rules. In some respects, this was no more than a return to Immanuel Kant's distinction between determining and reflective judgment. Determining judgment works from fixed or basic rules to actual events (as games might be thought to do). Reflective judgment works from the particulars of events towards indefinitely revisable rules. So at the point of Cicourel's intervention, it seemed as if the everyday involved reflective judgment, while formal games were a matter of determinative judgment.

But that was a long time ago and in another country, and besides. . . . So now we might consider the question of how sports are actually done – as everyday events. The work of Anne Freadman (1988) sheds some light on this. She distinguishes between game and ceremony, a distinction that leaks. If the game is formal play within basic rules, then the ceremony is the frame that surrounds it: spectators, broadcast, interviews, drinks after the game, and so on. But, as Freadman shows, we can't have the purely ruled game on one side of the coin and everyday unruly ceremonies on the other. Both are ruled and unruly, and each is mutually dependent on the other. Still, there is a difference.

Both games and ceremonies have basic and preferential rules, some of which are shared. For example, the toss of the coin (in tennis) and the pre-race for pole position (in motor-racing) are both inside and outside the basic rules of the supposed game-as-such, suggesting that sports are both inside and outside the everyday. How can this peculiar double exist? May it have to do with such a strange (and also ordinary) event as a swimming coach saying 'We won! We won!'? Let's go back then to Lawrence's exclamations and look at how a pronoun ('we') hooks up the game to the ceremony, the sports event, and the broader everyday. If this is the case, then the much-honoured idea that games and sports are time-outs from the routine business of the everyday world will have some new question marks about it.

Sacks argues that pronouns have many different and distinct uses in addition to substituting for particular and known nouns. Dealing with the word 'we', he distinguishes between two distinct varieties. The first type is a 'listed' or 'summative' 'we', referring to specific persons, say Al, Dave, and Roger. In the case of listed we's, you get a contradiction if you say 'We do X' but also 'I don't do X.' That is, if you're on the list of persons who do such and such a thing, then, logically and practically, you've got to do it. If we can swim, where 'we' includes Al, Dave, and Roger, then it's false to say 'Al can't swim' (Sacks 1995a: 333–40; 568–77).

The second 'we', however, does not have this property. This is the 'categorized' use of 'we'. Here, 'we' refers to a social or cultural category of persons – a category, moreover, which cannot be reduced to a finite list. It's non-specific in that sense. 'We' might mean 'men', all men ever – dead and alive, and yet to be born. Then you don't get a contradiction if you say 'We're bastards' but also 'I'm not a bastard.'

Type 2 (the categorized 'we') is interesting, then, because it provides for exceptions, and talk of and around those exceptions can lead to all sorts of moral work. It can lead to talk of who's exceptional and who's not. So if we get 'Men are bastards, but my husband's not a bastard', there's a claim to positive status for the particular person in question. Likewise, if we get 'Lawyers are rich, but my lawyer husband is poor', there's a claim about the person's failings.

Interestingly enough, Sacks wants to say that these kinds of knowledge about members of a category are not strictly 'stereotypes' in the negative sense of that term (Sacks 1995a: 568). He argues that none of us can do without categorials as techniques for making the culture of everyday life run at all. Whether they're true or false, naughty or nice – and whether we're politically astute or drop-outs and bigoted – all of us work with the general things we know about 'we' and 'they'; on what we know about certain categories of persons in general; and on how we use them as explanations of ordinary and exceptional events. Type-2 knowledges, then, are 'protected against induction' (1995a: 336). Empirical evidence of contrary cases does not remove them from our vocabulary (or armoury) of cultural techniques. Indeed, contrary cases *cannot* do this *because* these categories are the very techniques that must already be in place for us to be *able* to find exceptions. Here and elsewhere, Sacks argues for this fundamentally technical nature of categories of person and their category-bound activities.

In fact, while still on the question of the correctness or incorrectness of these techniques, Sacks warns us that our political and moral will to destroy some of them because they can be morally negative may have more consequences than we know. To give his example: if you hear there have been eighteen breaches of civil rights in a particular state in the last year, involving unsolved murders of African Americans, then you can hear what category of persons it is that perpetrated the crime – in all likelihood, *ceteris paribus*, other things being equal. Or, if you hear that twelve women have been sexually assaulted in a particular suburb in the last month and that the guilty party is still at large, then you can assign that person at least a gender category and perhaps some others. Knowing the category of person who did it, in advance of inductive knowledge, provides an *explanation* once the category of actor is empirically revealed: it was a redneck; it was a man – because rednecks do that; men do that.

Moreover, these are not just something akin to moral stereotypes, according to Sacks, because they are not always used to do moral work. They can have quite practical import – for example in the course of careers advice and self-help: 'it's important to know that lawyers are rich so as to permit somebody who wants to be rich to know what to do with their lives' (1995a: 339). The argument, then, may be that these aren't actually stereotypes at all – that there may be no such things – but techniques in common use, components of a culture. The moral will to delete them (or *a fortiori* to legislate against them) is unsatisfiable: 'It might pay to examine what else would happen once you changed one of them, and consider whether you would like to change it' (1995a: 340). That is, if you somehow managed to change one that you found to be morally degrading ('Women are fickle'), you might affect a counteracting one that you wanted to remain as it is ('Men are power-hungry'). An Aboriginal colleague recently remarked something to the following effect: 'The Wedjelas [non-Aboriginal Australians] are always saying we get drunk or abuse women or steal, and stuff like that; so when they see a black guy, they say "Must have been him did it".' So if you get rid of the categories that 'they' (whites) use, you may also have to get rid of those that 'we' (Aborigines) use *about* them; things like 'They're always saying such and such.' A device in a culture, then, is nested within neighbouring devices: it cannot be singly deleted or counter-legislated.

Most of this extreme moral work, though, applies to cases of 'they'. Naturally enough, in such cases, category-bound activities are applied to persons other than the speaker. The upshot is not quite so problematic for 'we's'. But there is, nevertheless, a moral consideration. That is: 'we's' have to be done 'on behalf of' a list or a category. In the case of listed 'we's', there's some likelihood of a problem: the speaker may either be on the list or not. In the case of categories, the problem can be compounded. And this might, for example, show up in Sacks' own frequent use of Jewish examples. Does his own membership of the category make him somehow exempt from moral judgement? Either way the question of 'license' (being on-behalf-of), or 'representativity,' as Sacks calls it (1995a: 344) can be a problem when it comes to categorial 'we's'.

Some quite peculiar instances of this may be unique to sports. 'We' can do both listed and categorial work at the same time. Contrast these two examples from Sacks: 'A little boy announces "We're playing the Rams today!" You say, "Are you going in as fullback or tackle?" ' (1995a: 335). Here the joke works because the little boy intends a categorial 'we' while the (adult?) hearer provides a hearing based on listing: as if the boy were actually a specifiable and named member of the team. Contrast this example: 'A member of a football team can . . . say *in both senses* "We're playing the Rams today"' (p. 336; our emphasis). An actual player, then, can use 'we's' to do both listed work (via his team membership) and categorial work (via his affiliation with the club). In a sense, then, sports fans do categorial 'we's' and actual players do both types. This has a number of consequences.

First, it might explain a number of fan phenomena such as wearing replica team shirts. If fans are limited to categorial 'we's', they may still have a desire to be licensed to do the listed variety; in effect, to be closer to the team, to make their identification visibly greater than the mere rank and file entitled to categorial 'we's'. So, in that case, they may try to borrow predicates from the category of persons licensed to do listed 'we's'. If we [listed] wear red shirts, then 'We [listed-wannabes] wear red shirts' will distinguish the loyal fan from the others. And this is interesting because very few forms of identification outside team sports permit 'we'. For instance, even the most loyal fan of, say, the Rolling Stones, will not say 'We played well tonight' after a particularly successful gig. It will always be a reverential 'they'. Sports teams may be unique in this respect. They effectively up the ante for pronominal distinction among supporters. The only comparable case would be national identifications: such that it is possible to say 'We cleaned up in the Gulf War' without actually having seen active service. Going so far as to wear the uniform, however, would be another matter entirely.

Secondly, this unusual quality of team sports does not apply to solo athletes. 'We' (now meaning a list of helpers and so on) may be used by an individual. But few situations actually allow it. For example, on winning the Canon Golf Challenge in February 1997, Peter Senior reported the following incident of crowd heckling: 'I don't really know who he was, but he said I was gone as I walked up the 10th fairway. . . . After that I really got going. It spurred me on' (*Australian* 24 February 1997: 32). Now while a translation into 'we's' is just (if very barely) possible, it would be a very peculiar way of speaking. In fact, because it would have to consist of listed 'we's', it would seem to demand an explicit listing – or risk emulating royalty.

Thirdly – and here we come back to swimmer, coach, and broadcast – some sports lie between team and solo sports with

ne, normality and subjection'). They utilize the new forms of
dge to multiply and intensify the expression of power over
For example, adults who lack the ability to narrate their
and struggles to the satisfaction of psychologists are incar-
for failing the duty of disclosure that is the corollary of
enment freedoms (Foucault 1979a: 193, 224, 296; 1987: 23;
977: 152).

ult regarded madness as 'the Absence of Work'. And
culture is often thought of as intellectual, bodily, and ethical
, '*at a distance* from madness but *within distance* of it'.
culture is frequently condemned for enfeebling and distract-
public, and psychology gets hauled in to pronounce on col-
nd individual maladies supposedly caused by it. In turn, the
itself feeds on psy-discourse. The 'grey morning of tolerance'
med to be dawning for diverse sexual practices in the 1970s
essarily marked by anxieties over sudden change and the
ility of cheapened commodification: Foucault's 'movement of
consumption-tolerance' (Foucault 1982a: 73–74).
stance, US women's magazine articles on marriage shift in
0s towards sexual pleasure and high romance – though not
ily in combination – and away from self-sacrifice and
But such shifts bring their own disciplines and loyalties, their
rs and vocabularies of consent and orthodoxy. Far from
llyana-ish accounts of domestic bliss, the magazines of the
nd 1950s had depicted the household as a site of struggle
appiness and intellect were awkwardly exchanged for stabil-
conformism; perhaps a more realistic version of the hetero-
ontract than today's mantra, 'You can have it all.' Women
etail about incredible drudgery, not fantasies of professional
ntic fulfilment (Foucault 1995: 292; 1988b: 15; 1982a:
Cancian 1987: 163; Cancian and Gordon 1988; Moskowitz

gs are often held to exist in a state of grace, as 'true',
tionalized forms of understanding and realness. But emo-
known and spoken. They are part of signification, and as
ject to historical, spatial, economic, and cultural forces, just
planes or cable companies. Feelings are discursive con-
etermined by certain conditions of definition and response:
y and pity shift in meaning in accordance with changes in a
's view of 'victimhood, poverty, and the social contract'.

respect to 'we's'. Swimming is a case in point. Swimmers mostly
compete singly against one another, but they also swim in teams
(actually in relays and aggregatedly in terms of national competitions). In this respect, there is always the possibility that non-
swimmers such as coach, crew, and even family can get, as it were,
on the list. Categorial 'we's' may be available to fans, or indeed
(particularly in the case of the Olympics) to any person with the
same nationality as the swimmer. A swimmer is particularly entitled
to use listed 'we's' and may even do so to avoid the above-mentioned
problem of ego-references. But this then logically entitles others: if a
swimmer does a listed 'we', there has to *be* a list – with other
members. So this, finally, is what we think the coach is doing with
'We won! We won!' as he leaps into the pool. It's not merely the
excitement of the moment that makes him temporarily identify with
the man who has actually swum the race. To be sure, his usage is
problematic in terms of representativity (Sacks 1995a: 344) or
licensing. It is, perhaps, on the edge of legitimacy. Audiences bring
these complex, everyday, cultural knowledges to bear in viewing the
swimming event. Is the coach licensed to do listed 'we's'?; is he
speaking (even screaming) without licence?; or is he, just like one of
us (and no doubt the commentators and every other one of 'us',
poolside or back home), simply exercising his common right to do a
categorial 'we'? And on our decision, our interpretation, hangs his
moral character. Is he a legitimate team member, is he usurping that
right, or is he just like the rest of us?

Because this is where our moral decision hangs, the everyday
techniques of the sporting arena – in this case, its 'we's' – are, at one
and the same time, identical with the remainder of the culture, yet
also unique to sport. Sport is neither completely separate from
everyday life; nor is it quite *ordinary* life as usual. Rather, the two
leak into each other on particular and specific occasions; and where
they do, we're called upon to exercise line calls, to make decisions
and interpretations. Some of us enjoy such small controversies. But
the enjoyment is no escape from 'real-world' controversies; sporting
life as usual.

4

Self-Help/Therapy

[P]eople will regularly pick up on items that weren't specifically addressed towards them. It's a matter about which you have to be really sophisticated because people are vastly smarter than you'd ever imagine about these sorts of things. I offer you a sort of thing I found in my favorite magazine, *Cosmopolitan*. It's the most extraordinary magazine; it's been taken over by Helen Gurley Brown and turned into an unmarried girls' technical manual. And what I mean by sophisticated is advice of the following sort. How do you meet a rich guy in New York? A cheap way is, you put an ad in the *New York Times* for a slightly used Aston-Martin. You get phone calls from guaranteed rich guys, and you say, 'Gee I'm sorry, I sold it,' at which point the conversation can go wherever the conversation goes. Now that takes ingenuity. (Harvey Sacks 1995b: 131)

We believe that feelings are immutable, but every sentiment, particularly the noblest and most disinterested, has a history. (Michel Foucault 1977: 153)

'Your shrink?' I said, amazed. 'What the fuck? Can't the third world enjoy the benefits of analysis?' 'I, ah, just assumed you natural folk weren't in need of that sort of witch doctoring.' (James Crumley 1994: 129)

To carry a concealed weapon here in Texas, a person must pay a $140 application fee, have no history of major crime or mental illness, demonstrate an understanding of use-of-force laws and pass a shooting proficiency test with a .38 caliber revolver or a 9-millimeter semi-automatic handgun. And one other thing: the applicant must be in touch with his or her inner child. (Sam Howe Verhovek 1995: A1)

Real men don't get on the couch. (Spokeswoman for George Bush, quoted in Forbes 1994: 250)

This chapter is divided between an examination of advice books and therapeutic discourse, popular genres of self-help and ther-

apy that make a person 'subject to so dependence; and tied to his own identi knowledge' (Foucault 1982b: 781). Suc human sciences, which divide the subject cile those divisions. The human scien material production, and bodily mechar the subject within itself and from oth conduct; and the subject identifies as su of Jerome K. Jerome's 1889 novel *Three* medical manual and diagnoses himself a illness it describes, apart from housema akin to the internalized discipline discu

These practices typically accompany tion: the speaking subject (defined a working subject (from economics); ar natural sciences, especially biology). Pr internally riven or separated from oth the mad, the criminal versus the we versus the sick. These categories are p istrative decisions and apparatuses of i scientific knowledge. And self-directed a subject: gay versus straight, privat versus lear*ning*. Struggles for power tal individual: on the one hand, they asser they underline everything which make On the other hand, they attack eve individual, breaks his links with oth forces the individual back on hims identity in a constraining way' (Fouca

The raw stuff of human beings, th *become* individuals through discourse see in a specific instance at the close rites of passage from traditional so They are increasingly displaced, su symbolic by scientific accounts of pe join measurement and confession, as guilt and state authority. Epistemolo pretations deriving from experimen authority. But even as this looser moc hospitals and psychologists (Foucau

discipl
knowl
bodies
feeling
cerated
Enligh
Albee

Fouc
popula
lazines
Popula
ing the
lective
popula
that see
was ne
inevitab
growth

For i
the 196
necessa
loyalty.
gramma
being P
1940s a
where h
ity and
sexual
read in
or rom
73–74;
1996).

Feelin
uninstit
tions ar
such sub
like aer
structs,
sympath
given er

English-speakers in the Middle Ages, for example, experienced a feeling called 'accidie', now gone. Where English today has over 2,000 emotion-words, with tiny shades of meaning, and Dutch has 1,500, Malay has 230, Taiwanese Chinese 750, and Chewong just seven, while the Yoruba do not have words for depression. Translation and back-translation analysis suggest that even seemingly equivalent terms actually describe quite distinct states. Bedouin Arabs, for example, do not inquire about feelings or request line-by-line retellings of conversational exchange (Russell 1991: 426, 428; Russell and Sato 1995: 384–85; Albee 1977: 153; Pinch 1995: 100; Abu-Lughod 1990: 24–25). Are we to regard such languages and nations as more repressed than the English?

Nor should we accord the discourses of feelings a universally gendered status as the special province of women. German Romanticism of the 1800s enshrined Friedrich Schlegel's 'tender manhood', which conceived of men as sensuous, emotional creatures, unlike his ideal of 'independent femininity'. The Enlightenment era of rationality had its double in *Empfindsamkeit*, or spiritual sensitivity amongst intellectuals of both sexes. This called for the expression of feelings and attention to the passional. Men were encouraged to record their emotions in diaries and discuss the results with others. In short, they textualized and voiced what was required in a way that was historically and geographically specific. Closer to our own time, we might consider changes in the management of the American infant. Between the 1940s and 1960s, manuals on domestic paediatrics moved from describing the child as a machine that should be handled only when broken, to endorsements of spontaneous physical affection as sources of bonding and development for babies and parents. Anthony Synnott references the alternately contradictory, separate, and isomorphic influences on such developments of 'Freudian theory, psycho-therapy, primate research and anthropology . . . the Hippy movement, sensitivity training, somatopsychic theory, existentialist philosophy and, especially, the women's movement' (Schlegel quoted in Trepp 1994: 132 n. 25; ibid.: 132–35; Synnott 1993: 161).

The history of loss and grief in the United States is also illuminating. After the Second World War, public discourse over grief was muted. It encouraged people to overcome the strong, potentially disabling emotions associated with the death of others. This was quite different from the reaction after the First World War, when there was much noise about the appropriate means of responding to such powerful experiences. Death was not discussed as often in the late 1940s, especially when compared to the Victorian love of intense melancholy. Mourning was disrespectful to the dead in war, who had lost their lives so others could move on. Grief was to be transcended as part of accepting the many moments of separation that characterize life. Today, by contrast, we find intense therapeutic investments in the generation of new identities amongst the bereaved, enabling them to display full adjustment to new circumstances. Similarly, there wasn't much empathy around in the United States before the turn of the century: the word didn't exist in English until psychologists coined it in the 1920s to describe a technical response to emotion. Within a few years it had come to signify a form of aesthetic response to works of art, but only in the 1950s was it transformed into everyday language as meaning: to identify with the feelings of others. Today, psychologists struggle to identify and understand the mechanisms of empathy, even as commonsensical norms suggest it is a natural part of life. Empathy developed as a concept at the same time as psychotherapy developed as a profession, endowing an historical event with timelessness. There is a similar history to 'agoraphobia', a word which was invented to deal with new forms of public life and morality in the late nineteenth century. As European restrictions on women's freedoms were loosened by urbanization, the means of coping with this innovation in gender relations provoked new anxieties (Stearns 1994: 158–59, 250; Duan and Hill 1996: 261–62; de Swaan 1990: 146–47).

Early North American Puritanism stands alongside the frontier as a defining characteristic of the New World via control of the self, moderation of appetites, and calibration of the correct means of conduct, all achieved through devotion to a higher being who transcended base human desires. Mortals who wrestled with their hungers and drives might attain a life-world of the spiritual through proper behaviour which, in turn, would compensate for disappointments they might experience in material life. Individuals might even feel liberated by establishing and maintaining an alternative universe to the secular. Puritanism also connotes collectivity, of course, and a decidedly secular domain of law and community. The earthly universe expressed the divine universe. But the notion of a collective good was equally experienced as authoritarian oligarchy and plutocracy by those at the bottom of the social order. Puritanism's ethical technology takes on deeply pre- and pro-scriptive form that ramifies and intensifies secular law with a duty to obey God's (heavily interpreted) word. This code rarely made sense in terms of an improved everyday life for those subject to it, but appeared to be imposed from above. Lastly, Puritanism became a monetary technology, an index and guide to thrift and self-actualization via utilitarian calculation (Susman 1984: 41–45).

This decidedly material mode of salvation stressed the propensity to work, save, and invest rather than consume goods. It supported the formation of capital and the disciplining of the workforce. In the hands of apologists for and heralds of US nineteenth-century capitalism, dominant Puritanism endorsed labour and savings as the keys to building an earthly heaven and ordering individuals through the material rule of law and the interpersonal rule of belief. But from the late 1880s to 1940, Puritanism was held responsible for the personal and social alienation experienced by intellectuals. Writers began to wonder about other forms of self-expression than those mandated by the narrow corridors of the Puritan home. Freudian discourse made desire an inevitable and valuable corrective to the anal retentiveness of prevailing ideology. Aesthetic discourse contributed to notions of expressive totality and sensuous response rather than tightly buttoned shirts. Temperance and censorship were seen to favour certain categories of person over others. Secondly, a middle class was forming between 1870 and 1910, consisting of folk who were neither property owners nor proletarians. An intellectual class with managerial and scientific knowledge appeared. Science defined corporate health via the discovery of truths that could be tested rather than magically revealed from hermeneutic readings of great books. The corollary to this intense rationalism was a notion of human quintessences that should emerge in art: desires were to be expressed, not denied or displaced. Since the Second World War, Puritanism has enjoyed a revived status, perhaps as a reaction against corporate life and permissiveness, with excessive personal behaviour obsessively chronicled and decried (Susman 1984: 41–48).

There are analogous shifts today to the role of this Protestant work ethic in the nineteenth century. At that time, with the rise of capital privileging labour, the economy, and men (all in search of transcendence from the social relations produced by birth), self-help ideas emphasized love, family, and women. But this time, the transcendence is from social-movement politics rather than ecclesiastical bonds, as stockbrokers and parsons are supplemented by 'emotional investment counselors'. The 'ascetic self-discipline which the early capitalist applied to his bank account, the late twentieth-century woman applies to her appetite, her body, her love' (Hochschild 1994: 1–2, 13).

Many writers, from both left and right, are critical of self-help and therapeutic cultures (perhaps forgetting that the greatest number of these groups are devoted to coping physically with disabilities, not learning how to feel). Each revels in denouncing the solipsistic absorption and selfish individualism of those derided by Bill Clinton in 1994 as 'the worried well'. For radicals, the taste for therapy and personal growth is a bourgeois phenomenon, a luxury of commercial interiorization unavailable to those preoccupied with subsistence living which manifests middle-class guilt at the ravages of capitalism (though North American polls show growth-group members are three times more likely to describe themselves as conservative than liberal, Wuthnow 1994). It is also a reminder of the 'Red Scare' of 1919, when the US government was assured that psychotherapy could defuse the appeal of Marxism to the urban poor, and the later rise of behaviouralism, a model of person-as-machine that promised to manage individual conduct. Youth-culture critics argue that the pathologization of young people is part of the way social order and disorder are psychologized. Feminist critics object that the discourse of self-help encourages women to adjust to domestic care-giving. (Radical feminists occupied the offices of the *Ladies' Home Journal* in the 1970s in protest.) For conservatives, therapeutic culture represents the decline in spiritualism and the rise of secular selfishness, an elevation of self over service. According to this view, monumental self-absorption overrides obligations and responsibilities. Alternatively, self-help can be a badge of qualification for high office: the 1992 Presidential election found both Clinton and Al Gore sharing with the electorate their group-therapy encounters and past triumphs over familial alcohol, gambling, and cocaine use. Bush declined to participate in this confessional ritual. (He also lost the election.) Serious supporters of self-help link it to the mutual-aid societies of the eighteenth century, including trade unions, that provided citizens with buffer zones (self-selected ones at that) between church, state, and capital. Four out of ten Americans today belong to groups that are autonomous from their employment (church, sport, local improvement, group-grope and so on), again something taken as a sign of the strength of civil society by its proponents. These included Bush, whose administration sought to push back the work of government in educating, housing, medicating, and assisting poorer citizens on to 'the community' (Mäkelä et al. 1996: 13; Irvine 1995: 150; Moskowitz 1996: 66; Wuthnow 1994: 336, 71, 4; Musto 1995; Stenson 1993: 43; Prilleltensky 1989: 795, 798; Forbes 1994: 249–50; Riessman and Carroll 1995: 12, 176).

Lasch, whose views on sport we looked at in the previous chapter, claims that the failure of radical popular politics in the 1960s is evident from a retreat to the personal: 'psychic self-improvement' has displaced faith in popular democracy and collective endeavour and reward. Health food, recovery groups, learning the discourse of feelings, thumping drums, believing in Jung, not 'beating myself up', and 'having difficulty valuing you at the moment' may be perfectly reasonable activities – until they are 'elevated to a program and wrapped in the rhetoric of authenticity and awareness'. At that point they 'signify a retreat from politics and a repudiation of the recent past', as the New Left's struggles through youth culture and the horrors of Vietnam get displaced on to 'growth'. History is forgone: not merely the collaborative American past, but any sense of participating in the making of history. Unlike the returns to spirituality that characterize American religious cycles, this era lacks a sense of its own origins or the drive towards collective renewal. Confessing to large groups of people, be they readers, group members, cyber-pals, or therapists, suggests a self that depends on the attention and approval of others. Far from the 'rugged individualist' destined to build culture, this narcissistic subject relies on informal institutions for validation. Concerns about economic and social inequality are displaced by the therapeutic apparatus on to individual emotions and psychological histories (Lasch 1979: 29–32, 38, 43, 63).

Jane Shattuc, conversely, defends this move to the personal as a new form of politics. Two-thirds of daytime talk television focuses on psychological questions. In addition to the testimony of the public and the mediation of presenters, the genre makes significant use of social workers, therapists, self-help writers, and psychologists. The terms of trade vary between discourses of Freudian repression and unconscious drives and twelve-step recovery programmes (for which see more below p. 117–19). Free association, vital to the project of psychoanalysis, is off the menu, however; the unconscious must express itself directly in order to fit the TV format: a set number of segments, commercial breaks, and studio apparatus. And the psychologization of social problems has itself been brought into doubt by Phil Donahue's regular ironic intervention: 'All she needs is to go into therapy and everything will be nice?'; while populist appeals to experience debunk some of the very authority figures called upon to explicate topics of the day, as self-actualization encounters the psychological establishment. This is not to claim a comprehensive opposition, but a negotiation. The cognitive strand of US therapizing is well represented in lists of how to behave: Oprah Winfrey's patent guide to gender-sensitive schooling is a renowned instance, as rational emotive therapy is deployed to detect and treat hidden failings. Shattuc maintains these programmes are 'an arena of collective feminine experience' that promises 'a utopian vision of female equality', connecting women to one another and immunizing them against 'the stultifying nihilism of Foucaultian skepticism' (Shattuc 1997: 111–13, 116–17, 120, 122; Donahue quoted ibid.: 115). We'll encounter these tensions as we make our way through other such genres.

But first, a word on our own preferred method. A basic premiss for both ethnomethodology and cultural studies is that the world is criticized in terms of sociocultural affairs. For all their differences, this puts both at odds with the psy-complexes (psychology, psycho-therapy, psychoanalysis, psychiatry, and psychic healing and advice). These disciplines, by contrast, overwhelmingly assume that the ordinary world's fundamental units are an individual person's inter-nal states; what is social arrives, as it were, after the fact. It is an agglomeration of personalities. The psy-complexes explain or pre-dict (diagnose/prognose) social practices as functions of persons and their interior states.

Sociologically speaking, this is a category mistake where the unit in question is not a particular person or 'mind', such as when people are simply operating with standard inferences and predictions. This mistake covers a vast number of cases; so that what psy-help discerns is not what it identifies ('minds') but 'the way that society goes about building people', to use Sacks' phrase (1995a: 117). That 'way' is, however, enormously complex: everything covered by the term 'socialization'. But, as Sacks shows throughout his lectures, it is an apparatus that even provides for exceptions to whatever might be thought of as 'normal' socialization – wherever, and for whomever, 'normal' operates.

So our argument here is that the psy-complexes *add to* ordinary inferences that anyone in a society can make: the inner peculiarities of individual persons, consisting of their personalities, motivations, pathologies, traumas, neuroses, and so on. Then, these complexes delete the ordinary inference and offer a more mysterious account as the primary explanation or prediction. In this way, they work very similarly to conspiracy theories, alternative New Age sciences, alienology, and so on. The point, however, is not to show the psy-complexes to be 'wrong' – much as they may offend the sociological imagination; rather it is to show how, prior to the introduction of *extra*ordinary inferences, perfectly ordinary and mundane inferences must be in place, just as they are for people in everyday life, regardless of disciplinary specialization. At the end of the chapter, we sketch three cases in point. But first, some notes on the different genres of self-help texts and the culture industry most concerned with 'help'.

INTERPERSONAL MANUALS

There are three forms of interpersonal manual: general etiquette, sex education (including child-rearing) and lifestyle. General etiquette books advise on everyday living, specifically politeness and how to be popular. Sex-education books use medical discourse to describe people's bodies, moving between primers on manners and more technical treatises. Less aesthetic, such texts are alternately technicist and emotive. Lifestyle books reject grand divisions of art from science in favour of a holistic approach, seeking 'holes' in the person in order to reintegrate them into a 'whole' person. They present all problems as arising from internalized social expectations.

Publishers Weekly has charted the top-selling non-fiction titles since 1917. We have taken a random sample from each decade, and annually since 1990. In addition to war books, the inaugural list is dominated by biographies and autobiographies. The same is true ten years later, although history emerges along with *Why We Behave Like Human Beings*, at number nine. Since that time, these genres plus cookery, self-help, humour, and diet books have remained on the list. By 1937, self-help is a regular. Dale Carnegie's *How to Win Friends and Influence People* is in first place (sixth the following year) and his *How to Stop Worrying and Start Living* is popular after the war. A decade on finds *Peace of Mind* at number one, whilst in 1957 Norman Vincent Peale's *Stay Alive All Your Life* is in third spot, continuing a string of best-sellers since 1948, including *A Guide to Confident Living* and his massively successful *The Power of Positive Thinking*. *Games People Play* by Eric Berne, MD is third for 1967 (the third year in a row), while 1977 has *Looking Out for #1* at number two and Dr Wayne W. Dyer's *Your Erroneous Zones* fourth. Erma Bombeck's *Family: The Ties That Bind . . . and Gag* is third for 1987, by which time one out of every three Americans has bought a self-help tome. Generic twelve-stepper John Bradshaw's *Homecoming: Reclaiming and Championing Your Inner Child* is sixth in 1990 (a year in which he gave 200 speeches at a $5,000 per day rate); *More Wealth Without Risk* and *Financial Self-Defense* (both Charles J. Givens) are seventh and tenth in 1991; 1992 sees *How to Satisfy a Woman Every Time* by Naura Hayden at three and Gail Sheehy's *Silent Passage* at number nine; in 1993, Deepak Chopra's *Ageless Body, Timeless Mind* is at five, *Women Who Run With the Wolves* by Clarissa Pinkola Estes is seven, and *Men Are from Mars, Women Are from Venus* (John Gray, PhD) ninth. Gray moves up to second for 1994 and to number one the following year, as well as having *Mars and Venus in the Bedroom* at seven, while Chopra reappears at number four with *The Seven Spiritual Laws of Success*. In January 1997, the hardback edition of *Men Are from Mars* had been on the best-seller list 196 weeks in a row, and *The Seven Spiritual Laws* for thirty-nine weeks. Gray's first book had sold 10 million copies. In paperback, Stephen R. Covey's *7 Habits of Highly Effective People* celebrated its 308th week on the hit parade early in 1997. By 1994, over 300 US bookstores were exclusively devoted to 'recovery' prose (*People Weekly* 1996: 308–24; Hochschild 1994: 20 n. 2; Maryles 1997: 47; 'Paperback Bestsellers' 1997; Weber 1997: 29; 'Hardcover Bestsellers' 1997; Mäkelä et al. 1996: 223; Wuthnow 1994: 118).

This vast process encapsulates the 'commercialization of the individual'. It is also a *technologization* of the individual; for just as books are sold and group-gropes exchanged, the persons within them learn new forms of conduct under the sign and tutelage of multiple institutions and discourses. Gray, for instance, turned his best-seller into a successful Broadway question-and-answer show in 1997, when his *oeuvre* comprised five books, twelve videotapes, twenty-two counselling centres, thirty weekend seminars per year, and two web sites. Oprah Winfrey exposure catapulted to fame Ellen Fein and Sherrie Schneider's *The Rules: Time-Tested Secrets to Capturing the Heart of Mr Right*, a 'retro husband-snagging guide'. It recommended women hold out on sex, never telephone men for a date, and refuse to go out on a Saturday night if requested later than Tuesday of that week. Eight hundred thousand copies were on sale in the last months of 1996 and film rights had been bought by Paramount. A similar movie deal was done by Tristar for rights to an unwritten answer, *The Code*, which was announced as offering men 'time-tested secrets for getting what you want from women – without marrying them'. The entertainment audiovisual industries were synchronized for the first time with the interpersonal manual! Lest we view this as an exclusively 'New World' or 'New Age' phenomenon, it should be noted that Germany saw the number of self-help groups double to 60,000 during the 1980s, while the ten best-selling non-fiction books in South Korea for 1996 included three titles on sexual relationships for the young and three on defeating adversity to study at university. This references another key to the genre: directing workers to some mixture of toil, entre-preneurship, manipulation, and displacement of success on to leisure (Gerhards 1989: 740; Quinn 1996; 'Congratulations' 1997; Mäkelä et al. 1996: 25; 'What' 1997; Biggart 1983).

The etiquette book

This genre of publishing is often said to have begun with Erasmus' *De Civilitate Morum Puerilium*, or *On Civility in Children*, in 1530. Translations followed into English, German, Czech, and French. The book was adopted as a set text in schools and reprinted thirty times over the next few years. By the close of the eighteenth century, it had run to 130 editions. The subject matter of *De Civilitate* is proper conduct: how to look at others, present and maintain clean nostrils, dispose of spittle, and eat. Overt staring at other people becomes a key monitorial manoeuvre: sight is now the principal measure of character, with speech carefully subordinated and subjected to for-mal turn-taking rules. The same period ushers in, what we might now call, auto-invigilation, a requirement to evaluate one's own actions and appearances. In the late eighteenth century, the genre is named: 'etiquette' is a neologism standing for *une petite éthique*, or mini-ethics. This mini-ethics is a shift from the manners model of earlier. What began as a guide to courtiers became a more wide-spread model of new class societies: Reinhart von Knigge's 1788 work on courtesy is a break in the literature because it addresses the bourgeoisie as well as the aristocracy (Elias 1978b: 53–56; 1978a: 78, 82; Arditi 1996: 421; Wouters 1995: 120). This process gathers pace across Europe, most spectacularly in the nineteenth century, via 'new fields of social management in which culture is figured forth as both the *object* and the *instrument* of government: its object insofar as the term refers to the morals, manners, and ways of life of subordinate social strata' (Bennett 1992: 26).

In the US, the etiquette book began during the early nineteenth-century Republic, with extensive church involvement and direction. It developed into a combination of technically 'correct' instruction and a more utilitarian form of advice that was about making an impression in order to advance one's material prospects. Cas Wouters' (1995) longitudinal study of the US and Western Europe indicates that etiquette literature plays down differences in expected conduct between classes with the advent of welfare societies in the mid-twentieth century. Rules become rules for all, rather than markers of elevated position. Nineteenth-century etiquette manuals empowered women by declaring domestic conduct a key social grace. Authorially, the genre underwent a major change. Up to the 1890s, men had been the dominant givers of written advice, whereas women emerged as equal players from the turn of the century. By 1923, Emily Post's *Etiquette* was the top-selling non-fiction book, and Frances Benton's volume of the same title was fourth in 1956 (Lichterman 1992: 421; Arditi 1996: 417; *People Weekly* 1996: 309, 316).

Many etiquette books explain spatial and occupational differences: the announcement in the mid-1970s that the Germans and Dutch would henceforth accept 'social kissing'; how to behave as a tourist; how not to give offence; how to be an anthropologist; how to drive; how to drink alcohol in a restrained manner; how to act in court or Congress; how to avoid sexual harassment, and how to recognize it. Consider the experience of retiring for the night on the second evening of a visit to someone's home and finding on the bedside table a copy of an etiquette book, with the page dog-eared at the chapter 'On Staying the Night at Another Person's House' – what a useful pointer to how you are getting along with people, as one of the authors of the book you are reading found out some years ago! Alternatively, these works may be directly applied to economic advantage: social psychology claims that waiters who draw a smile on the back of their customers' bills receive a larger tip than otherwise if they are female, a smaller one if male, which rapidly attains institutionalization in the lore of employees (Rind and Bordia 1996).

The etiquette primer can be about having a relationship with oneself as well as others, concerned with fulfilment more than politeness. Arnold Bennett's *Mental Efficiency and Other Hints to Men and Women*, first published in 1920 and reprinted forty years on, gives instruction in 'mental callisthenics', 'expressing one's individuality', how to marry and collect books, and the distinction between success and contentment. The idea is to treat the mind like a body with less visible muscles – it too needs exercise, via 'culture'. This will 'round off our careers with the graces of knowledge and taste' through 'the cultivation of will-power, and the getting into condition of the mental apparatus'. Bennett's book is based on his response to letters from concerned readers who wish to improve themselves. He recommends reading to increase concentration. Learning poetry and prose by heart is a ' "cure" for debility', just as stretching in the morning is for the ailing physique (1957: 9, 13, 18–19, 26–28, 35).

Sex education

Contemporary sex educators identify sexuality with humanness. Sexuality becomes the truth of the person. It holds hidden verities that can be brought out and moulded into sociable conduct. Hence the turn in education towards explaining pupils to themselves – making them parent their future adult identities. This presumes that child sexuality has long been repressed by conventions and strictures. Sexuality is the basis for people's relationships, so parents, churches, governments, and schools must deal with it in the openness and freedom of the classroom. Another way of figuring this development is to discern a growing and powerful network of psy-

experts circling the child, analysing and provoking sexualized interpretations of conduct as a means of discovering 'truth'. This
alternative view of sex pedagogy does not see sexuality as a particularly privileged form of understanding people, but as one more
discourse in need of having its history catalogued. For sexuality is
new. Sex, of course, is old, as old as biology. But deriving whole
accounts of the person from limited observation of such acts is
recent; it needs Freud and anti-Freud, plus humanistic, experiential
feminism, behaviour modification, and a raft of other disciplinary
practices to sustain it (Hunter 1984; Hochschild 1994: 3).

Sex Fulfillment in Marriage is a typical artefact of this discourse. It
was written in the 1940s by a lot of people named Groves. First
comes Ernest R. Groves, a professor of sociology and marriage
guidance counsellor who is also 'Director of the Annual Conference
on the Conservation of Marriage and the Family'. He is credited
with having taught the first American university courses on how to
prepare for marriage. The second Groves is Gladys Hoagland
Groves, also a marriage guidance counsellor and author of marriage
preparation texts for college students and 'the general public'. The
third and final author is Catherine Groves, who has written *Get
More Out of Life*, 'a book telling how troubled people can find
help'. Social worker and marriage guide, she has 'had to deal with
many instances of domestic difficulties of various types', whilst as
'the wife of a newspaper man and the mother of two children' her
travails are self-evident (Groves et al. 1945: n. p.). Together, the
many Groves produced a book with endorsements from the *Journal
of the American Medical Association* and the *American Sociological
Review*.

The 'Preface' describes the book as part of the search for 'a
harmonious, progressive and character-making fellowship'. The
'Introduction', by Duke University obstetrician and gynaecologist
Robert A. Ross, declares '[w]hat a relief it is to find emphasis placed
on the normal!' in a way that meets the needs of those 'anxious to
know and practice normal things'. The combination of case-notes
and blood relations (the authors are revealed here as husband, wife,
and daughter) elevates *Sex Fulfillment in Marriage* in the eyes of
Professor Ross. The work is interdisciplinary, producing an amalgam of the duties of 'educator, sociologist, physician, biologist,
sexologist' in a study of the science of 'impulses' and 'innate good
taste'.

The Groves identify sexuality as the culprit in marital breakdown. Presiding over both 'a general sense' and one's own 'past', sexuality holds the keys to pleasure and individual history. It works against much of the labour of civilization, but that is also its wonder: '[m]odern men and women, healthy in body and mind, can taste all the flavor of the cruder forms of physical sex and much more besides'. But sex has been stigmatized into darkness, a space where everyday knowledge is inadequate. It is no longer instinctive, but 'an even more complex drive in the civilized human being'. To uncover the personal history that gives birth to and parents the present-day adult, we must enter into a dialogue with ourselves, a therapy without the social worker or shrink, where we come pre-shrunk, ready to read ourselves for hidden facts that lie beneath a surface of control, in the murky depths of desire. We must undertake exercises of the con-science, in the following form: *What were my sex experiences in very early childhood?*', *What was the influence of my home upon my sex development?*', *How did school influence my sex development?*', *What influence did my church and religion have on my sex develop-ment?*', *How was I trained in modesty?*', *What were my sex experi-ences during youth?*', and *What effect has masturbation had in my sex development?*'. These seven questions concern issues of social management, positioning 'sexuality' at the epicentre of everyday individual and collective life: the family, education, religion, man-ners, development, and confessional self-absorption.

The other side to these concerns is the science of sex, its physical aspects, where the 'arts of love' can be supplemented by knowledge of what the Groves refer to as 'sex equipment and its functioning'. Women are criticized for having 'vague ideas' about 'their own sex equipment' and are recommended to explore themselves with a mirror. By contrast, men are 'franker,' and their 'equipment more obvious'. Nevertheless, even a strong awareness of their 'equipment' frequently leaves '[t]he American husband . . . criticized as a poor lover'. Sexually incompetent men must learn the gift of variety. As the Groves tell us:

The great musician does not endlessly play over and over the same composition. His preferences change. He is a great artist because he makes what his skill produces accord with his inner feeling. Thus it is with the true lover.

This is a liberal document, typical of the 1940s: it recommends the selection of sexual positions on the basis of pleasure, and acknowledges the importance of women having financial independence from men. Physical abandon is taken to signify a successful marriage. The negative side to this is the increasingly heterosexist discourse that accompanies it, attacking same-sex love with vigour, as the divorce rate and open homosexual activity grew. Post-Second World War experts connect these developments and attribute them to sexual maladjustment. The solution is to rearticulate sex and love, rather than keeping them apart as in the Victorian era.

Attempts to scientize sex in the popular mind are fully achieved with the publication of the Kinsey studies in 1948, when *Sexual Behavior in the Human Male* is the fourth biggest non-fiction seller; 1953 sees *Sexual Behavior in the Human Female* at number three. Helen Gurley Brown's *Sex and the Single Girl*, ninth best-seller for 1962, combines the new findings on pleasure (and dissatisfaction) with an interest in evoking and charting a new morality, while William Howard Masters and Virginia E. Johnston's *Human Sexual Response* legitimizes clitoral orgasm *en route* to number two four years later. By the end of the decade, finding a way to understand and satisfy is on the agenda: 1970 has David Reuben, MD's *Everything You Always Wanted to Know about Sex but Were Afraid to Ask* and *The Sensuous Woman* by 'J' in first and third spots respectively, whilst 'M''s *The Sensuous Man* is first the next year and Dr Reuben's *Any Woman Can!* comes fifth, with *The Joy of Sex* by Alex Comfort charting in 1973, and its successor *More Joy* the next year. A survey of adult sex manuals to 1980 finds three basic models for women and sex: 'different-and-unequal, humanistic sexuality, or sexual autonomy'. Women move from finding sex an unpleasurable duty, through seeing sex as a required essence of personhood, to the idea that pleasure can be achieved without submission to, and indeed without the presence of, men. Sex changes from an anthropological and social topic to a biological and autotelic one (Weinberg et al. 1983: 312, 315; *People Weekly* 1996: 314–15, 317–20).

We can see these trends in such books as *Woman's Orgasm: A Guide to Sexual Satisfaction* (Kline-Graber and Graber), from the mid-1970s. This could easily be read as an example of the tentacles of medicine and the psy-complexes making their way across women's bodies. Alternatively, we might understand it as a technical tool dealing with issues that cannot be safely and easily left up in the air, as women's orgasms *are* routinely problematized (by definition, frequency, or method). The fetishization of sexuality has recently turned itself on to men's bodies in politically fascinating ways. John Davidson's *Cleo* article, 'Does Penis Size Really Matter? One Guy Gets Honest', comes with a measuring apparatus to determine whether a man's penis is 'SMALL' (1–10 centimetres), 'AVERAGE' (11–20 cm), 'IMPRESSIVE' (21–25 cm), or 'OUCH' (26 cm and counting) (1992: 69). In January 1996, the magazine's TV campaign comparing penis sizes was criticized by the Australian Advertising Standards Council. These developments replicate the lines of force long drawn over women's bodies that specify 'correct' measurements of breast, waist, and hip and 'healthy' sexual response.

Lifestyle

That leads us to the third and last of our categories, the lifestyle book. It derives in part from the moment in the 1960s when sex and love are partially disarticulated in advice literature, as casual sexual encounters increase along with birth control and political activity by gays and lesbians. These supposedly greater freedoms do not produce happier marriages or less worried people, despite efforts to use sex as a vehicle to wellness. That failure does not, however, serve to question the concentration on sexuality as a key to happy living. Instead, more and more publications focus on the topic, albeit moving beyond directly sex-related matters to interlace those concerns with psychologized versions of early manners manuals, as per Erasmus. In the 1930s, European and North American etiquette books begin an epistemic shift of great proportions: by the end of the 1960s, an exuberant efflorescence of feeling is prescribed in place of restraint in search of correct behaviour (Gerhards 1989: 176–77).

This awkward change really starts with singer Pat Boone's memorable *'Twixt Twelve and Twenty*, in which he endorses the maternal beatings received during his teenage years. This caring and sharing family history propels the book into second spot in US best-seller lists for 1958 and first the following year (the follow-up, *Between You, Me and the Gatepost*, is tenth in 1960). The message is that feelings are important, if somewhat inscrutable – and who could pass up a damned good thrashing from a devoted parent when suffering adolescent confusion? By 1965, a cross-over between etiquette and emotional interiority has made psy-complex texts into regular sales leaders. Following the success of *Games People Play*, Thomas Harris' *I'm OK, You're OK* is in the top-ten sellers from 1971 to 1973, and Nena and George O'Neill's *Open Marriage* posts good figures (close to two million sold over the decade). By the mid-1970s, the US offers 164 different brand-names of therapy. Twenty years on, the transactional analytic theory of ego states must be parroted by applicants for gun permits in Texas, who are instructed that the 'Make my day' line from *Sudden Impact* (Clint Eastwood 1983) exemplifies aberrant 'inner child behavior' (*People Weekly* 1996: 316, 319; E. Ross 1980: 109; Gerhards 1989: 77; Verhovek 1995).

The media have been critical bearers of the therapeutic message. Consider multiple personality disorder (MPD). As Ian Hacking puts it, '[i]n 1972 multiple personalities were almost invisible'. But books and TV talk shows about multiple personality disorder, along with its (disputed) clinical uptake, led to an explosion within people: the average US number of 'multiples' was twenty-seven personalities per body ten years later. The disorder became tied to rising interest in child abuse (1961–) and child sexual abuse (1975–), while the late 1980s concern with Satanism provided additional stimulus. Final acceptance of MPD followed the 1990 conviction for rape of a Wisconsin man following sex instigated by a woman, on the grounds that he was aware of another, 'motherly' side to her than the one that consented to and claimed to have enjoyed sex with him. Each of her personalities was sworn in by the judge to testify. Gloria Steinem mused about the pleasures of having several different menstrual periods each month, arguing that the 'disorder' should be renamed a 'gift'. Subscribers to *Dissociation*, journal of the International Society for the Study of Multiple Personality and Dissociation, receive a diploma with instructions to 'display your professionalism. Be proud of your commitment to the field of multiple personality and dissociative disorders' (Hacking 1992: 3, 8–9, 17; Nathan 1994; 77–78, 82, 85, 103; Society quoted in Hacking 1992: 5).

More routine problems have also proved popular. Robin Norwood's 1985 manual on *Women Who Love Too Much*, a book about addictive relationships (medicine meets friendships and families), sold close on three million copies in two years. Related titles include *Men Who Hate Women and the Women Who Love Them* (S. Forward, 1986), *Women Men Love, Women Men Leave* (C. Cowan and M. Kinder, 1987), and *Smart Women, Foolish Choices* (C. Cowan and M. Kinder, 1985). Their message is that women should be less obsessed, easier and lighter in their touch, less emotionally demanding, and not endeavour to change men. In his study of the communities that read these books, Paul Lichterman finds middle-class people with clear ambivalences about their purchases. They neither embrace nor resist the messages, but assimilate them along with numerous other inputs into their lives, forming a 'thin culture'. The precepts of popular psychology are 'adopted loosely, tentatively, sometimes interchangeably, without enduring conviction'. When Lichterman asks his sample of readers who would be unlikely to join them in consuming such objects, the responses are: 'someone who is afraid to be open . . . someone who is not willing to face up to their problems [and] . . . still in the dark ages'. Such texts and their readers characterize non-readers of the genre as ethically incomplete. But these willing explorers of their psyches are not very reliable narrators of what they read, recalling very little content. The books are emblems of an attitude, signs of a willingness to think about inner truths. They do not present a route to salvation via their subject-matter. As one reader spectacularly says: 'you could read *War and Peace* and that's self-growth in another way'. These are limited technologies, or matrices of popular reason, used by their readers to deal with specific problems. They are not elevated to holy writ and are understood as consumer objects circulating in the sphere of merchandising and product differentiation. The loose affiliation of the readers is a sign in part of their multiple demographic backgrounds. At the same time, the fact that readers generally come to the genre after emotional relationships have broken up indicates a search to understand personal failure (Jimenez and Rice 1990: 16–18; Lichterman 1992: 444 n. 1, 421–22, 426, 428–30, 439).

The readership is clearly gendered. One publisher that sold three million books on codependency in the US in 1990 claimed women were 80 per cent of the market. These books are often said to divide between '*the psychological and the retrofeminist.*' For critics, each represents a retreat from, or at least some compromise of, feminist principles of equality. As per *The Rules*, many such books operate with an infantilized model of masculinity: men are isolates, hope-lessly lost in fantasies of independence, who must be tricked into commitment through denial and manipulation. Women, by contrast, are aware of their fundamental neediness and are encouraged to get their way through a combination of psychological theories about gender difference and turning against feminism in favour of com-forting and exciting men. Consider codependency, Melody Beattie's 1986 invention in *Codependent No More*. It explains why the intimates of alcoholics, workaholics, shopaholics, and countless other compulsive types remain with them rather than walking out. There are now over 3,000 Codependents Anonymous (CoDA) groups throughout the US. CoDA manages an interesting dialectic between politics and the psyche: on the one hand, subservience to others' needs is condemned as unequal and damaging; but its explanation is resumed to interiority, to psychological disposition rather than social subjectivity. The discourse is marked out by its anti-institutionalism: churches, schools, and families made these problems, and they cannot solve them – only the company of our fellows can take us away from codependency. Bradshaw's patent causal phrase is 'poisonous pedagogy' (Irvine 1995: 145, 147, 149; Rice 1992: 337, 344; Jimenez and Rice 1990: 8, 12; Bradshaw quoted in Rice 1992: 349).

Something very similar to the call for an unyielding commitment to physical fitness (noted in Chapter 3) is happening: women are endlessly in need, according to this literature, of advice on feelings. The supposedly direct line between the self, intersubjectivity, and happiness that comes from the supposedly natural connection of women to the realm of emotion paradoxically requires massive training, an unending intellectual guidance that sees readers and clients always in need of the next publication or therapeutic session (Hochschild 1994: 8–9). The new masculinists among us hunt enviously for similar unities between body and self, places for 'reclaiming your original potential'. The 'development and integra-tion of body, mind, and emotions' will restore the natural aptitudes and tastes distorted by modernity. *Accessing the King in the Male Psyche* (Moore and Gillette 1992) can be done, for example, via *The Warrior Athlete* (Millman 1979). The contemporary era is full of passive men claiming they want to be emperors, but their weakness drives women away. *Newsweek* announced 'the first postmodern social movement' in 1991: Robert Bly's followers looking within for the lost monarch. As Carol Gilligan says, where the 'feminist movement has held men responsible for their violence and privilege . . . [, t]he mythopoetic men's movement has embraced men as wounded' (Moore and Gillette 1992: 25–27; Millman 1979: viii; E. Ross 1980: 118; *Newsweek* quoted in Boscagli 1992–93: 71; Gilligan 1997).

Some of this is rooted in Jung's uptake of Greek and Roman mythology as a universal, transhistorical truth about masculine and feminine bases to personality, a 'collective unconscious' that animates everyone. Other accounts derive from middle-class re-actions against feminist challenges to male authority and privilege. Sometimes this has been extremely misogynistic and anti-feminist; at other moments, it has been expressed as envy of women's 'feelings' discourse, their unity, and their claims to expressive totality. One wing became 'Men's Liberation', the other 'Men Against Sexism'. Both sides are liable to stress the difficulties of being a man, the pain of leadership, the confusion of roles 'under' feminism, the vacuum of authority and direction, and the need to 'share'. Of course, there are revisionist positions on this: Francesca M. Cancian argues that what counts as loving conduct has been erroneously feminized in the US by identifying love with the announcement of feelings rather than the instrumental expressions of helping or fucking. She favours equal value being placed on both sides to love (Cancian 1986: 692).

THERAPY DISCOURSE

What of professional therapy? Psychiatry has twice announced breakthroughs that appeared to guarantee its stature, during the nineteenth century and again in the 1960s. First, moral treatment and the 'talking cure' (named by a patient of Freud's, Bertha von Pappenheim), then pharmacology and community care (JFK's promise of 2,000 community mental health centres and the American Psychiatric Association's in-house 1963 declaration that the profession was ready to 'inherit the earth') were thought to offer deliverance. This has been a shift – winding, incomplete, and frequently circular – from religious judgement and confessional technique to medicalized chemical intervention and deinstitution-alized help, from bucolic surrounds and elongated couches to pill-dispensing hospitals and returns to nature (Musto 1995; Shattuc 1997: 114).

Whereas most academic psychology maps mental processes on to behavioural conduct in an empirical way, psychoanalysis focuses a priori on desire as the driving force of all acts, whether consciously or otherwise. It depends on two developments: the elevation of confession beyond its religious and penal origins and the 'medicalization of sexuality'. The contradictory dialectic of inhibitions on speech (etiquette) and 'strong incitations to speak' (recovery sessions) gets worked over in the notion that what is repressed – desire – finds ways to speak up no matter what forms of silence are favoured. The truth of sex is routinely associated with confession. Protestantism, the pedagogy of the eighteenth century, nineteenth-century medicine, and psychoanalysis combine to move confession from the special rituals of the Catholic church to fully governmentalized and commodified forms of talk and understanding. When psychiatrists are deciding whether to hospitalize someone on the grounds of madness, they frequently ask questions and receive answers rather than administering physical or written tests, with patients indirectly instructed in what counts as madness and sanity by the direction of these queries in what Kevin Stenson calls 'talk among *as if* equals'. It requires clients to account for themselves via linguistic markers such as 'I mean' and 'so', which are just as crucial as narrative drive or historical validity (Frosh 1989: 250; Foucault 1979b: 73; 1988c: 16; 1984: 63; Bergmann 1992: 137; Stenson 1993: 53; Gerhart and Stinson 1994).

What of all this desire? Psychoanalytic 'talk' is 'intimate', something that 'socially independent' persons 'must conceal from other people'. Our desire to have 'a homogeneous personality' means we fail to 'admit' this truth even to ourselves. Psychoanalysis is constructed around 'psychological defence', a self-protection that fails to deal with particular difficulties in the present and so must be encouraged to disclose travails buried in history (Freud 1982: 42–44; Foucault 1987: 36). Freud insists that 'mental processes are in themselves unconscious'. He argues that 'psychoanalysis cannot avoid raising this contradiction; it cannot accept the identity of the conscious and the mental'. Feelings, thoughts, and desires are mental, to the extent that they can be known consciously. But they have unconscious components as well. A constant struggle is under way between 'the pressure of the exigencies of life' and 'the satisfaction of the instincts'. For Freud, 'civilization is to a large extent being constantly created anew, since each individual who makes a fresh entry into human society repeats this sacrifice of instinctual satisfaction for the benefit of the whole community' (1982: 46–47).

Dreams are Freud's principal means of 'finding a hidden sense in something'. The chances are that a man confused as to the meaning of a dream '*does* know what his dream means: *only he does not know that he knows it and for that reason thinks he does not know it*'. Interpretation imbued with analysis is essential to deal with the 'strongly emotional thoughts and interests' informing the 'unconscious', which Freud called 'complexes'. Interpretation combines the 'manifest' and the 'latent' to produce an integrated account of dreams (1982: 115, 119, 130, 138, 150–51).

The 'Oedipus complex' is the key to forming adult sexuality and conduct. It explains the rivalry between people of the same sex, which derives from each son's 'special affection' for his mother, to the point of believing he owns her. This then casts his father in the role of a rival. For her part, a daughter regards her mother as an obstacle in the way of an 'affectionate relation' with her father. The complex refers to a Greek myth in which a son kills his father and marries his mother, despite trying to avoid doing these things – he has been warned of them by oracular decree. When he discovers that he has made the prediction come true, Oedipus tears his eyes out. Freud did not presume that the Oedipus complex provided a total understanding of parent–child relations, but saw it as a necessary moment in each child's 'mental life' (1982: 243–44, 373, 375). After an initial belief that the daughter is literally seduced by an incestuous father, Freud claims such memories are fantasies (the announcement in the early 1980s that he had secretly changed his mind was crucial to the formation of Recovered Memory Syndrome, a popular way of retrieving lost memories of parental mistreatment).

The 'castration complex' is the child's reaction to threats aimed at stopping early sexual activity. It relates to little boys' disturbance when they discover little girls lack what Freud calls 'such a precious portion'. This discovery soon turns into a threat; the little boy might lose the organ of delight. 'He comes under the sway of the castration complex' at this time. By contrast, little girls 'feel greatly at a disadvantage' and 'envy boys'. They 'develop a wish to be a man' (Freud 1982: 245, 416, 359–60).

These bizarre assumptions about all children derived from case histories of grown-ups. As Foucault has said, 'psychoanalysis believes that it can write a psychology of the child by carrying out a pathology of the adult'. Academic psychologists chastise psycho-analysts for leaping from the reminiscences of a handful of adults about their childhood to rules about what children universally experience, especially since that experience is allegedly unconscious. Theorists reply that the analytic encounter recreates the tensions and struggles of childhood, with clients transferring negative feelings for their parents on to analysts. These powerful emotions, frequently at work in a hidden way, can then be directly encountered and changed. Psychoanalytic therapy wants nothing less than a compre-hensive restructuring of the subject, in accordance with this totaliz-ing Oedipal account. Psychological therapy, by contrast, is limited in its design and claims, concentrating on behavioural techniques to cope with familiar discomforts or a cognitive focus to combat ill-feeling through rationality (Foucault 1987: 19; Frosh 1989: 67–69, 254–55).

In addition to these models, there are therapies that draw upon the principal debates in the area of child development and the acquisition of gendered conduct. Two theses predominate. One argues that the absence of fathers from child-rearing leads girls to identify with mothers and boys to 'identify' with themselves, becom-ing anomic, wandering subjects in the process. This is then said to generate adult sexual difference: where women find individuation and separation from men difficult, men experience the reverse, fleeing intimacy and togetherness. Different intersubjective ethics of everyday life supposedly follow from these distinctions. Women have an 'ethic of care' whereby they assume responsibility for others. Men function via an 'ethic of justice', preferring abstract principles of rightness to the guidance of embodied human experience. And of course there is volunteer therapy, where non-professionals are given basic non-directive, client-centred skills of conversation and are encouraged to break down the walls between client and service generated by the institutions and discourses of professionalism. The common result is 'helper's high', when counsellors report heightened pleasure from being helpful, along with improved personal health

(Jimenez and Rice 1990: 14–15; Riessman and Carroll 1995: 159–60).

SELF-HELP

Self-help is somewhere in between psychology and psychoanalysis. On the one hand, like psychology it privileges the empirical, experiencing subject, favouring the expression of feelings without any necessary mapping of them on to the unconscious. But it is equally caught up in narrative form, as per psychoanalysis: self-help, like Freudianism, likes nothing better than a good story.

Critics write off the 'awareness movement' as a money-making venture that takes a particular theorization of the self as a guide to improvement and growth. Again, it sees a long-term process at play. Consider a recent analysis of Dutch and German magazine advice columns over four decades. Until the mid-1960s, they recommended silence on the subject of feelings, shifting gradually from that time into a directive to 'own' emotions at all costs. We can see a process that codifies rules for self-conduct to formalize a training in how to be 'natural'. This even extends to instructions on how to discover what is 'already' there (Gerhards 1989: 740, 742–43). There are important connections here to 'the subculture of psychotherapy', which seeks to 'facilitate self-growth, self-understanding, and a . . . change in self-perceptions and functioning'. It is worth noting that such practices are conventional in the bigger US urban centres, as well as in Paris, Buenos Aires, and Sydney. But you'd go a long way in search of them in Ireland, India, or Iran, where religion would seem to do that job ('Now' 1997).

One of the high priests of populist feeling and experience is Carl Rogers. He is associated with the 'uh-huh' school of helping people in distress, known as non-directive client-centred counselling. This form of psychic management takes the view that therapists have no greater stability or innate qualities than their clients, but are simply not currently facing intense difficulties of the type confronted by the person in front of them. Rogers works from Freud's basic dictum that all people speak and understand at some fundamental level what the nature of their problem is and how to deal with it, but resist acknowledging the answer in straightforward ways. In a conversation-analytic sense, Freud is looking for repair of others' remarks; in an interpretative sense, he holds to their statements as intrinsically important. Unlike Freud, Rogers does not understand these psychic conflicts as related to a set series of sexual narratives across time and space, and has no desire to do more than encourage both sides in the counselling event to exchange their sense of their environment in language that relates directly to feelings and experience. He rejects the behaviouralist idea that people are simply clusters of individual conduct, instead divining basic human qualities and abilities to change (Prilleltensky 1989: 798). Rogers offers the following precepts for helping others:

(i) *In my relationships with persons I have found that it does not help, in the long run, to act as though I were something that I am not.* It does not help to act calm and pleasant when actually I am angry and critical. . . .

(ii) *I find that I am more effective when I can listen acceptantly to myself, and can be myself.* . . .

(iii) *I have found it of enormous value when I can permit myself to understand another person.* . . . Our first reaction to most of the statements which we hear from other people is an immediate evaluation, or judgment, rather than an understanding of it. When someone expresses some feeling or attitude or belief, our tendency is, almost immediately, to feel 'That's right'; or 'That's stupid' . . . when someone fully understands those feelings, this enables them to accept those feelings in themselves. Then they find both the feelings and themselves changing.

(iv) *I have found it enriching to open channels whereby others can communicate their feelings, their private perceptual worlds, to me.* . . .

(v) *I have found it highly rewarding when I can accept another person.* . . .

(vi) *The more I am open to the realities in me and in the other person, the less do I find myself wishing to rush in to 'fix things.'* . . .

(vii) *I can trust my experience.* . . .

(viii) *Evaluation by others is not a guide for me.* The judgments of others, while they are to be listened to, and taken into account for what they are, can never be a guide for me.

(ix) *Experience is, for me, the highest authority.* The touchstone of validity is my own experience. . . .

(x) *I enjoy the discovering of order in experience.* It seems inevitable that I seek for the meaning or the orderliness or lawfulness in any large body of experience.

(xi) *The facts are friendly.* It has interested me a great deal that most psychotherapists, especially the psychoanalysts, have steadily refused to make any scientific investigation of their therapy. . . .

(xii)   *What is most personal is most general.* . . .
(xiii) *It has been my experience that persons have a basically positive direction.* . . .
(xiv)   *Life, at its best, is a flowing, changing process in which nothing is fixed.* (Rogers 1977: 16–27)

While social factors are important, the opportunity to develop and be happy lies within. Life is a series of encounter groups that can produce equality and community for all by focusing on feelings (Prilleltensky 1989: 799).

We could usefully compare these concepts with twelve-step programmes of self-improvement, which derive from Alcoholics Anonymous (AA) and have been redeployed in a series of social, intersubjective, capitalistic activities: borrowing, gambling, shopping, sex, and eating among them, along with the splendid WATCH ('Women and Their Cheating Husbands') and MAD DADS ('Men Against Destruction Defending Against Drugs'). In 1990, 13 per cent of US adults had attended a twelve-step meeting, often connected to the 'inner child': a critical component in recovering from these dependencies is recognizing and celebrating repressed infancy, permitting it to parent the adult (Wuthnow 1994: 117; Riessman and Carroll 1995: 117; Mäkelä et al. 1996: 216; Forbes 1994: 233–34). The list is:

1   We admitted we were powerless over alcohol – that our lives had become unmanageable.
2   Came to believe that a Power greater than ourselves could restore us to sanity.
3   Made a decision to turn our will and our lives over to the care of God *as we understood Him.*
4   Made a searching and fearless moral inventory of ourselves.
5   Admitted to God, to ourselves, and to another human being the exact nature of our wrongs.
6   Were entirely ready to have God remove all these defects of character.
7   Humbly asked Him to remove our shortcomings.
8   Made a list of all persons we had harmed, and became willing to make amends to them all.
9   Made direct amends to such people whenever possible, except when to do so would injure them or others.
10 Continued to take personal inventory and when we were wrong promptly admitted it.

11   Sought through prayer and meditation to improve our conscious contact with God *as we understood Him*, praying only for knowledge of His will for us and the power to carry that out.
12   Having had a spiritual awakening as the result of these steps, we tried to carry this message to alcoholics, and to practice these principles in all our affairs. (quoted in Forbes 1994: 237)

AA emerged from a combination of Britain's 1930s Oxford Group, a homosocial Protestant evangelical movement, and American temperance movements (though it avoided their moral fervour) which called on *all* drinkers to stop. Over sixty years, AA has spread across the world to comprise over 90,000 groups. We are especially interested in the performative aspects of AA, its intersubjective declarations and establishments of truth and fellowship as achieved in the daily meetings that enact and specify these precepts. They tell us not only about the very Christian nature of the ritual, but also how it does and does not relate to other customizations of AA ideas, and therapy more generally. For we are at the crossroads of medicalization here: persons are labelled alcoholics by others when they are held to be unable to 'meet social obligations', whereas the self-definition encouraged by AA requires people to acquire and recognize a personal and spiritual disease (Cain 1991: 211, 213; Mäkelä et al. 1996: 14, 117). We show later how a social condition can be transformed into a disease.

AA is fascinating for its huge cross-cultural reach and the fact that it is independent of church and state, not-for-profit, and not a charity (no donations or grants are sought or accepted and its only revenue comes from people at meetings and the sale of literature). It must also be one of the few enterprises whose world governing body has a rule that at least two-thirds of members must be alcoholics. AA also has special cells for professionals whose work lives would be placed in jeopardy if their alcoholism were known: 'Anesthetists in Recovery', 'International Doctors in AA', and 'International Pharmacists Anonymous' are favourites, along with the shadowy AA group for airline pilots. It has successfully internationalized: a third of all members live in Latin America, while the decline of state socialism in Central and Eastern Europe has opened up major possibilities for expansion (Riessman and Carroll 1995: 85; Mäkelä et al. 1996: 4–5, 20, 65).

When AA members speak at meetings, they must demonstrate

sensitivity to the context, its recipient design, and the subjectivity expected of the site as defined by the moral standards of AA talk, many of which are 'known' but not formally codified. Rules only emerge explicitly when someone breaches them and then seeks to repair this transgression. Ilkka Arminen (1996) has identified three styles of repair in AA life stories: 'corrective formulations' either resile from or explain away prior statements that imply deviation (say, holding others responsible for one's alcoholism); 'ordinary word replacement' substitutes correct-line speech for errors; and 'more factual' descriptions are replaced by 'more subjective ones', encouraging identification from others by tailoring stories to a universalist discourse of emotions. One might add that the perform-ance of mistakes and their repair models the very fallibility followed by redemption that is integral to membership. This redemption requires an endless process of negotiation and work. It is never completed: Protestant performativity wants repetition. In fact, a vast array of people employed in private, state, and community mental health organizations are former clients – the 'professional ex-' phenomenon – where self-designation as ill becomes a qualification for occupational mobility: former addicts claim a special relation-ship to clients that goes beyond clinical understanding. Over 70 per cent of employees in the 10,000 substance-abuse centres across the US are former abusers, and the academic who collects these statistics and analyses the phenomenon is an ex-professional ex-, a former 'deviant drinker' and former 'primary therapist'. This is part of the romance that asks us to regard 'ten million alcoholics as potential help givers – *a resource rather than a problem*', and a money-making resource: AA provides a huge international network for business relationships, a place for people to meet across professional cultures and generate economic ties (Brown 1991: 219–20, 223, 226; Riessman and Carroll 1995: ix; Mäkelä et al. 1996: 69).

Self-help attains spiritual endorsement and technical application in the cross-gendered marketing of transcendental meditation: in 1975, *TM: Discovering Energy and Overcoming Stress* (Harold H. Bloomfield) enters the best-selling lists. It is not long before IBM, Mitsui, General Motors, the Pentagon, and Mitsubishi are hiring TM experts to lower executive blood pressure. Caring and sharing are popular throughout business. Today's collection agencies deal with recalcitrant debtors by sending them videos that describe the therapeutic benefits of talking over their problems with account staff: 'We work to make your calls to us a positive experience . . . you'll feel so much better because you've taken control.' A third of recipients – long-term defaulters all – make at least one payment (Frosh 1989: 244; Segal 1990: 280–84, 289; *People Weekly* 1996: 320; Mills 1989; 'Now' 1997).

How can people pay money to receive this message, or sit in silence as it is delivered? There is a tendency in industrial societies to look wistfully on present projections of imagined pasts, to see 'natural humanity' as a source of true personhood that can shine through 'civilization's artificial rationality' (Lutz and White 1986: 409). A projection back to Eden is integral to the longing of the contemporary to know itself through a differentiation from the 'primitive'. Put another way, the use of indigenous life to illustrate the teleological motion underlying advanced industrial societies has always contained its share of melancholic nostalgia for simplicity, a utopian model of personal, environmental, and collective harmony that can come only with organic, subsistence social organization and everyday spirituality. Of course, Freud and Jung were very dependent on the Romantic elevation of indigenous peoples into model psychic subjects: lower Fifth Avenue therapy owes a great deal to desert cosmology.

Whilst he is critical of New Age politics, Andrew Ross differs from the attack mounted by Lasch. He sees value in contesting dominant medicine, science, and psychology. This may not amount to a coherent political opposition, but it is a popular alternative to conventional rationalism and religion, in keeping with its 1960s antecedents and the intense solipsism and acquisitiveness of individualism. Alternative lifestyles meet middlebrow concerns in the happiest of encounters, but personal responsibilities and rights – the dance of the citizen – are worked through in interesting ways (although explaining food shortages as a problem of attitude, or one that will be alleviated for sufferers in the next life, would be tough to support).

Perhaps the advent of the talk shows that began this chapter is not a symptom of mass triviality, but a new point in the history of truth and communication. What is endowed with the status of infotainment by TV producers becomes a complex morality play about social structures for TV audiences. This would situate the current moment of popular culture as one of generic change, akin to the period ushered in by *The Life and strange and surprising Adventures of Robinson Crusoe* (Daniel Defoe, 1719). Much of the book's early negative reception derived from two competing senses of truth-telling then in circulation. One of these was bound up with epistolary letters, confession, and the self, and the other with the emerging novel and its publication (Gans 1993: 31; A. Ross 1992: 532–33, 536, 545; Hunter 1988: 219). A moment of epistemological rupture produced a new textual form, guaranteeing its prototypes a difficult reception. New classifications of writing (the novel) and subjectivity (the calculating self) were intermingling. So it is with the genre of self-help. Arnold Bennett's 'flapper-age' search for 'the graces of knowledge and taste' is refined by new moves in commodification, publishing, and self-revelation.

FREQUENCY BECOMES OBSESSION

What does this mean in the everyday? Time is a crucial orientation to the everyday world; so much so that the philosopher Heidegger analysed *Dasein* (everyday being) in terms of its temporal constitution (see Heidegger 1962). Competence in the everyday consists, in large part, of routine orientations to time. This can be particularly the case with arriving at meetings, catching public transport, and making significant dates. But it also applies to frequency. An important consideration in proving one's normalcy is: how many times ought something to be done? Now this is going to depend on the activity itself. If it is washing out a domestic lavatory bowl, then zero times per year would be a remarkable frequency, as would five times per day. However, the latter count might be considered unproblematic in institutions demanding high sanitary standards, such as the acute infection wards of hospitals. Variation is noticeable, but only in local circumstances.

By comparison with train timetables, frequencies do not operate by strict rules (see Chapter 3 on basic versus preferential rules). Sacks (1995a: 57–65) handles such matters in terms of everyday measurements, which are distinct from scientific and clinical measurements. He argues that everyday life consists of measuring devices with 'directional differences'. These directional differences are occasioned rather than absolute. In fact they are MIRs (Membership Inference-rich Representatives). The frequency MIR allows us to find perceivedly normal latitudes. It allows us to say on a particular occasion, for example, that someone who is ten seconds late for a meeting was 'on time', that someone who is ten minutes late was not, and that someone who is ten hours late wasn't there at all. Hence:

> Variations from 'normal' are noticeable phenomena. They're noticeable by reference to whatever it is that's 'normal for me.' And it's the fact of the variation which is relevant to some state being noticeable, and *not* what the state's features are. That is to say, if you sleep four hours a night normally, that doesn't make how much you sleep noticeable. Two hours may be 'poor.' That would make it noticeable. Six hours may be 'poor' for somebody else; that would make it noticeable for them. You don't have an equivalence. (1995a: 58)

If this is the case (that everyday frequencies of such things as sleeping, washing, or having sex are MIR-governed rather than matters of absolute measurement) then the psy-version has a set of normal frequencies. Variations from them, instead of being explicable in terms of their ordinary inference-rich character, are explained as deviant. By contrast, in everyday life, frequencies are not noticeable just because of a state's features; and there is no strict equivalence involved in MIRs. The psy-complexes assume the utter centrality of a state's features and the equivalence of frequencies, turning variations into 'character defects' and 'anxiety disorders'. In the case of frequencies, one likely transformation of this kind is called 'obsession'. Hence, observed shifts from 'normal' equivalents can actually become a disease: Obsessive-Compulsive Disorder (OCD).

OCD is popularly applied to persons with the following characteristics:

> She's convinced she's going to 'catch' AIDS. Terrified of contamination, she washes her hands seven times on one side, seven times on the other, up to 50 times a day. She shampoos her hair for 30 minutes morning and night, more on weekends, and showers for at least an hour at a time. . . .
>   Obsessed with germs and contamination, Leanne washed her hands constantly until they were raw and bleeding, and refused to touch any object unless she wore rubber gloves or used a paper towel. (Cox 1997: 23, 25)

Notice the order of reporting here: the 'inner' pathological state now appears to *precede* the over-frequent practice. 'Terrified of contamination' → much washing. 'Obsessed with germs' → constant washing and over-protection. In this way the extraordinary psychologistic explanation appears to precede the quite ordinary inference that, for a large number of people, but not all, fifty times per day is 'noticeable' when it comes to hand-washing. The *Concise Oxford Textbook of Psychiatry* lists the following as '[c]ommon themes of obsessional thought': dirt, orderliness, aggressivity, illness, sex, and religion (Gelder et al. 1994: 15). Quite clearly, the extent to which one thinks regularly about these activities is social rather than psychological: priests are supposed to think about religion, hospitals are supposed to be concerned with health, the military with order, and so on.

But for the psy-complexes, the next stage is a clinical practice aimed at removing what appears to be the underlying root of the noticeable activity – the neurosis, disorder, pathology, or whatever – even though there are still no grounds for its existence:

> The danger signs
> Worried a friend's acting a little strangely? 'Be on the lookout for any sort of repetitive behaviour, such as a girlfriend who parks her car and spends 25 minutes checking the doors are shut,' says Rocco Crino, a clinical psychologist and deputy director of Sydney's St Vincent's Anxiety Disorders Unit.
>
> If you suspect a friend is suffering from OCD, bring up the subject casually. Say you read an article about it in a magazine or newspaper and then leave it [this very text?] around for her to read it in private.
>
> If she's admitted she has OCD, don't be tempted to 'help' by dashing out at midnight to buy shampoo so she can wash her hair a strand at a time. Instead, encourage her to seek qualified help. (Cox 1997: 24)

In short, the reader is being told to leave her to confess the (non-existent) inner state that the psychologistic explanation produces – and then she's supposed to cope with that account.

By this point, we have moved from a very vague set of frequent behaviours (and they must be vague, for that's how MIRs actually work) – including washing the body and locking doors, but not, say, smoking or using a keyboard – to an underlying disorder, and thence to a 'condition' (via a medical analogue) and its 'delicate' treatment, which ultimately becomes the responsibility of someone who is now a patient. We have come a fair way from anything that might count as 'reasonable inference'. 'She has OCD' is, then, as good an inference as 'Jesus makes her do it.'

INFERENCE-MAKING BECOMES INTUITION

In a remarkable lecture on the 'inference-making machine', Sacks (1995a: 113–25) refers to the following data:

(1) A: Yeah, then what happened?
(2) B: Okay, in the meantime she [wife of B] says, 'Don't ask the child nothing.' Well, she stepped between me and the child and I got up to walk out the door. When she stepped between me and the child, I went to move her out of the way. And then about that time her sister called the police. I don't know how she . . . what she . . .
(3) A: Didn't you smack her one?
(4) B: No.
(5) A: You're not telling me the story, Mr B.
(6) B: Well, you see when you say smack you mean hit.
(7) A: Yeah, you shoved her. Is that it?
(8) B: Yeah, I shoved her. (1995a: 113)

Sacks suggests this exchange works because inferences *go backwards* from categorial explanations to describe events. In Chapter 3 on sport, we saw how categorials work in everyday life: a category of actions is held to obtain for a general category of persons in the society; if an activity takes place but the actor is not known, the actor can be inferred from 'types of persons who do that'. In this case, the categorial is slightly different – something like 'the types of activities we all know can lead to the police being called'. If there is (a) an argument between spouses + (b) unknown action + (c) a call to the police, we can reasonably infer that (b) is an action warranting (c). Given, then, that the wife's sister makes the call (and not, say, one of the neighbours) it is likely that the husband has been noticeably violent action towards the wife (and not only that they both screamed). The inference-making machine then goes through possible actions of this type and, as it turns out, reaches the correct one on second try: shoving.

While the categories of person-in-general are relevant to the mundane inference (husband, wife, wife's sister, child, and police) *no particular person's* interiority must be comprehended in order to draw the correct inference. As Sacks puts it:

> [I]t is an awesome machine if one needs to know that it is 'my wife' and 'her sister.' And you can do this because *that holds for every like unit in society*, such that you don't need to ask for example, 'Well tell me some more about your wife's sister, is she elderly? Is she prone to hysterics?' which is something that would be absolutely essential in psychology. (1995a: 117; our emphasis)

'[E]ssential in psychology' – why? We suspect psychology works in the following way: it turns normal inferences based on categories of person (like the one above) into questions about the characteristics of an individual involved: matters that are redundant to the inference. It then 'explains' the (ordinary) inference in terms of its (extraordinary) assessment of the individual. It works something like this: the man steps between the wife and the child; the sister calls for the police. The inference is: he has done something that warrants a sister's call to the police; so it is a violent action. Then: this particular man is prone to violent actions – was he brought up by a violent father? If so, the harsh upbringing explains the shoving.

Although psy-professionals rarely make such procedures explicit, in pop psychology the process is plain. For example, it can turn inference into something much more mysterious – intuition:

> As a teenager I could always tell when my parents were due home from work. Minutes before their arrival our family cat sat expectantly at the window above the driveway. Animals often have a finely-tuned sense of perception. (Osfield 1997: 58)

The ordinary inference is visible: parents return from work at more or less regular times; if they have animals, that is when the animals get food and affection. Animals are not without a sense of time, if only the regular timing of food and affection. *Ergo*, the cat waits for the sound of the returning car. A perfect inference, then, until 'intuition' is super-added as a quality of this particular cat (or indeed of cats in general). Then the 'analyst' can add 'expert' testimony:

'Unfortunately, rational society tends to trust only what people can see, hear, taste, touch, smell. We tend to disregard our sixth sense and rely completely on our thinking minds,' says Simon Turnball, President of the Australian Psychic Association. 'Most people live disconnected from their intuition until it fights its way out from the subconscious.' (Osfield 1997: 58)

So, on this account, some individuals have a particular inner capacity that resides in the 'subconscious' and is a psychic corollary of the bodily senses. Almost anything that is explicable by normal inference or is generated by probability (such as getting a call from someone you were just thinking of) can then have 'intuition' super-added to it. But at the same time, the super-adding process (which may, in some circumstances, be a kind of analytic dishonesty) is quite ordinary, if not utterly commonsensical:

What is intuition?
Intuition is not as mysterious as you might think. It mixes life experience with commonsense and a willingness to tune in and find out what you are *feeling* about something, as well as thinking. It's a good idea to try out your intuition on relatively trivial matters before using it to make big decisions. (Osfield 1997: 61)

Do I really feel like chocolate, or is it just what I *think* I might feel? And if I really felt like it, how many cases of such a feeling would it take before someone arrived here with some for me? But then people bring me chocolate all the time. So: how many times is the reception of chocolate a normal thing? Maybe it is not intuition – maybe I just get too much.

The cat, then, may well be in the driveway window waiting; but it's also out of the bag. Intuition is no more than the inference-making machine used by every member of 'rational society'. The psy-help account of it, cast in relation to particular persons' internal states and capacities, turns it into something extraordinary.

THE CAUSATION DEVICE BECOMES NEUROSIS

We want now to use Sacks' idea of sociocultural devices to explain how the psy-complexes arrive at extraordinary explanations grounded on personal states rather than mundane actions. Sacks' best-known device for analysis concerns MCDs or membership categorization devices (see Sacks 1972a, 1972b), but his lectures are studded with other examples and a great diversity of devices. One of these, which he does not name, could be called a 'causation device'. It has to do with the fact that we roughly divide causality into two classes and, moreover, that certain persons (especially children but also infantilized adults) get the classes confused. Sacks writes as follows:

> It's rather well known that very young children have, from the per-spective of adults, a rather poor notion of causation. They don't know how things happen to happen. Now, among the ways that adults go about formulating rules for children, are two which it's important to distinguish. Call them Class 1 and Class 2. A prototype of Class 1 is, 'Don't stick your hand on the stove.' Prototypic of Class 2 is 'Honor thy father and mother' – and such things as 'If you want people to love you, you should love them, be thoughtful of them, etc.' belong in that class. (1995a: 77–78).

These are not only causal but injunctive. They have to do with the idea that x will cause y, such that if you do x, y will eventuate, which might be positive or negative. So putting your hand in the fire will cause burns (negative); being caring towards people will cause them to love you (positive); and vice versa: no stove, no burns, positive result; no caring, no love, negative result. So right from the start, for Sacks, causation is tied up with moral injunction (with what should and should not be done). But, as he continues his analysis, the two classes of cause-and-injunction become quite distinct; people routinely distinguish 'natural' from 'moral' types of causation. Hence only Class 2 types produce normative sanctions, where someone has to determine whether a positive or negative sanction is due, while Class 1 types produce immediate effects, positive or negative. As Sacks puts it: 'If you stick your hand in the fire, you get burned. Whereas for Class 2, that is not so . . . somebody has to do something to you for you to get the negative consequences.' Hence, 'You can "get away with" things of the Class 2 sort' (ibid.: 78).

Where is the device? Psy-theory says there is a general human capacity for distinguishing between natural and social causation, which it identifies as a mental capacity. For Sacks, the division into

Class 1 and Class 2 *is itself the device*, an element of social being. The division is the device, and the assignment of instances to the division is not algorithmic but problematic. If we produce the division as you do, then we recognize it that way. But there is always the possibility that we recognize it differently. Neither the division nor the device is stable; they are neither mathematical nor axiomatic. That is, armed with the device, we do not generate an instant foreknowledge of its operations. Everyone in a culture makes the division and they only more or less make it in the same place; just as not everyone has the same 'normal' period of nightly sleep and so on. Children (who are learning the culture) do not make the division in the same place as adults, and 'mad persons' do not make it in the same place as 'the sane'. The device therefore provides for types of persons such as 'initiates' and 'the alienated'.

Moreover, not only do 'adults' and 'normals' make this division in a certain place, but they can also 'exploit' that version of the division to get certain effects. The effects that Sacks documents are far-reaching in their consequences. He shows how adults use the device to control children:

> [they] formulate a whole bunch of those rules for which the consequences occur only when somebody does something, as though the consequences occur as a natural fact of life apart from anybody's doing anything. . . . So that parents say to children while giving them a spanking, 'I do not want to do this, it just had to be done,' retaining thereby the relevance of Class 1. (ibid.)

The exploitation of the device in this way leaves a greater possibility of confusion on the part of some children. If parents deliberately present Class 2 rules as though they were Class 1 types, then we might reasonably expect children to be unclear as to where the division lies. Sacks suggests this accounts for what, in other forms of analysis, would be discussed as 'disturbances' or 'neuroses'. For example, it might explain reports (attributed by Sacks to Bruno Bettelheim) of:

> kids in Chicago who do things like get into a barrel and roll down a hill on to a main street where there is [*sic*] fantastic amounts of traffic, just checking out whether it's so that you get hurt. And seriously disturbed

children are those who go about checking out the causal properties of the world as though they were normative properties in the sense that Class 2 rules are. (ibid.)

A further effect of the operation of such a device could be that some adults remain unclear about the two class types. Sacks mentions a possible instance: when adults do not put a time limit on the supposed arrival of sanctions. That is, they can live their lives continually awaiting the arrival of a sanction. The psy-complexes might call such behaviour 'neurotic'. But Sacks puts it this way:

> What they tend to do by not putting a time-bound upon the operation of these rules; by not saying if at some time the consequences haven't occurred then these must be Class 2 not Class 1, is to formulate these sets of rules as 'prophecies.' So when their parents had told them 'If you do not change your ways no man will ever love you,' then you'll find forty or fifty year old people who eventually can give as an account of the failures of their romances that indeed they never changed their ways, and their parents were right. So they live out their lives under these rules as prophecies of what it is that will happen to them. (ibid.: 79)

Sacks goes on to describe 'whole paradigms in the history of the culture' for this sort of thinking, where the ideas of 'rise' and 'fall' are held to betoken the deservingness and non-deservingness of caused consequences – a kind of paranoid historicism. In particular he mentions 'Sodom [and] the decline and fall of Rome', going on to describe the idea of a supposed 'success syndrome' in the same terms.

His conclusion is characteristically modest; but it contains a potentially devastating critique of the psy-complexes and their idea that social practices are a function of personal dispositions and/or deeply hidden psychological traits:

> So that just gives, I think, a sense of what it is that the psychotherapist is talking about when he says that neurotic adults do not have a good sense of reality. And also when they say that they remain children, and that the projected operators in their presumptively adult lives are always parents, you can see what it is the psychotherapist is seeing. (ibid.: 80)

The psychotherapist is seeing culture at work – or more specifically, a cultural device. 'Having or not having a good sense of reality', 'growing up', or 'remaining children' are predicates applied to persons not in terms of their ingrained psychological condition, but how they operate the 'causation device'. The predicates generate a subsequent second-order search for psychological conditions. This causation device is a materially available technique that produces what come to count as certain types of subject: 'well-adjusted', 'badly adjusted', 'pro-social', 'anti-social', and so on. To that extent, it also provides the basis for psychoanalytic tropes of parental reference: the Oedipus complex, for example. That is, there is nothing essential or fundamental about everyday life that can be explained by 'loving one's mother' or 'hating one's father'. Rather, the psychoanalyst's source of these tropes is identical to the patient's: the causation device, a material feature of social being.

If we return briefly to Sacks' reason for working through this device and its broader cultural operation (from Sodom to Freud and beyond) we can see that it has to do with a purely empirical (some would say banal) question. The lecture begins with Sacks trying to account for a feature that crops up in several calls to a suicide prevention agency, which often involve such exchanges as:

A: This is Mr Smith. May I help you?
B: Well, I do not know. My brother suggested that I call you. (ibid.: 76)

Sacks wants to know how people who call in this way – saying that someone else told them to, or suggested they should – sound dependent or infantile. The causation device gives an answer. And the analytic perspicacity of the device extends to many other cases – Sacks' answer to the 'so what?' challenge often issued to ethnomethodology. His answer is a demonstration. To put this another way: one might think an exchange like the one quoted above was trivial, a mere fraction of everyday life. Any analysis of it would be equally trivial, confined to such a fragment and its immediate context. However Sacks treats 'a friend told me to call' as a device that solves a generally occurring problem, escaping traditional psychologistic analyses of guilt and neurosis. In this sense, the derivation of material devices from supposedly micro-situations can turn out to be 'something real and something finely powerful' (Sacks 1995a: 246).

CONCLUSION

This methodological point is of crucial importance for a de-psychologized analysis of culture. One must begin with actual materials and proceed to ask, perhaps as a heuristic only: what socio-logical problem is solved by this talk and action? A cultural object is not inspected for its representational capacities. We do not begin by asking, for example, what deeper thing this micro-object represents, looking into the supposed subjectivities of cultural speakers and actors with the question 'What does this mean to them?' nor into speculative collective 'minds' as per 'worldvisions' and *Zeitgeist*. By turning instead to cultural practices as problem-solutions, we look for devices that are the very being of a culture, material forms of production in their own right rather than representations of something else. These can then be run through other cultural objects, general or specific, to see whether (and how) they could be equally responsible for those further objects.

If cultures consist of collections of devices, then micrological analysis is an entry-point to a more general 'deviced' culture. And if this is the case, then the venue or context of the empirical and micrological beginning is more or less irrelevant: for any 'deviced' culture ought 'not . . . to be found only by aggregating all of its venues; it is substantially present in each of its venues' (Schegloff in Sacks 1995a: xlvi). Sacks puts this theory of 'order at all points' in the following way:

> it would be extremely hard, given the possible fact that there is over-whelming and detailed order, to not find it, no matter how you look. . . . Such that, for example, any Member encountering from his infancy a very small portion of it, and a random portion in a way (the parents he happens to have, the experiences he happens to have, the vocabulary that happens to be thrown at him in whatever sentences he happens to get) comes out in many ways pretty much like everybody else, and able to deal with pretty much anyone else. (ibid.: 485)

This may seem like no more than rejigged depth analysis, where a cultural object (say a practice or an utterance) simply stands for or betokens an underlying general culture (which Sacks calls 'an order'). The cultural analyst's task would then be just to derive the latter from instances of the former. But we think Sacks is pointing to the intrinsically material property of all cultural practice – Garfinkel's 'reflexivity' or 'incarnateness': that methods for the production and recognition of a cultural object are identical and consist of devices (Schegloff in Sacks 1995a: xxxix). This is what Sacks means when he refers to a culture being substantially present in all its venues. Neither he nor Garfinkel is referring to a ghostly (let alone psychologistic) thing 'represented' by a cultural object. A good instance of the omnipresence of social order comes from Wes Sharrock:

> Social order is easy to find because it's put there to be found. When you go about your actions . . . you do them so that (or in ways that) other people can see what you're doing. You do your actions to have them recognized as the actions they are. When you stand at the bus stop, you stand in such a way that you can be seen to be waiting for a bus. People across the street can see what you're doing, according to where and how you're standing. . . . [Y]ou're standing at a bus stop and somebody comes and stands next to you and they stand in such a way that eventually you can see that these people are standing in a line and that one person's the first and another is the second, and some person's at the end. People stand around at bus stops in ways they can be seen to be waiting for a bus. (Sharrock 1995: 4)

The question of what a cultural object stands for or represents (as it were, deep down) arises *as a question* only when we inspect the subjective capacities of persons or posit objective mysteries – cultural systems, *Zeitgeist*, mythologies, and so forth. But if cultural recognition is possible because of cultural production (rather than because of representation) and if, moreover, the methods for the two (production and recognition) are both identical and material, then culture is (a) fully empirical and analytically inspectable even from minute fragments, (b) 'finely powerful', and (c) something that exists despite rather than because of personal or collective minds. It produces those things that come, *after the fact*, to be described as personal and collective minds. This is why, throughout this book, we propose an analysis of culture turned to empirical instances, to the devices for their production and recognition, and also to some parts of the array of other cultural objects that those devices might be seen to generate, as opposed to previous analyses of them from inside any essentially 'mystical' version of cultural analysis. Our concluding chapter focuses on a range of such devices.

5

Cultural Devices: Talking

I'm trying to suggest a picture in which lots of things are happening in the world, out of which people are catching the way in which it happens, happens just to them. Where the world is arrangeable nonetheless to have that be a vehicle for the culture reproducing itself in terms of its body of knowledge. That is to say, one kind of problem a culture faces is getting its known things kept alive. A basic thing it uses is people's heads. Where people's heads are not just to be repositories for known things, but they have to be repositories that are appropriately tapped so that those known things get passed to others. And, having been put in some others' heads, there need to be ways that those known things again get tapped and put into yet others' heads. (Harvey Sacks 1995b: 468)

Standard conceptualizations of popular culture assume that producers send messages to audiences. But there is no definite point of commencement or conclusion as suggested by the notion of a discrete sender, message, and receiver – the movement of meaning is 'continuous and cyclical' (Michaels 1990: 12). These categories are inexorably intertwined, defining and informing one another, as per the notion of textual technologies from Chapter 1. This chapter inspects the cultural devices used by audiences to make sense of the popular. We are using some examples from our own experience to illustrate how such devices can be identified, along with an audience test of a popular TV series.

There are three crucial sites for defining and refining popular culture: the culture industry, the state, and criticism, which construct audiences as part of their *raisons d'être* (Hartley 1992b: 105). In other words, the audience is called into being by a variety of actors in search of points to make in public discourse: TV executives invoke it as a category they seek to engage, regulators use it to organize broadcasting administration, psychologists to produce proofs, and audience lobby-groups to change programming. In short, 'the audience' is not available in pristine form, but scarred by its origins in discourses and institutions (Ang 1991: 46; Fiske 1992: 353; Hartley 1992b: 105). These entities act upon their creation to exercise social power:

> The energy with which audiences are pursued in academic and industry research bespeaks something much larger and more powerful than the quest for mere data. The TV audience is pervasive but perplexingly elusive: the quest for knowledge about it is the search for something *special*; literally, knowledge of the *species*. (Hartley 1992a: 84)

Paradoxically, the cultural audience is not a specifiable group within the social order, but the principal site *of* that order. Just as people are citizens as well as individuals, so the moment of being an audience is the textual connection linking society and person. It is both collective and singular: viewing television is an act of both solitary interpretation and collective behaviour (Hartley 1992a: 85). Hence the link to panics about educational under-attainment, violent behaviour, and political apathy supposedly engendered by the popular that is investigated by the state, psychologists, the left, conservatives, religious groups, liberal-humanist feminists, and others. The audience as consumer, child, criminal, voter, and idiot engages such groups.

Take ratings and shares. Ratings compare the number of all radio and TV sets to those tuned to channels at a given moment. Shares compare the number of sets switched on across channels. They derive from the need of commercial media, advertising, and public broadcasters to know whom and what they are 'producing' outside the text itself. And in addition to knowing the size of that group, they want to know how it relates to the population as a demographically sliced formation of sexes, ages, races, tastes, patterns of consumption, and politics. Such systems arose as a consequence of the rash of methods for measuring consumer activity that were developed across the United States over this century out of a desire to know as much about the targets of mass-produced goods and services as possible, to *control* through measurement as well as to *sell* through measurement.

Consider this anecdote. It is New Year's Eve, the cusp of 1991–92. A woman is listening to 2KY, a Sydney commercial radio station set up by the New South Wales Labor Council. (In the 1920s, this station had announced plans for a Brechtian choral-response system, a two-way relay between central transmission and the people's voice, rather than one-way broadcasting.) The 1991–92 listener rings on the request line and asks to hear 'Stand By Your Man'. The station plays the song. She calls back, complaining that instead of the Tammy Wynette version, 2KY has provided a parody by the Chipmunks. The woman threatens to kill herself: result unknown. A moral panic emerges in the newspapers about the maudlin nature of country music. University tests are cited: country music's sombre tales of grief, solitude, and liverish excess are liable to drive people 'at-risk' to a stage beyond. Competing university tests are cited, attributing the incidence of suicide to social factors rather than ethereal ones. 2KY's rival 2SM, then owned by the Roman Catholic church, announces it will not play depressing music. Shortly afterwards, the Catholic management of the station is in legal trouble, and the church dispenses with the business after decades of ownership. Country music continues.

What might we make of this? In terms of genre and knowledge, we are witness to a moral panic that ties the popular to preserving life, and a debate over ecological fallacies versus the individual experience of suicide. This difference divides sociology from psychology as intellectual communities: a debate that correlates white suicide with divorce, with gun ownership, and also with country-music lyrics about loss and drink (Maguire and Snipes 1994). In financial terms, ratings overdetermine the cultural and political history and ownership of both 2KY and 2SM. And textually, we are aware of how fragile the phone-in system is as a marker of active listener participation, something brought into sharper focus when we contrast it with the same frequency under the same ownership in the early history of radio, when radio was thought of as a turn-taking device that made everybody into both broadcaster and listener. In the remainder of this chapter, we walk away from the dominant modes of understanding audiences, but take our cue from the radio-audience relationship. In place of psychological, commercial, or citizenship models, we want to know how people use cultural devices, handle talk and texts in actual settings. Our instances come from radio, television, and the crossword puzzle.

Our argument will be that the links between audiences and producers are remarkably tight, though complex and distinct in each case.

LISTENING

Listening is surprisingly crucial to the consumption of popular culture, including films and TV programmes. We tend to think of film and TV as requiring a purely visual literacy – some theorists even insist the camera can 'write' in isolation from other factors. Yet as noted film editor, director, and theorist Walter Murch says, 'we do not *see* and *hear* a film, we *hear/see* it' (1994: xi) – having designed the sound to *The Conversation* and *The English Patient* he should know. And when UN Security Council delegates were shown videotape of Israeli border guards killing Palestinians gathered at the Al-Aqsa mosque in Jerusalem, the screams for help and medical supplies made as big an impact as the visuals (Jayyusi 1993: 51 n. 25). As Rudolf Arnheim argued sixty years ago, radio's lack, the absence of vision that stands between it and documentary status, gives it the drive to go beyond mimesis (1969: 160). From all points of the spectrum, the medium's special strength and dependency – its sound – imposes the 'severe code of radio's discipline', a code requiring all changes in diegesis to be earmarked: radio decodes and encodes other sign systems as aural pictures painted by a promiscuous social tourism (Rodger 1982: 10).

It is conventional to differentiate three types of sound in the culture industries: dialogue, effects, and music, which are further divided by volume, pitch, and timbre. Volume is determined by the amplitude of vibrating air, pitch by movements along the scale, and timbre through the harmonic effect of tone. Such an approach works with the grammar of musical notation. But sound includes grunts, belches, avalanches, silence, streetscapes, vibration, compression, and frequency modulations; in short, sound 'at work' is part of an event, and usually recorded at a different time and place from any visual action. Sounds that can be written down as identical have different values according to what is taking place around them. Put another way, sound is narrativized and edited. It varies from the focused to the omnidirectional, with consequent changes in direct and reflected impressions on the eventual projection (Bordwell and

Thompson 1996: 318–20; Altman 1992a; Mancini 1985: 366, 361).

Sound design in the cinema, for instance, involves coordination with the sound editor and musical composer, assistance with the sound mix, and evaluation of theatrical presentation. With the rise of action-adventure, the role has increased in significance: the 1994 film version of *Wyatt Earp* credits thirty-nine people with post-production sound work (Weis 1995: 56). Realism in continuity-system cinema functions via arbitrary conventions – song lyrics refer to what is happening visually, and the ratio of shot-length to sound is 'impossible'. Most swashbucklers of the 1930s and 1940s, or action-adventure high-concept vehicles of the 1980s and 1990s, rely on music to keep their fight or chase sequences moving, both rhythmically and in terms of continuity. We should note that, by the late 1930s, realist actuality based on a notion of aural space had been drowned out by the requirement of intelligibility. The scale of image and sound no longer needed to be identical. Close-ups moved to medium shots with a visual cut, but remained intimate on the soundtrack. Sound was independent of image: it had to remain audible. Ease of spectatorial comprehension was the expectation, not a relationship between the profilmic subject's distance from the lens, or real life's confused jumble of sounds (Altman 1992b: 51, 53–54, 57).

Hence Michel Chion's concept of '*added value*', the information and expressivity that sound brings to pictures, fully achieved at moments of '*synchresis*', when there seems to be 'an immediate and necessary relationship' between what is seen and heard, an organic one-on-one correspondence of visual and aural signs that produces empirical faith in the listener-watcher (1994: 5). Audiences domesticate this jumble of signs, assembling and testing inferences from characters and making their own meanings. In order to see how sound works, we are going to investigate sound first on radio and then on TV.

RADIO ENCOUNTERS

The field of writing on radio is neither large nor worthy. As an object for behavioural research panics, it was quickly overtaken by the advent of cinema and television. As an object of textual analysis, it was less easily recuperated from archives than the visual media. As a casual part of everyday life, it was held to occupy less *real* attention than, for example, the newspaper. But radio training manuals, audiological research, and governmental policy documents are now being supplemented by critical academic study. As the everyday becomes a site of contestation and valorization in cultural theory, so Umberto Eco's use of the 'radio that is turned on but not tuned' as a model of phatic communication may offer new life to a site that had seemed insignificant (1987: 164). At the same time, the medium is expanding: there are over 11,000 radio stations in the US, using forty different formats.

Radio has a unique reputational history. Unlike television, which began as a reception-only device and is becoming interactive, radio started life as an emblem of innovation and activeness. The (mostly male) ham operators of the 1920s battled technological difficulties on a daily basis, exemplifying self-reliance and innovation. This 'proper' life of initiative was replaced in the 1930s by the supposedly lazy, dependent listenership of women. The appearance of the loudspeaker made radio an effortless listening medium. A device of consumption rather than mastery, it had been feminized, with the will to buy advertised goods becoming its defining quality. Noting this trend in a more positive vein, the Television Broadcasters Association in 1944 stressed avoiding 'any repetition of the errors that marked radio's beginnings' (Stavitsky 1995: 81; Association quoted in Boddy 1994: 114): those errors had situated the audience as a participant, not a recipient.

Ideally, radio both 'speaks to the public' and 'lets the public speak'. Its extraordinary variety calls for a more specific theoretical and analytic treatment than much cultural theory will allow. For example, the same commercial broadcasters who translated radio into a site of listening-to-prompt-purchasing also viewed it as a nation-binding medium that would, as NBC President Merlin Aylesworth put it in 1930, 'preserve our now vast population from disintegrating into classes' by producing equivalent, sometimes identical, cultural experiences (Potts 1989: 172; Aylesworth quoted in Boddy 1994: 109).

For Adorno and Horkheimer, radio is a turn away from the precious artistic and social traces of authentic intersubjectivity, because it is dedicated to the 'control of the individual conscious-ness' through the absence of any 'machinery of rejoinder' (1977:

349–50). Professionalism masked this suppression of spontaneity by engaging audiences under predetermined conditions of its own choice. C. Wright Mills refers to a lament for 'the simple democratic society of primary publics' that interacted via face-to-face communication, supposedly superseded by enlarged and centralized institutions of government and culture (1970: 581). Left critiques position radio as a 'mediator of the attentions of the state and of capital at the hearth' (Lewis and Booth 1989: 187). On the right, it is derided as an 'alternative to the whole problem of thinking what to do . . . defusing the moral atmosphere' through lowest-common-denominator appeals to 'the "law of optimum inoffensiveness"' (Abrams 1973: 119, 103, 107–8).

But for college footballer Taft Robinson in Don DeLillo's novel *End Zone*, turning the radio off and on is 'almost a spiritual exercise. Silence, words, silence, silence, silence' – a practice for disciplining the body, as per Maguire's ideal types encountered in Chapter 3. Alternatively, we might see talk radio – the particular concern here – as a reaction to the power of television, transforming the older medium from its focus on 'entertainment' to 'a kind of nervous information system', as Marshall McLuhan termed it. Critics argue that talk radio has become one more 'slick format' in response to commercial pressures. But for others it is 'the last bastion of free speech for plain, ordinary citizens' (DeLillo 1987: 239–40; McLuhan 1974: 318; Liddicoat et al. 1994; Higgins and Moss 1982: 1, 29; Munson 1993: 1).

Seven decades on, it is much more divisive than that. As DeLillo's *White Noise* narrator Jack Gladney says – in a family driving ordeal characterized by his son's obsessive privileging of weather forecasts over personal observation – '[j]ust because it's on the radio doesn't mean we have to suspend belief in the evidence of our senses'. Jack is wrong. Our senses *include* listening to the radio, as he realizes later, sensing his family may be developing symptoms of illness through hearing about them on-air (1986: 22–23, 125–26). This echoes the public and professional debate over therapy and treatment, which we looked at in the previous chapter.

Talk is central to the broadcast media, especially interviews. News and current affairs radio, in particular, rely on it as much as first-hand reportage, and more than actuality recording. The interview is radio's phenomenological mode, a record of sense-making as much as empirical information that brings outsiders (like audiences) 'into' the station. Philip Bell and Theo van Leeuwen allot four histories to the genre. The first history is transformed into the presenter as a source of access for these listeners, using *vox populi*. The second history sees a movement of the interview away from its original location in entertainment programmes towards offering light, shade, and humanity to current affairs. The third history is linguistic. A speech genre emerges, mixing orchestrated, monologic, authoritative pronouncements with the spontaneous, dialogic provisionality of everyday talk (prior to the advent of tape, and during wartime, interviews were scripted so that they could be censored before being read on air). Finally, this mixture is itself brought within manageable norms of length, topic, and enunciation (Bell and van Leeuwen 1994: 37–38). Contemporary discourse analysis inspects 'naturally occurring' pragmatic sites such as the radio interview. While certain conversation analysts deny the generic dictates of forms of communication, insisting on talk as the defining mode of interaction, others place social structure, medium, genre, and talk in a dynamic interrelationship. That type of pragmatics is obviously most amenable to our approach (Schegloff 1978: 81; 1992: 110).

Conversation analysis is helpful in finding the second-by-second properties of exchange by attending to the accomplishment of paired parts (questions and answers, for example), turns at talk, corrections and repairs, interruptions, pauses and silences, and the insertion of such short sounds as 'um' and 'eh'. These accomplishments are ordered at the moment of their achievement, rather than being incidental effects of externally imposed meaning and organization. In this sense, all practical, everyday actions are locally produced. The reference points of language and action are determined not only by their location alongside other words, their correspondence with specific objects being described, or a macro-political determination, but by the very *occasion* and *setting* in which they appear, the *use* to which they are put, and the *means* of their reception.

TALKING BACK

Interview radio is a major phenomenon of our times. In 1989 there were 300 talk-radio programmes across North America; by 1994, the number had grown to over 1,100. Deregulation permitted owners to run formats without news or current affairs journalism and removed the requirement to offer competing views on contro-versial topics, while satellites offered simultaneous or time-delayed transmission across the country. (Many of the 600 US stations carrying Rush Limbaugh in the mid-1990s did so because they were facing bankruptcy and could not afford local talent: they were given the show for free in return for sharing advertising revenue with Limbaugh's owner.) Numerous hosts run for political office and organize listeners to act beyond the airwaves. The political right is absolutely straightforward about this orchestration. Around 70 per cent of talk-show hosts declare themselves conservative, which led Bill Clinton to characterize talk radio as 'just a constant, unremitting drumbeat of negativism and cynicism', and former US Federal Communications Commission chair Reed Hundt to denigrate its distorted account of politics. Conservative presenters outnumber liberals two to one, and they have been unrepresentatively negative about Clinton when measured against public opinion surveys. A 1990 report by the Center for Media and Public Affairs on ethnic discourse in talk shows from New York, Chicago, and Philadelphia found the material divisive. And it's now quite apparent that Limbaugh and other talk hosts were crucial players in organized attempts to claim a White House conspiracy in the death of Clinton aide Vincent Foster (Nye 1994: 10; Egan 1995b: 22, 1; Lewis 1995: 60; Brudnoy et al. 1994; Walsh 1994; Munson 1993: 4; Gopnik 1994: 98).

Limbaugh enunciates opposition to what he claims is a liberal hegemony exercised over 'the mainstream media', citing the follow-ing endorsement from Ronald Reagan: 'Now that I've retired from active politics, I don't mind that you've become the number-one voice for conservatism in our country.' Limbaugh refers to criticisms from *Time* and *USA Today* as proof that 'every corner of liberalism' is against him. He characterizes the talk-radio audience as believers in 'God, American ideals, morality, individual excellence, and personal responsibility'. Paradoxically, these people, who 'do the right thing', are under attack from liberals for selfishness and greed. In place of such assaults, he offers this group of 'intelligent, enraged citizens' a mix of 'information and inspiration'. His listeners are those who 'subscribe to conservative periodicals and read classic conservative books, teach their children at home, write letters to the editor, run for school boards, and volunteer to work on local political campaigns or with a local charity', and who are enlisted by

Limbaugh telling 'The truth' about liberalism. For Limbaugh, the 'explosion of talk radio' presents a distinctive 'cultural challenge' to the country's dominant institutions (Reagan quoted in Limbaugh 1994: 4; ibid.: 4–5, 10).

The *New York Times'* notion that talk radio is just banally oppositional, that it automatically reaches out against clusters of institutional power and therefore will change under Republican administrations, is reassuring but improbable. Racism is the lodestone of the medium. Whilst Limbaugh may have ceased his mockery of African-American speech on air, that remains a staple for many of his colleagues, and he continues to make mention of 'feminazis', 'environmental wackos', 'long-haired maggot-infested dope-smoking pansies', and 'the spaced-out Hollywood left'. At the same time, even liberal hosts point – they think positively – to his and others' criticisms of Zoe Baird, Clinton's first-choice Attorney-General, for illegal employment practices that caused disgruntled citizens to push politicians (and many conservatives favoured her pro-corporate positions) into opposing her nomination. And when conservative New England host David Brudnoy revealed he was gay and living with AIDS in late 1994, the audience reaction was positive (Egan 1995a; Page and Tannenbaum 1996; Rich 1995).

So there are ambivalences and ambiguities here. For Hollywood, the genre provides a metatextual space to deliberate on the horrors of genuinely interactive popular culture: the host is murdered in *Talk Radio* (Oliver Stone 1988), the caller suicides in *Pump Up the Volume* (Allan Myle 1990), and the lonely heart accepts Jack Lucas' suggestion to shoot barfly 'yuppies' in *The Fisher King* (Terry Gilliam 1991). On the other hand, Taiwanese pirate talk radio provides a distinctive oppositional voice for dissidents. Nelson Castro, a popular talk-show host in Argentina, regularly features Loony Radio, broadcast by patients at Borda Psychiatric Hospital, which brings their concerns into the public domain. And in Singapore, the government's normalizing morality has been comprehensively queried by Radio Heart, especially by Xiu Mei's programme, *Night Train of Emotions* and imitators on the Singapore Broadcasting Corporation. Xiu Mei introduced listeners to public discussion of rape, child abuse, and homosexuality ('Messiah' 1994; Sims 1996; Birch 1992: 94–95).

The term 'talk radio' becomes a misnomer for a tightly organized, multi-generic format that is ultimately directed and authorized by station management, production, and on-air staff. An agenda is set by the person behind the microphone and then worked with by the callers, much as Limbaugh told a 1995 Museum of Television and Radio audience that 'My show from the beginning has been what I care about, not what the callers want. . . . The purpose of the caller is to make the host look good.' And this is so not merely of the topics discussed, but also of opportunities for taking conversational turns, interruptions from the studio, the technical capacity to over-ride callers, the seven-second delay between callers speaking and going out on air, intonation, and so on. A whole series of editorial and proprietorial strategies of control is exercised from the station. Let's again examine a fragment from Australian radio:

Caller: Good day Howard, how are you going?
Sattler: Good Bradley.
Caller: Answer a quick one about the Waugle [Nyungar Aboriginal word for Rainbow Serpent]
Sattler: Yes.
Caller: Um, what do Waugles and pink elephants have in common?
Sattler: What do Waugles and pink elephants have in common?
Caller: You've got to be drunk to see either of them?
Sattler: Now now, now now, now now, Bradley, you shouldn't be like that. Well, I can't account for everyone. (Quoted in Mickler 1992: 2, 3)

This comes from 6PR's morning radio show, *The Sattler File*, in 1991. 6PR is a Perth-based talk and racing station, then owned by the West Australian Totalizator Agency Board (an instrument of the state government). At that time, federal broadcast regulations prohibiting 'gratuitous vilification' of particular social groups were unsuccessfully invoked by complainants against Sattler. In his account of the programme, Steve Mickler maintains that although the broadcaster's individual utterances may have been outside the official definition of vilification, the programme itself constitutes a unity of words voiced, turns taken, editorial strategies implemented and rejected, voice-tones, and intellectual frames that are discriminatory, with Sattler representing the ideas of callers he likes as expressions of public opinion in general. Sattler effectively edits and broadcasts the 'raw material' he selects from a pre-known pool of callers. 6PR's listenership is solidly ancient and quite unrepresentative of the Perth population in general. Those callers who dissent from a populist derogation of land rights, or seek to debate police treatment of Aboriginal people, are routinely interrupted or contradicted.

James Ridgeway calls the American audience to talk shows 'the electorate that sits alone in cars, alienated, resentful, and pissed off' (1994: 27). Over half the voters surveyed during the congressional elections of 1994 were in that audience, with regular listeners supporting the Republicans by a ratio of three to one. One in six citizens tune in regularly, including a high proportion of registered voters. The constituency is disproportionately white, male, well-off, and retired. This leads some critics to explain the advent of hate radio in terms of an end to the Cold War. An audience that had cheerfully seen themselves as citizens of a vast military apparatus in the name of capitalism and the American commercial empire now finds the international division of labour a threat and peacetime government alienating. The coercive state, once so welcome, is derided as a creature of liberalism (Egan 1995b: 22; Kohut and Bowman 1995: 46, 48, 50; Page and Tannenbaum 1996: 45; Media Studies Center 1996). So this is an enormously complicated genre, with audiences routinely invoked by left, right, broadcasters, and indeed themselves, as signs of civic participation, extremism, and everything in between.

As raw material, we are going to use an interview exchange between a radio announcer Kevin Hume (K) and Toby Miller (T):[1]

1   K: . . .at twelve tuh *six* .hhh now to our *sensitive*
                  cultural commissar who joins us each tuesday ev'ning
                  on Dri::ve, Toby, Mi?ller .hh putting at least er
                  seven intriguing levels 'v meaning tuh th' mos'
                  commonplace of or'nary be*hav*iour in our pop culture
                  slot .hh like >f'r example< getting z:*app*ed .hh or
                  z:*app*ing as it is sometimes caused er called uh a
                  >ref'rence o' course< to er *arcane video* behaviour
                  Tobe >is 'at right?<
                        (.)

2   T: .hh it may well be Kevin but as usual you've caught
                  me totally off guard with your - *charming*
                  description of me, sensitive, when did I suddenly
                  get this appellation

3   K: Well it w's - after you::r grov'ling 'nd er before
                  the altar of post *feminist feminism*:: las' week er
                  where you w'r reproving me fer not being politic'ly
                  correct Tobe s'l thought .hhhh obviously th- here's

```
          a man who's er .h chasing after >shall we say< er
          .hh sensitive new age s::kirt.
                 (2.6)
 4    T:  I'd like tuh say th't Telecom's cut in here and
          there's some kinda communic(    )ns breakdown
                              [    ]=
 5    K:                       .hh
 6    K:  =hahk y'k hah
                [  ]
 7    T:          (  ) -ing like tha' 'n we all know I'm thee –
          authentic f:eminised male 'v thee: – early nineties=
                              [                    ]
 8    K:                       (hh)    hah
 9    K:  =hah    hah
               [   ]
10    T:          Let's get serious
```

Toby's moral position is challenged to the point where complicity would – to use a term from ethnomethodology – membership him in ways he finds politically abhorrent. Under these circumstances, is it sufficient to remain within an exercise of the self, or should disruption be projected into the public event itself.

Toby was being interviewed by phone, live-to-air. The audience hailed by the programme had middle-level cultural capital, was interested in local and national politics, and formed part of a labour force characterized by credentialism *and* a sense of radio as distraction and information. Understanding this made Toby concentrate on three relatively discrete forms of talk. The first brought into play the knowing subject, a respectable public speaker and an 'interesting' on-air voice engaging in a certain amount of confession to leaven academic discourse. The second form centred on a topic, alternating between policy, institutional, textual, and popular understandings. The final form of talk acknowledged the indefinite capacity of texts to be remade through interpretation, stressing the partial nature of the account given and offering *it* up as interpretable. By contrast, cultural studies' endorsement of openness was evident in his decision to pick up on a specific subjectivity within texts, such as gender, class, or race. This in turn needs to be understood inside the discourse of radio sound and discussion itself, which are themselves generic and rule-governed.

Regular listeners to the programme knew that Toby's interviewer, Kevin Hume, often engaged in verbal 'sparring'. As the interview began, such listeners also knew he had ended a previous encounter by doubting the authenticity of Toby's pro-feminist politics. That session concluded – right on the regular time, after several signals from Kevin that it was time to end – with Toby making the sound 'Hm::::?', marked by an upwardly rising contour in place of the usual closing procedures (Schegloff and Sacks 1973). As the transcribed session started, this topic was taken up again: the turn-pause that lasted a week!

The interesting conversational phenomenon here is the gap between turns three and four. By any standards, this is very long. Since it occurs at a transition relevance place, it is clearly Toby's gap rather than Kevin's. Toby was expected to speak here in response to the implication that his pro-feminism is a sexual ploy. At line four, Toby jokingly offers a technical hitch as the reason for his silence. But this was clearly not what had happened – Toby held his tongue to give himself time to form a response. And remember that talk radio, whilst intimate, is *designed* to be overheard (Cameron and Hills 1990: 53). Silence gave Kevin's show a dose of what professional broadcasters fear: dead air. It worked as a reprisal-without-content: no explicit objection was voiced. Once the gap was over, Toby could use the 'Telecom' explanation as a polite excuse, with the word 'communications' conveniently blipped across by a tiny patch of broadcast silence, then get on with his riposte.

A technical requirement (minimizing gaps, one of the major components of turn-taking) was passed over, though not breached, in favour of a moral requirement for Toby to express community membership allegiances and differences from Kevin. At the same time, Kevin was clearly attempting – in the other direction – to membership Toby as a fellow-misogynist by inviting him into that community: 'here's a man who's chasing after [. . .] sensitive new age skirt'. Off air, verbal abuse might be the only available and effective reply, followed by a termination of the talk. On air, such a tactic would mean only one thing to listeners: Toby was arrogant. Suitable on-air language would sound like a compromise, and the station's contract required him to continue performing. Temporary but extended silence had an artful design-consequence. It generated dead air and space to formulate an over-emphatic and parodic riposte, reminding Kevin of the programme's purpose: 'we all know I'm the authentic feminised male of the early nineties [. . .] Let's get serious.' As with Toby's earlier 'Hm::::?' sign-off, this marked a deep-seated difference despite, and perhaps because of, its resistance to interview conventions. Political differences were signified by substantive irony and the manipulation of silence, in ways both required by, and subversive of, the norms of radio, using the positions of general knower and specific 'personality' to make a parodic point.

The effect is produced through techniques of talking, not talk itself; at least, not in any spoken words. The tactic involves communication through non-talk, a precision-timed move at the limits of conventional radio conduct. Without speech, it says: 'any further, Kevin, and you have to improvise for the next few minutes' – in other words, the audience will know you have erred. Now whilst we might not all think in conversation-analytic terms while talking or listening, we know – like the producers – about such conventions as *badinage* between regular participants, pausing in order to distance oneself from an interlocutor, and so on.

Having looked at sound and the micro-politics of conversation, we want to turn down the political volume a little, as it were, and see what information is handled by audiences in the context of television drama. What happens to sound when vision enters the mix?

WATCHING AND LISTENING

For the purposes of this section, we tested the centrality of sound by dividing student groups in two. One cohort watched an episode of a well-known television series with the soundtrack turned off. The other listened with the screen blank. When we administered a standard comprehension test (designed with neither verbal nor visual bias) the sound-only cohort routinely achieved higher scores. So our purpose below is to examine how, in the case of a popular TV series, dialogue and other sounds are critical components of everyday 'watching'. We will be looking at *The X-Files*, a programme known for its depiction of investigations of 'unknown' phenomena (unidentified flying objects, government conspiracies, extra-sensory perception, the supernatural, and so forth). In some ways this 'baseline' description already encapsulates a paradox: how can what is in effect 'unknown' be watched? For surely: if *watched* – at least according to empiricist theories of knowledge – then *known*

– rather similar to the conundrum facing would-be audience counters and controllers more generally.

We can see how pertinent this paradox is to science fiction writers and readers. For one of the unique qualities of science fiction is that it works by building up a puzzle and, at least in some cases, offering a solution in the course of the narrative; or else, in other cases, leaving the reader or viewer with a conundrum to solve in the form of a reading or interpretation. In many cases this is achieved through a disjunction between what we may call *agents* and *activities*.[2] Agents are participants in a drama, the character types – for example, police officers. Activities are what such types are routinely *known* to do – for example, wear certain clothes, carry certain weapons, make arrests, keep the peace, investigate criminals, and so on. But in science fiction, leading agents, often antagonists, can be 'unknowns'; no routine, everyday knowledge clearly ties them to particular activities. Nothing about them can be taken for granted. Ever since the early masters H.G. Wells and Jules Verne started to refer to 'the thing' or 'the creature' to describe peculiar events that could have no earthly agent, science fiction has worked in this way. And *The X-Files* is no exception to this technique for referring to the unknown.

With visuals aiding the process, agents and their activities in *The X-Files* can be made suitably mysterious – until we find out how, in the end, such a one (or ones) could do such a thing (or things) – or else we can be left, as before, with only guesses. Agents of a suspected alien or paranormal type can be seen through mirrors, from their own points of view (thus not revealing them), or from a victim's distorted point of view. Actually filmed frames can be skipped (as they were to great effect in the *Alien/s* movies) – or the 'thing' can be seen from the rear – or through speed-ups or blurs – through incomplete scenes, half-views, and so on. On the other hand, we might see the effects of their activities, but not the method of perpetration. So in 'Humbug' (*X-Files* episode 2.20 – numeration as per Lavery, Hague and Cartwright's 1996 'Appendix') the first shot of the mysterious creature terrorizing Gibsontown is shown through a heavily greased lens. In this case, the unknown agent could actually be any of the many possible suspects, from The Conundrum to the fabled FeeJee Mermaid; and its relevant activity could involve anything from the victim being eaten to . . . well, whatever it is the Mermaid is supposed to do to its victims.

But over and above these remarkable televisual effects, the speculations of FBI agents Scully and Mulder, as they talk about possible
weird agent-types and their activities, add a considerable amount to
the viewer's sense of a problem – and, where relevant, its solution. In
fact, as we hope to show, the dialogue is crucial to such matters.

Routine dialogue

Science fiction stories and films, then, work with puzzles or problems about 'unknown' agents and their activities and, moreover,
with how these two are bound together. They pose such questions as
'What's been done?' and 'What did this?'; along with 'What's the
connection between the two?' This is quite specific to science fiction
and horror genres. For in most other spheres of everyday life, such
questions are few and far between. In fact, in routine situations, if
we are given a description of an agent, we can usually hear along
with that description the sorts of activities in which she or he
engages. And vice versa. So if we describe someone as a postal
worker, you will hear, immediately, the activities they routinely
undertake: sorting and delivering letters, wearing a certain uniform,
and so on. Then again: if we tell you that someone exhibits their
intimate parts on street corners while attempting to seduce passers-
by, you will be able to tell us which agent-description is most
plausible for that range of activities. For routine dialogue there is a
loose rule: if we have the agent-description, we know the activity;
and if we have the activity-description, we know the agent. That is
how life-as-usual proceeds. I'm a bass player (agent-description) – so
you know what I *do*. You dig flower beds and prune roses (activity-
description) – so I know what you *are*. And in both cases, we can
hear these things without being told in so many words. In ordinary
talk, the doing tells us the being, and the being tells us the doing.
Examples of such routine inferences from activity to agent (or vice
versa) can be found in *The X-Files* itself. In 'F. Emasculata' (2.22),
Mulder is on the trail of two escaped convicts. The trail leads to a
gas station where the two have been holed up, and the cop leading
the investigation is puzzled as to where they should look next.
Mulder draws on a routine agent-activity connection and reminds
the cop of how such commonsense techniques work:

2.22.2 'F. Emasculata', 28 April 1995
Mulder ((of the escaped convicts he's tracking)): If they had girlfriends
   they probably tried to call them.
   ((Walks to phone booth to check the last number dialled))[3]

The agent-activity connection is simple enough in this case: if the agent is 'boyfriend' or 'girlfriend', a routine and expectable activity is that they will call each other, especially if they are apart and there is news to tell (in this case, that the boyfriend is out of jail).

The same thing can work in reverse: an activity can be *dissociated* from a type of agent if it is not routinely connected to that type. So when Scully and Mulder discover that Sheriff Hamilton was once 'Jim Jim, the Dog-faced Boy' and then find him burying something in his garden at night beneath the full moon, they decide to see what he has buried. But just prior to this, Mulder cautions Scully about the assumption they are making by connecting a particular agent-description ('hairy-faced person') with a possibly non-routine activity for it ('lycanthropy', 'aberrant behaviour'):

2.20.3 'Humbug', 31 March 1995
Mulder: Y'know Scully hypertrichosis does *not* connote lycanthropy.
Scully: What are you implying?
Mulder: We're being highly discriminatory here. Just because a man was once
   afflicted with excessive hairiness we've no reason to suspect him of
   aberrant behaviour.
Scully: It's like assuming guilt based only on skin colour isn't it?
Mulder: ((nods))
   ((They start digging))

This instance has a number of interesting features. (1) The agent-activity connection is both announced *and put in doubt* by being made explicitly through such terms as 'connote', 'imply', 'assume', 'suspect', and their negations. (2) If actions speak louder than words, neither Scully nor Mulder actually believe in the doubts they raise, since they do try to exhume what the Sheriff has buried. (And this leaves them somewhat embarrassed when they find that the Sheriff has merely buried a potato as a superstitious cure for warts.) (3) The example shows how what may or may not count as a 'normal' agent-activity connection can be the basis of claims and struggles about political/moral correctness and incorrectness. We cannot go from skin colour to guilt (or innocence) and we cannot go from gender to, say, strength (or weakness) and so on. But it is not entirely clear whether we can go from hirsuteness to lycanthropy. What counts as an acceptable agent-activity inference, then, is not always fixed once and for all, but can be part of a particular historical conjuncture between descriptions, morality, and politics. The ways persons are discursively categorized tell us not only about *their* moral positionings; they also tell us about those who make the categorizations. We shall see another aspect of this later in the case of the 'Fresh Bones' episode (2.15).

As soon as we move even slightly outside this sphere of life-as-usual, things get more complex. And they also get more puzzling and alluring. For example, newspapers would not be able to sustain themselves if they reported only routine conjunctions of agents and activities: 'Dog bites man' is less interesting (news-wise) than 'Man bites dog.' Another of our favourites is the magazine headline: 'Killer Nuns!' What is going on here – and it brings us close to *X-Files* territory – is a disjuncture: nuns might do all sorts of things but kill; and killing might be done by almost anyone but a nun. Hence, throughout 'Humbug' (2.20), Scully reminds the Sheriff that even though he regards his 'freakish' townsfolk as 'normal', they may be killers – and she cites the fact that most relatives of serial killers think of them as perfectly normal persons until the truth comes out. Only in retrospect can the tell-tale activities ('peculiarities') be seen – and then they are seen as having been there 'all along'.

The question in science fiction is similar to news reportage: what is the activity, and who is its agent? Or: if one is supplied, how can the other be possible? These are the sorts of questions that *The X-Files* poses to viewers: the episodes are just such puzzles. Though it is also true that certain episodes are quite disappointing if viewed this way: for sometimes both agent and activity are known to the viewer very early on. The only interest then resides in seeing how Scully and Mulder manage to arrive at the same connection. And given *The X-Files* format, this usually means just after the often mysterious opening scene and the initial credits. At that point, we usually see Scully and Mulder in the lab or the morgue examining the evidence, or at the scene of the crime. At these crucial points, they set up – through their dialogue – the main pieces of the puzzle to be solved. They start to ask who and what agents and activities are involved, and speculate as to how they can be related, thereby establishing the main narrative interest for the rest of the episode.

X-dialogues

A brief but typical instance of the kinds of conjoint inference made by Mulder and Scully comes near the start of 'Fresh Bones' (2.15). Following the death of a Marine working at the Folkstone resettlement camp, Jack McAlpin – the audience knows that he crashed his car into a tree while hallucinating that a strange disfigurement was overtaking his face – Mulder and Scully investigate the crime scene. They notice a strange marking on the tree itself.

> 2.15.1 'Fresh Bones', 3 February 1995
> *Mulder*: Most of the refugees at Folkstone are Haitian.
>   ((Long pause))
> *Scully*: Mrs McAlpin believes that voodoo is behind her husband's death?

The suspect agents in this case are Haitian refugees, and the suspect activity is what they may have done to cause McAlpin's mysterious death. Accordingly, Scully and Mulder have to find an activity tied to the relevant agent-description that will render a plausible account of the Haitians' possible agency in the death. An obvious candidate, then, is voodoo: obvious as this agent's activity, but equally an 'unknown' quantity in terms of standard versions of cause and effect. This 'discovery' gives Scully her chance to deliver what has now become a standard line of scepticism in the face of Mulder's belief in aliens and the paranormal: 'You don't mean to tell me that you think X [agent] is responsible for Y [mysterious event]?'; or variations on that trope. We shall see another example of this in connection with the 'Calusari' episode (2.21). For now we can note an interesting variation on the format. Instead of charging Mulder with the expectable-but-weird agent-activity solution, Scully attributes it to the dead man's wife, Robin McAlpin. We can only speculate as to why this may be; but there is at least one candidate reason here: namely that the Haitians–voodoo connection has more than a slight element of 'racial' or 'ethnic' incorrectness about it. It is one of the possibly politically incorrect agent-activity connections we noted above in the case of Sheriff Hamilton and his 'lycan-thropy'. By attributing the connection to a third party, Scully is able to get the (as it turns out correct) narrative solution off the ground while, at the same time, attributing any negative ethics to a minor character.

The next instance is the post-credit lab scene from 'Humbug' (2.20). Following the death of the Alligator Man in Gibsontown (a haven for practising and former sideshow acts), Mulder notices a trail of such inexplicable deaths around the country. When he shows Scully a selection of photographic evidence, he goes on:

2.20.1 'Humbug', 31 March 1995
Mulder: The victims range from all different age groups, races, both male and female. The mutilations appear so motiveless that one would suspect some form of ritual. Yet they adhere to no known cult. No known serial killer would have been expected to escalate the level of violence of these attacks over such an extended period of time. So what do you think Scully? What are your initial thoughts?

This again is a typical trope for (what many think are the best) episodes in which neither the FBI agents nor the audience under-stand a set of events. Mulder describes the evidence, looks for patterns in it, and then invites Scully to speculate on the possible agent-types that could have brought about those events. In this case, as well, he rules out lists of candidates on the basis of his pro-fessional knowledge of the kinds of criminals to which the practices in question can be tied. Hence, the activity-description 'ritual killing' goes with the agent-description 'cults', and the activity-description 'low escalation of violence' goes with the agent description 'serial killer'. These, among other things, can be ruled out. Scully is invited to speculate. As is often the case, she refuses to be drawn into paranormal agent-activity solutions. Instead she turns to the photo of the Alligator Man and comments: 'Imagine going through your whole life looking like this.'

Since the scene-setting in this episode does not yield a plausible agent-activity connection, Scully and Mulder probe more deeply. They visit Gibsontown itself. On the way with Sheriff Hamilton to the shop of one Hepcat Helm, Mulder wants to check an illustration from one of Helm's manuals:

2.20.2 'Humbug', 31 March 1995

Mulder:	Just hang on. I wanted to ask you about this manual illustration. I recognise most of the historical portraits you've drawn here. But what's *this* here?
	((pause))
Hepcat:	It's duh FeeJee Mermaid.
	((pause))
Hamilton:	Is *that* what that thing is?
	((pause))
Scully:	What's the FeeJee Mermaid?
Hepcat:	The FeeJee Mermaid — it's it's the FeeJee Mermaid.
Hamilton:	It's a bit of er humbug Barnum pulled in the last century.
Hepcat:	Barnum billed it as a real live mermaid. But — people went in to see it, all they saw was a real *dead monkey* sewn on the tail of a fish.
	((pause))
Mulder:	A monkey?
	((pause))
Hepcat:	A *mummified* monkey.
Hamilton:	It supposedly looked so bad he had to exhibit it as a *genuine* fake.
Hepcat:	Ah but see ((pause)) that's why Barnum was a genius. You never know where the truth ends and the humbug begins. He came right out and he said this FeeJee Mermaid thing is just a bunch of BS. That made people want to go and see it even more. So I mean — who knows. Maybe for box office reasons Barnum — hawked it as a hoax — but in reality . . .
Mulder:	The FeeJee Mermaid *was* a reality.
Hepcat	((shrugs))
	((Then a little later))
Hamilton:	. . .what's all this about?
Mulder	((showing him a photo)): These tracks were found at several of the past few crime scenes. They've defied exact identification. But one expert speculated that they might be *si*mian ((pause)) in nature.
Hamilton:	You don't mean to tell me you think these tracks were made by the FeeJee Mermaid?
Scully	((to both men)): D'you recall what Barnum said about suckers?

Here a suspected agent gets inspected for the kinds of activity that might be tied to it. Since 'the FeeJee Mermaid' is a complete unknown (except to sideshow insiders), its possible range of tied activities is unknown. It is effectively 'the thing' or 'the creature'. The question is: could one such activity be strange murders? Mulder, finding a suitably informed insider (presumably, as we find out a little later, because he has his suspicions about a possible 'simian' agent) mobilizes the agent-description: 'But what's *this* here?' Scully attempts to solicit an activity-description: 'What's the FeeJee

Mermaid?' The answer does not make the required connection. On the contrary, as is almost typical of this episode (cf. Dr Blockhead's several assertions to the effect that some mysteries are better not cleared up), the answer is of the 'maybe yes, maybe no' variety: perhaps it is a fake, perhaps it is real, who knows? It is left to the Sheriff to articulate what is usually Scully's line: 'You don't mean to tell me . . .?' This allows Scully an even more sceptical position, addressed to both men: 'D'you recall what Barnum said about suckers?'

'The Calusari' (2.21) is more typical of the narrative structure. The audience has a fairly good suspicion of who the agent is and what the strange activity is – even though we cannot guess the connection at first. The episode begins with a fairly direct suggestion that a young boy, Michael Holvey, has somehow 'willed' the death of a toddler, Teddy Holvey, to whom he is related. The 'somehow' sets the narrative puzzle. Psychic powers are suggested, along with a barely visible 'attacker' whom Michael seems to control. He appears to 'think' the infant on to the track of an oncoming showground train. In the lab, Mulder spots a helium balloon behaving strangely in a photo taken just before the death.

2.21.1 'The Calusari', 14 April 1995
Mulder: You see this is a helium balloon here and the one thing I did learn in kindergarten is that when you let them go they float up up and away but you see this is moving away from him – horizontally.
Scully: Did you learn about wind in kindergarten?
Mulder: Well I called the National Weather Service and they said on the day that Teddy died the wind was blowing *north* but you see the balloon is moving *south*. As if it's being pulled against the wind.
Scully: Pulled? By whom?
Mulder: Well I don't know. That's why I came to Chuck, the king of digital imaging.
    ((Then a little later))
Chuck ((pointing to a shape holding the balloon by a string)): Here it is. ((pause)) It's clearly a concentration of electro-magnetic energy. ((pause))
Scully: Uh so you're saying that er a ghost killed Teddy Holvey? ((pause)) Has anyone checked the camera that took this photo?

Here, unlike the audience, Mulder and Scully have only an outcome: a toddler who has escaped an apparently escape-proof harness and, it would seem, 'wandered' on to a train track. (Did he wander or was he led?) They have no candidate agent and no possible activity which could bring about the event. In this computer-lab scene, again immediately following the credits, they speculate first on the activity. It is somehow connected with a helium balloon which we (although they do not) know Michael Holvey wanted, having lost his own. It effectively becomes a substitute agent, something which has 'led' the toddler to his death. As an agent, it has a set of typical predicates which everyone knows: 'when you let them go they float up up and away'. But this agent description defeats those standard preferences (as per the headline 'Killer Nuns'). It has done something helium balloons cannot do: drifted horizontally against the wind. *Ergo*, another agent is responsible for its movement, for 'pulling' it along, presumably to lure the toddler on to the track. Enhancing the image, the computer scientist Chuck is able to get a further visual unknown on to his screen and ours: 'a concentration of electro-magnetic energy'. So a possible quasi-human agent has been found, and Scully can introduce her by now completely expected 'You mean to tell me?' line, plus the equally expected dismissal of what she thinks Mulder might have in mind: 'Has anyone checked the camera that took this photo?'

As a final example, there is an interesting twist to these agent-description conventions in 'F. Emasculata' (2.22). More than one X-phile has noticed and complained that this episode is egregious to the series, containing neither paranormal nor alien activities. It is a straight conspiracy narrative based on a big pharmaceutical company that secretly experiments on captive live populations. Given that this part of the story is 'outed' very early in the episode, the main puzzle does not have to do with peculiar events or 'beings' at all; rather, the agents in this case are literally the agents, Mulder and Scully, themselves. And the unknown activity is: why are they on this case? – apparently one in which two 'mere' convicts have escaped from the state pen.

The episode begins with a bio-diversity scientist in the jungle who finds a dead animal body with strange pustules that are crawling with peculiar insects. Investigating, he is squirted in the face by one of the pustules. Later, a similar-looking piece of meat is delivered to a penitentiary. Some infected prisoners manage to escape and Mulder and Scully are called in – but only with a brief to aid in the recapture of the convicts.

2.22.1 'F. Emasculata', 28 April 1995
Mulder: I thought this was about escaped prisoners.
Scully: It is.
Mulder ((indicating a medical crew in an adjacent room)): Then who are
          the men in the funny suits?
          ((pause))
Scully: I don't know – it looks like some kind of decon. situation.
          ((Then a little later))
Mulder: Where did this case originate Scully?
Scully: Came out of Skinner's office.
Mulder: Did he say why he gave it to us?
Scully: No – why?
Mulder: Well this is not the type of thing the FBI normally gets called in
          on – I have a feeling we're not being told the entire story here.
Scully: I've got the same feeling.

Mulder's first line is interestingly self-reflexive. It could just as easily refer to the episode itself as to his own narrative situation within it. Then there is a side-puzzle: what agent goes with wearing funny suits (decontamination outfits)? Scully speculates. Then Mulder gets to the main point of the puzzle: if the agent is an FBI agent, then getting called in on a fairly normal prison break is not appropriate. On the contrary, that is no solution to the question 'What are we doing here?' It must have to do with some other, more FBI-like, activity, presumably connected with the side-puzzle, the men in funny suits. So while the audience can have pretty good suspicions about 'the entire story' (and this makes the episode far from the best ever), Mulder and Scully are not 'being told the entire story'. Once they find out, of course, there is nothing much to do other than pursue it to its inevitable conclusion, which leads to one of the series' continuing puzzles: who is the Cigarette Smoking Man and what does he have to do with the X-Files? The solution to this master agent-activity puzzle may (or may not) have to wait until well into a further season, or the feature film.

Either way, this remains a continuing instance of what each episode does with varying degrees of success: talking the unknown into existence. Here, as in so many cases, we can see that popular-cultural texts, even when dedicated to the spectacular, offbeat, or hyper-normal, rely on techniques and devices found and used in everyday life. Otherwise, they would make no sense. Our next case turns us to perhaps the ultimate case of the audience as an agent that brings the unknown into existence: from *X-Files* to x-words.

CROSSING WORDS

Aptly capturing the ways we ease into leisure after periods of work, the Australian crossword expert, Noel Jessop, writes:

> You've had a trying day at the office, shop or factory. Now you're heading home. Navigating a course through the throngs of your fellow afternoon escapees, you board your train, bus or ferry, and with the goddess of good fortune smiling on you, you find a seat and settle back with a sigh of relief. Now you unfold your evening paper, glance at the depressingly sensational headlines, turn to the back page and groan at the glum report of the latest Aussie cricketing debacle (or maybe exult over the glowing accounts of the team's latest phenomenal success), then in desperation turn to the only thing in the newspaper worthy of your time and attention . . . the crossword. (Jessop 1994: 1)

What actually occurs from this moment on – once the puzzle is before us, the pen poised, the white squares ready to be filled? In the section below, we try to access the 'lived experience' of this everyday sequence of events, to show the commonsense technical knowledge-in-action of crossword puzzle solvers. In the section following it, we look at the practices of compiling crosswords. While, of course, our interest here is specifically in crosswords and the work they require as leisure activities, our analyses exemplify how to break down mundane event-sequences to display the techniques that constitute them. Here and throughout this book, we are concerned to show that culture is constituted *procedurally* – by its techniques – as much as *substantively* – in terms of its contents.

What the solver does

Because crosswords are mostly done by people acting alone, and because the solver detailing his procedures here is one of us (Alec McHoul), we shall move into the first person singular. As part of the analysis, however, we invite readers to follow the solver's steps and write the answers in sequence into the blank grid provided below, in order to see at first hand how these practices work.

1. First I see a 15×15 square grid, white on black, with numbers marking the start-letters or 'initials' of each 'light' – a light being an answer or, more strictly, the 'across' or 'down' spaces where an answer can be written. I peruse the grid before looking at the clues beneath it.

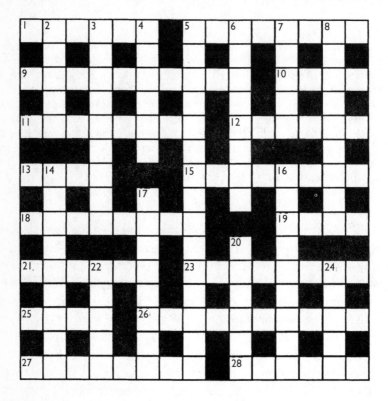

Source: *Times* puzzle no. 4624, *The Australian*, 21 April 1997, p22; originally published in *The Times* (London) as puzzle no. 20,433

2. I notice first that the grid is only just a fair one. That is, of its 29 lights, about one third (ten) have 'orphaned' initials – their start-letters stand alone, unconnected with other intersecting lights. I also notice that eight of the ten orphans are on the extreme left of the grid, so this means I shall not get a large block of 'across' initials by solving the 'down' clues at the far left.

3. It is time to look at the clues. I look at 1A. My normal procedure is to look there first. If I cannot get the answer and fill the light, I read the clues through until I get one. Today I know that 1A is not as crucial as usual, because it is not going to allow me into 1D and a group of initials on the left-hand side – there is no 1D today. Still, the clue, perhaps in compensation for the grid, turns out to be easy enough: 'Part of shoe conforming with others (6).' I quickly parse the clue as a double synonym: so I need a single word for both 'part of shoe' and 'conforming with others'. With 6 letters in the light, the answer is almost certain to be INSTEP. The compiler is allowed a little licence here: combining two words, 'in step', to make one.

4. Now I have a letter N at 2D, a T at 3D, and a P at 4D. I turn first to 2D. The clue reads: 'None of relay team have set off in this direction (5).' Because clues almost always have a synonym of the answer either at the start (in theme position) or the end (rheme position), I take 'this' to point to 'direction' as the synonym. Primary compass directions (if that is what we are dealing with here) only have four possibilities, one of which begins with N. So the light probably requires NORTH. This checks out from the initial letters of 'None of relay team have.' So it is almost certainly NORTH, though I'm puzzled as to why 'set off' is trying to tell me to take only the first letters. 'Start off' might have made more sense. But it would be ungrammatical and pretty much a giveaway. I move on without further thought.

5. Next in my self-selected sequence is 3D, starting with T. The clue gives me the following: 'Where cobbler should stick throughout life (2,3,4).' My experience with 'split' clues – clues with multiple word answers – suggests I may be dealing with a well-known phrase that has a double meaning, one denotative and the other connotative. I go looking for puns and the like. The first word is T*, so it is pretty much got to be TO. Followed by a three-letter word, we are most likely looking at TO THE ****. Now I need something to do with cobblers, taking up four letters: AWLS? No, it is LAST. So the answer's going to be TO THE LAST.

6. Although the previous step has given me a number of inter-sections, and 9A is looking especially interesting, I stick with the plan of going to 4D: 'Englishmen in Perth rapidly firing gun (3-3).' Now, being an Englishman who lives in Perth, Australia, I am

immediately suspicious: this clue must have nothing to do with Englishmen in Perth (Australia or Scotland); it must be some kind of red herring. And because I have an initial P, I look for partial anagrams of 'Perth', wondering how 'Englishmen' could give the missing sixth letter. However, the split clue alerts me again to the possibility of a double synonym. So much for the 2D, 3D, 4D plan then. I draw a blank at 4D and look instead at the rather promising 9A.

7. The clue is: ' "R" for "Reckoning" (10).' With a *R*T beginning I suspect something like WRITING (as one of the 'three Rs'), but am unable to take it any further.

8. Then it occurs to me that 'Perth' in 4D is just an instance of an Australian place, such that an Englishman might be a 'pom'. If this is plural, then POM-POM is a possibility. *Chambers* dictionary has 'pompom' as a machine gun, but the word has no hyphen. Still, it is too good not to be right. So now I know that 9A is unconnected with WRITING, since it runs: *R*T*M****.

9. Now the nice set of intersections, *H*E*O**, takes me to 11A, where the clue is 'Garden tool has cut round – it helps to put heel in (8).' The letters I already have suggest that 'hoe' is the garden tool in question – sheer serendipity, because putting that word in, I get *HOE*O** and this leads to a strong suspicion of a word beginning with SHOE **** because of the connection with 'heel'. What puts the heel into a shoe is a shoehorn. And so I write out SHOEHORN and find that it consists of 'hoe' (garden tool) around/'round' the word 'shorn', meaning 'cut'. So the answer is complete.

10. Moving down the page to 13A, the clue is 'Singer, mid-morning, finally got out of bed (4).' Because 'singer' is in theme position, I suspect DIVA. But 'mid-morning' suggests the letter 'N' (it appears in the middle of the word 'morning') so I pass on, thinking it may be the name of a well-known singer rather than DIVA.

11. Given that not many helpful intersections are left, I decide to look at the 'big one', 5D. If I can get this, I'll have a new bank of potential intersecting lights available, plus the initials to 5A, 15A, and 23A. Also: the clue is split, so it is probably a well known phrase: 'When it is very cold, one may look sharp (3,4,6,2).' The last word, I guess, is most likely a preposition: TO, UP, ON, etc. And the four-letter component, as so often in crosswords, is likely to be

ONE'S or, less likely, YOUR. So I work with something like *** ONE'S ****** TO/UP/ON. This means that the start-letter for 15A is probably an S. But I cannot fill the light for 5D yet. Nothing comes to mind that can connect very cold weather (is it weather, or just the letters V and C?) with looking sharp (which may have to do with hurrying or else being observant). There are too many possibilities here, so I return to the idea of 15A starting with S.

12. The clue for 15A reads: 'Sallying out in striking fashion (8).' This is interesting because both 'out' and 'fashion' could signal anagrams. Moreover, 'sallying' and 'striking' have the correct number of letters. So it is either an anagram of 'sallying' meaning 'in striking fashion' or an anagram of 'striking' meaning 'sallying out'. Starting with S, the first option would suggest S**INGLY, but the A and the L won't fit the blanks. On the other hand, 'striking' yields the simple anagram SKIRTING. But this looks too simple and, more importantly, 'skirting' does not generally mean 'sallying out'. Checking the *Chambers*, however, the verb 'skirt' describes what a pack of hunting dogs does as it breaks formation. Sally out? So I decide to pencil in SKIRTING, though with some reservations.

13. Because I don't have much confidence in SKIRTING for 15A, I decide to move back over to the left, perhaps out of the habit of going there for important intersections, sadly missing from today's puzzle. The next cab off the rank there is 18A: 'Two coins (one new, one old) – this should cover stamp (8).' Again, the inclusion of 'this' appears to point to something that covers a (postage?) stamp as the answer. So I should be able to make this up from the names of two coins. The one intersection I have is: ***T**** and one obvious stamp covering is a postmark. It fits, and 'Mark' is certainly a coin – but 'Post'? I am a little more confident here, so I pencil in POST-MARK, just to look at the effect on 5D.

14. Returning, then, to 5D, the position of the K suggests the six-letter word begins with SK****. So now I have something like: *** ONE'S SK**** TO/UP/ON. The connection between cold weather and speed then occurs to me because of the SK**** – it is SKATES and the well-known expression is going to be PUT ONE'S SKATES ON.

15. This supplies me with the next intersecting letter for 9A: *R*T*M*T**. And, of course, I should have seen this all along:

the one of the 'three Rs' that is synonymous with 'reckoning' is ARITHMETIC.

16. But then I remember that 5D has also given me *entrée* into 23A, where the answer literally stares out from the clue: 'Capitalism, anarchism – both hold charm (8).' Despite the distracting comma between the first two words of the clue, 'hold' points back to them as including the answer: capiTALISM ANarchism. This is the type of clue known to some as the 'light inclusive'. As a matter of compiler etiquette, there is normally only one of these in each puzzle. I know I have that one for today and shan't bother to search for more.

17. 5D has furnished another starting letter, for 5A: 'Collapse under strain, having accepted a freebie (8).' I cannot get the parsing of this clue. The answer is probably a synonym of 'collapse' or 'freebie'. The only thing beginning with P that I can think of is PROLAPSE. But it is too close to 'collapse' in the clue. Nothing happening here, and so time to go back to the left.

18. I choose 27A because it will at least give me final letters for four other lights: 'Criminal takes two fools in (8).' Well, if 'Englishmen' in 4D can be 'pom' repeated, so 'two fools' looks like being 'ass' repeated. If this then takes the word 'in' at the end, we get ASSASSIN. This does not seem too hard and suggests a look at the new final letters I have got from it.

19. Reading the clue for 17D, I am simply at a loss again: 'Doctor visited Sanders' subordinate (8).' Who can Sanders be? 'Doctor' can mean a word has to be doctored, anagrammed. Or else it can be MO, DR, or MB. Again, I cannot parse this clue.

20. What is left? My guess at 15A, SKIRTING, and the answer to 23A, give one possible and one definite letter for 16D: 'Derived from forebears from parts of Lancaster (9).' With nine letters, this looks like an anagram of 'Lancaster' (my *alma mater*). So I write out the letters in a circle and underneath: T***S****. Now I need to insert the letters L/A/N/C/A/E/R into the spaces to get a word meaning 'derived from forebears'. It may be to do with genealogy, or else with wills and inheritances. After a closer look at the circle of letters, though, it looks as if it is going to be ANCESTRAL. After all, SKIRTING was wrong. Out with the eraser.

21. I know from the A of ANCESTRAL that 15A is going to be an anagram of SALLYING and will mean 'in striking fashion'. Again writing the letters in a circle to delete their linearity, giving each letter the same visual status, I find SIGNALLY.

22. But now I also have a new start letter – for 19A: 'Policeman putting mafioso finally inside prison cell (4).' With short (three- and four-letter) answers, the clue always looks too long! But 'mafioso finally' is just going to be the last letter, O, and 'policeman' rendered in three letters is pretty much going to be COP. Hence COOP can go into the light at 19A.

23. This gives me an O for the last letter of 8D – a fairly rare ending – which is now worth a look. The clue is interesting too: 'A jolly bad fuss about it – Kipling described how it started (9).' Now the word 'bad' again suggests anagram activity is going on, and 'a jolly' has six letters. So maybe I need those letters and a three-letter word for 'fuss'. That would be 'ado'. So I circle the letters A/J/O/L/L/Y/A/D/O. Because 'about' is in the clue, I assume the ADO part goes around/about the other letters. But I cannot get anywhere with this. The J seems to be a serious problem. Perhaps it is a proper name – some place in a Kipling story?

24. The next candidate in terms of intersections is, by now, 6D: 'Chap with a passion for church architecture (8)', **C***G*. The G* ending along with 'passion' suggests 'rage.' So: **C*RAGE. If the 'chap' is 'Vic', then it will be VICARAGE, so I revise 'passion' to 'a passion' to include the other A. That makes better sense. And the V looks interesting for the next step.

25. 5A has a curious and (in terms of English words, very delimiting) start: P*V*****. I can't think of any eight-letter words to do with 'collapse' or 'freebie' that start this way. In fact I cannot think of any words of this kind. No good looking here. But the top right is starting to look better.

26. I have the start-letter for 12A: 'Without you, as they say, what is left to settle? (6).' The question-mark may be there for grammatical reasons, or to signal a slight twisting of clue etiquette. Which could it be? Probably the former. So we probably need a word for 'what is left', and then we have to take the letter U from it ('you, as they say' → U). That's probably the parsing, but I cannot think of a synonym

for 'what is left'. I toy with REST, but nothing really works along that front.

27. So back to the final letters generated by the answer to 27A. The next going right to left (why that way?) is 22D: 'Steps taken to eliminate salt from cake (5)', five letters, ending in A. It probably means 'steps taken'; something to do with 'measures' perhaps. Too obscurely Brechtian? But then a word for 'salt' has to be taken out of a synonym for 'cake'. Could 'salt' be NA? No that is just sodium, the element.

28. I am really starting to run out here. 14D is a possibility, though. If POSTMARK is right for 18A, then it is **O* ****S. The clue reads: 'None the less, corrosion's ruined this medal (4, 5).' Could there be a typo, 'medal' for 'metal'? After all I am doing this in the *Australian* newspaper, which frequently mis-sets copy from the (London) *Times*. For some reason, I want 'rust' in here, but it doesn't go.

29. This is the first hiatus; though I am not sure whether that is the right word. More likely: I am just stuck as far as the stepwise procedure goes of moving from light to light, led by intersection values. All I can do is scan the remaining clues, especially including those I have passed on so far. The first of these is 13A which I wanted to be DIVA. How could that be? Well now I can see it. The N has to be *deleted* ('got out') and it has to come from the *end* of another word ('finally') and that word has to mean 'bed'. So DIVAN minus N gives us DIVA.

30. This means that the first, four-letter, word of 14D looks like this: I*O*. The only possibility here is IRON, and the 'medal' synonym means it is almost certainly IRON CROSS. No typo: it is a medal after all. But why that? I've missed it all along. It's an anagram of 'corrosion's' minus one of its letter 'O's (signalled by 'None the less' – that is, 'delete a zero'). But the clue is neat – and the answer lends some more weight to 18A being POSTMARK.

31. Getting the answer to 14D at least gives some (albeit non-initial) intersection possibilities: at 21A and 25A. The first of these reads: 'Creature once regarded as divine, namely horse (6).' We are prob-ably looking for a divine creature. Then if the word begins *C, the 'namely' could be 'SC' (or 'sc.', namely). That plus a four-letter

horse will get the light. 'Arab' comes to mind – a common synonym in crosswords for 'horse' – generating SCARAB as the answer.

32. This then gives us some intersections for the mysterious 17D which now reads: *A*B***S. Is it possible to use MB here (as in 'doctor')? If so, I can try *AMB***S. Perhaps Sanders' subordinate was LAMB***S. Or perhaps there is a hint of 'Dr Lamb' here? No breakthrough with this one.

33. I seem to have overlooked the start-letter I had all along for 24D: 'Plant arbours? (5).' It may be a double synonym with a 'twist' (marked by the question-mark), but I can't get a word with two such meanings – even with a twist.

34. This leaves the L intersection in 28A and the clue looks a bit easier: 'Join up broken lines, given time' (6). '[G]iven time' looks like just being a final T. So it is **L**T, and the 'broken' suggests an anagram of 'lines'. Therefore, ENLIST.

35. I am at another sticking point or hiatus. Time for an inspiration or epiphany, a stroke of luck or some accidental bit of thinking. I decide to go to a light with no intersections at all so far, something I haven't tried yet: 7D. The clue is: ' "A", for instance, stands for "Auspices" (5).' Soon I see that it is a straightforward charade made up of A + EG ('for instance') + IS ('stands for') so that the synonym for 'auspices' is AEGIS.

36. Now 5A looks very odd indeed: P*V*A***. Surely there is nothing like this in English; something must be wrong. It turns out to be 5D! After all GET ONE'S SKATES ON would be just as good an answer and that gives a much better set of possibilities for 5A: G*V*A***. This means the ultimate shame of getting out the correction fluid and altering something I was previously sure of. (This is quite different from pencilling in answers as tentative rather than certain.) Still it does yield an answer for 5A as GIVEAWAY: a synonym for 'freebie' made out of an expression for 'collapse under strain' ('give way') and the letter A.

37. I still have very little to go on. The top right is not making much sense at all. The Kipling clue at 8D seems to be holding things up, so I scan around again, to the point where it looks as if the method of rational progression has completely given way to: get anything you can. I move to new territory, 26A.

38. Here the clue reads: 'Spy or nark – 'e gets busily involved (4,6).' The apostrophe in e' suggests a cockney expression. But it is also the case that 'Spy or nark 'e' has the right number of letters, ten. So I try using an anagram circle on these letters, but to no avail.

39. For some reason, while I am doing this, working with the circled letters, my attention drifts to 25A: 'Wander around city, talking (4)': 'drifts' in the sense that I move up a clue on the page and also to the left on the grid. Here the 'talking' part suggests a simple pun, the kind of clue often marked by 'we hear', 'for auditors' and 'according to rumour'. And the city that sounds like 'wander around' is, of course, Rome – the light is ROAM.

40. Now I have all the intersects for 22D, R*M*A. That's pretty limited. I figure from the look of the letters (the way Scrabble players do) that it has to be RUMBA. That is a dance, so 'steps taken' seems a fair synonym. So the missing 'salt' is going to be AB, a sailor, an able seaman. If those two letters are dropped from 'rumbaba', a kind of cake, the light appears.

41. I still want the Kipling in 8D, and it occurs to me that Kipling wrote stories about how the so-and-so got its so-and-so. Animals! So the answer could be an animal involving the letters from 'ado'. Well that suggests the possibility of 'armadillo'. It fits. But now the retrospective problem of trying to find why. After a few attempts at parsing, it ends up looking like this: 'fuss' is ADO and 'bad' is ILL. Put the latter inside the former: ADILLO. Now where do we get the ARM? I suspect that 'A jolly' is a Royal Marine. Jolly-Jack-Tar? Now maybe I'll find out how the armadillo got its . . . armour? Out with the dusty old Kipling. The anagram was, after all, a red herring.

42. This makes 10A look very possible: G*M*. 'For instance, go for disabled quarry (4).' Sadly, the answer is GAME. This is Short Clue Overload Syndrome: the triple pun. OK, it is cryptic, but not very polite.

43. The Kipling answer also gives me the intersects for 12A. I have already toyed with a word for 'what is left' minus its letter U. Now it seems that word is 'residue'. Minus U = RESIDE ('settle').

44. Another quick look at 17D. Its current status is as follows: *AMB***S?? Or could POSTMARK actually be wrong? It is still

only pencilled because of my uncertainty over POST as 'coin'. Does it make more sense like this: **MB***S? Still nothing here.

45. I haven't paid any attention yet to 20D. Perhaps I have an aversion to bottom-right corners because they don't usually help with anything else. If we work left to right and top to bottom, then the bottom right is the most isolated corner. At 20D, there is 'Pass by the Spanish Church's eastern end (6).' I should have looked here earlier because 'the Spanish' is routinely 'el'. This gives me EL***E. Do I get that final E from 'eastern'? Or do I need a four-letterer meaning the eastern part of a church?

46. Still fascinated by 17D, I guess awfully (Scrabble-wise) at IAMBUSES!!!

47. Also 24D is proving strange. At least one thesaurus gives me 'axle' as a synonym for 'arbour'. Is 'axles' a kind of plant? Then what of the question-mark? But if I try that, it might help 26A. Sadly, though, that would give an L intersection in 26A and there is no L in the 'Spy or nark 'e' anagram – which I still cannot get.

48. The solution to 20D becomes clear. Hence ELAPSE (to pass by).

49. Now the second word in 26A runs P*R***. Taking out PARKER from the anagram, I am left, yes, amazingly, with NOSY!

50. So what are the 'arbours' in 24D: A*E*S. Could they have a question-mark because they are really 'harbours' with a missing H? Then I'd need another word for 'harbours' beginning with an H which, when dropped, gives the name of a plant. Perhaps 'harbours' is a verb? Thesaurus time again. *Roget* comes up with 'haven' and *Chambers* gives 'avens' as 'any plant of the hardy rosaceous genus *Geum*'. A sigh of relief here because it looked as if AVENS would be the remaining clue to be checked in tomorrow's paper; the word that would bother me all day; the word bringing the shame of incompletion.

51. Back to the POSTMARK. Perhaps 'post' just means 'old'? But then 'post-' usually signifies just the opposite: after. New?

52. I decide to retry the idea of LAMB*N*S for 17D but still cannot get a word here. Then the word 'visited', with respect to doctors in

particular, makes me think of 'saw'. So it is SAWBONES, a synonym for doctor. I still don't know where 'bones' comes from. Must have been some underling of someone called Sanders. Of the River?

53. That leaves POSTMARK. So I am just going to ink it in!

What the compiler does

Below is an exchange of e-mail letters between one of us and a well-known crossword compiler. In part, it shows the work of crossword compilation. But at one point it also alludes to the conjectures we have made about how crosswords are both made and solved and, moreover, how those making and solving practices may be related. We return later to our central topic, the question of the making–solving interrelation.

Letter 1

Dear ———,
[. . . preliminary lines deleted]
Would it be possible for you to send me a brief list of the basic stages you go through in compiling a cryptic? What interests me is the *order* of the procedure. I don't need loads of details *about* each stage – just a rough ordering of the stages. Would that be possible?
Cheers,
Alec

Letter 2

Dear Alec,
Being the maverick heretic of this cryptic game, I may not be the best person to ask about the procedure of creation, but you asked for it. I write cryptic clues for fun, without having used the word or phrase in an actual puzzle, but you know about my file of 45,000 plus entries. I compose only in 12 standard diagrams developed years ago to give a good cross-section of words of all lengths, and to conform to my own rigid set of rules concerning grid construction. On a work-sheet of empty grids I put an A in the top left-hand corner of the first grid, a B in the second and so on . . . or a P and Q if the last puzzle I completed started with an O. On the Mac-Dos machine I ask *Axword* (a

Windows programme) to show me the A words of the appropriate length and hunt through them for one that takes my fancy. On the other machine I ask *File* [a Macintosh database] if I have written a clue for that word or phrase, and if I have already used it in puzzles for the publication I am currently setting for. A bit of care needs to be taken here. I never put in an answer without checking to see if the crossing cells and the end might present problems with the intersecting words, but have done so many that it is rather instinctive now. You would just have to be steady as she goes. The 'fill' (there is a good Yankee cruciverbal term for you) gets built up in this way, using the wild-card search facilities of each program as more and more letters get set in the grid. Eventually I get a fill! Next I use *Crossword Magic* to enter the raw puzzle to the computer. *CM* is a piece of infantile software that just happens to have the best entry method of all the crossword software I have seen. *Crossmaster*, and now *Crosspuzzler*, both access puzzles made by *Crossword Magic*, so I convert the original to the new format and it is ready for cluing. On the top half of the [Macintosh] Performa screen I display the puzzle and arrange my Cryptic Clue file on the bottom. I ask *File* to list the words of the puzzle, and if I have a clue already written I type it into the puzzle. If not, I write one, adding it to the *CC* file and the puzzle. A bit of double-checking of one thing and another and print. Voila! A puzzle! Reading that back over, I feel it to be a bit simplistic, but then you didn't want a novel. If the above fails to quench your thirst let me know.
Cheers,

———

Letter 3

Dear ———,
Thanks a million. I didn't want to say what it was for – because that may have influenced your response. In fact, I suspect that compiler-competence is solver-competence in reverse (and vice versa!) What you've sent is invaluable to a wee thing I am working on right now. I'll get back to you with more later – I am being called to make the pasta sauce. A real man's job!
Alec

Letter 4

Dear ———,
This will, I promise, be my last bit of bothering. What I want to know about is how you construct a clue: that is, if you don't have one in

your database. Can I do the following: send you a short list of words and ask you to give the steps by which you arrive at the clue? This can be painful I know, because it may mean trying to explain something totally intuitive. But sadly that is what my awful discipline (called, would you believe, ethnomethodology) works on: how everyday events are brought off. At least some sketches of the *order* by which you make the clue would be handy for me right now. So, if you're willing, here are my target words:

SIGNALLY
TALISMAN
VICARAGE
SHOEHORN

Cheers,
Alec

Letter 5

Dear Alec,
This will be stream-of-consciousness and likely to be incomprehensible. SIGNALLY: Toss around definitions – settle on 'Remarkably' as correct enough but not too obvious – turn to secondary indication [. . .] – look at parts of words – Sally around a mixed gin, ugh, too clichéd – Sign + Ally seems okay – Toss around the many ways to represent these – 'Sign' a footballer = Engage – 'Ally' = Associate, of course. Make it gel – 'Remarkably engage associate' – Not brilliant, but beyond criticism. It'll do. TALISMAN: Amulet, charm, fetish, ju-ju all good definitions – Charm suitably ambiguous – What about an anagram . . . I think I see some animals in there, oh, there is a T left over – Okay, a partial . . . 'Charm wild animals' will cover the last seven letters – so, something for the T – Model, Tenor, Ton . . . no, they won't run – Back to the old shorthand list . . . back to front, beginning to tire, hasty heart, third of October . . . Yair, that's it 'Charm wild animals after the third of October (at the end of August).' VICARAGE: A clergyman's residence . . . that is sexist and too obvious. Am in a shitty mood so give the solver heaps . . . Residence, that is plenty for them – There is a car in there; a long time, a V for opposed or five . . . Oh, man, there is all sorts – whirl the whole thing round in the skull like clothes whizzing around in a washing machine and see what pops out – Give 'em a melange of bits – Opposed to (V) one (I) about (CA – Circa) fashion (RAGE) residence (definition) – does not make a lot of sense, but all the bits are accounted for. Take it. 'Opposed to one about fashion residence.'

SHOEHORN: Looks like a horrible thing to find a definition for without giving the game away by mentioning shoe or footwear – but the word can be a verb! I see a 'Shorn' around the outside, maybe 'Fleeced,' 'Clipped' or some such – and a hoe inside 'Garden tool' 'Implement' 'Weed' . . . ? Ah, but there is also an OEH inside . . . cannot see those letters without automatically thinking 'Old English Hospital.' Okay, what about: 'Clipped around Old English Hospital to squeeze into a tight space.' Let 'em see if they can make any sense of that, although why they'd want to defeats me. How the hell did you know I had already written clues for those words? Just don't ask me to write a cryptic clue for ephnodistemocophology, or whatever it is that is softening your brain these days. Win the Lotto!
Cheers,

———

Production and recognition

It should be evident from the above that there is immense overlap between the methods and techniques used by the solver and the compiler respectively. It is as if one, the compiler, carefully knits together an artefact stitch by stitch and then leaves cryptic instructions for the other, the solver, who can then unravel those stitches using very similar sets of implements. Putting this another way, we might say that compilation is a kind of 'progressive knotting into' the grid, to borrow a term from Thomas Pynchon, while solving is a progressive untying of the same knots (1973: 3). Compiling tightens or compacts; while solving loosens or decompacts. So the techniques remain reasonably constant between the two parties while the *ordering* of the techniques is, almost but not quite, reversed in each case. That is not unlike the relationship of *X-Files* writers to *X-Files* audiences. Let's explore this further.

The compiler's task is taken up mostly with the achievement of a fit. For some compilers (though not for the one in question here) the fit is achieved at the same time as the grid itself. In some crossword programmes, all the squares begin as lights. The compiler then enters an initial word followed by a dark square, as a punctuation mark or separator. The computer program then mirrors each dark in order to generate a half-symmetrical grid. This very raw method requires much trial and error and can sometimes mean scrapping a puzzle and starting again, when impossible intersection combinations arise. The problems that arise in this case are similar to those encountered by our solver at step 36 above: the combination P*V*A*** cannot produce an English word. For a compiler in this situation, the word has to be changed somehow. For the solver, though, the change has to be related to a 'mistake' in one of the intersecting lights.

Our present compiler, however, works instead with a set of given grids: '12 standard diagrams developed years ago to give a good cross-section of words of all lengths, and to conform to my own rigid set of rules concerning grid construction' (Letter 2). From previous correspondence on this matter, we know that the rules necessitate giving the solver a fair chance: not having too many orphaned initials, not having lights with fewer than half their cells intersecting and so on. Interestingly enough, the solver also sets out with a brief inspection of the grid according to at least one of these rules – the one concerning orphaned initials (see step 2). Here is a case where, briefly, the order of the setting and the order of the solving are the same. But from this point on things diverge considerably in terms of sequencing – though not the techniques that constitute each sequence.

For the compiler, as we have noted, the time-consuming question is the fit: the clues literally get tacked on at the final stage. But for the solver, the *clues* are the crux of the game. They generate the solver's sense of the 'correctness' of his answers, especially early in the proceedings. Eventually, the clues come to be supplemented by the already-entered answers so that the solver can work, as he says, Scrabble-wise, from the secondary hints given by the intersecting letters. At points, for example in the very final step, the grid is all the solver has to go on. So the rough sequence of operations for the solver is:

Solver: clues → clues + grid → grid only

We are not dealing with discrete stages but with an analogic progression, although our solver experiences a couple of episodes which he calls 'hiatuses' (steps 29 and 35) and alters his methods of attack. Then, for the compiler, the motion is reverse:

Compiler: grid → grid + clues → clues only

We can justify the inclusion of the middle term of the compiler's sequence here by looking at how he refers to the clue-relatedness of the fit as it builds up:

> I ask [the database] if I have written a clue for that word or phrase, and if have already used it in puzzles for the publication I am currently setting for. A bit of care needs to be taken here. I never put in an answer without checking to see if the crossing cells and the end might present problems with the intersecting words, but have done so many that it is rather instinctive now. You would just have to be steady as she goes. (Letter 2)

We take this to mean that a word can get selected for the fit *not just* in terms of its use in providing 'good' letter intersections (where 'good' would mean something like: likely to produce actual English words in the intersecting light), though this *is* an important aspect of word selection. But another criterion is whether the word has been used before in the publication. If it hasn't, then well and good, because the clue for it, from the database, can simply be entered. If it has been used before, then it is either discarded or a new clue written – presumably depending on whether the particular word is the *only* one that can fit into the grid, in this particular space, at this stage of the composition. The compiler does not want to alter a fit-so-far if it can be avoided, because each alteration has the potential to affect previously decided entries, and so on recursively until the fit might undo itself. As we have seen, he no more wants to do this than the solver wants to go back to *clues* to see whether or not a particular answer entry is right. However, this is not to say there is no revisability. The compiler feels obliged to make revisions if the fit starts to look impossible (grid-wise) or if the candidate word starts to look troublesome (clue-wise). For both compiler and solver, then, some entries are tentative (in which case the solver pencils them first) and some are firm. But it is also the case that such instances find the compiler looking back to the grid-so-far, while the solver looks back to the clues-so-far. Correspondingly, in these cases, while the compiler looks ahead to the clues-to-come, the solver looks ahead to the 'shape' of the grid-to-come.

In a sense, we have reversed temporal traversals of the same path and, perhaps at the mid-point of those two traversals, something like a 'meeting point' where solver and compiler, literally, *cross*; though each looks ahead towards his own, quite different, destination. As the compiler gets progressively locked to the grid, the solver gets progressively locked to clues. Then each must turn to the alternative: solvers to grids and compilers to clues. This is because, to some extent, the compiler side of things displays a sensitive dependence on initial conditions (SDOIC) (to borrow a phrase from chaos theory). He begins his grid with a letter A, for example, as he says in Letter 2. Given the grid, this locks him into, say, a seven-letter word beginning with A. Then he chooses whichever takes his 'fancy' from a computer-generated list. But the 'fancy' is constrained by the inter-sectional work ahead of him. The word ANXIOUS, for example, might be avoided because it leaves an X initial for its first intersect. And at least in theory, it must be possible for the first entry simply to be the 'wrong' word to start with: one that will prevent *any* possible complete fit. Hence, SDOIC. By contrast, the solver has a trajectory which is sensitively dependent on its *final* state: everything must end up not just with a *possible* fit (consisting of *any* English words) but with an *actual* fit such that the grid is filled with the specific words that the clues permit (in the first place) in combination with the grid intersections (as the puzzle progresses). Hence: at step 21, the solver finds that the word ANCESTRAL gives an A intersection with 15A. If the word at 15A contains an A, then it must be an anagram of 'sallying' and not of 'striking', though the sheer parsing of the clue allows both. We are now nearing the middle phase of the solution (21 out of 53 steps); the grid intersections are beginning to inform (for example, to disambiguate) the parsings of the clues. So how it is that the solver can tell that he is 'on track' or getting things right is that a definite *end* is in sight: an end, moreover, which has been predetermined, as the solver knows, by the compiler. For the com-piler, there is no such predetermination: the fit may take on any shape that it can and there are no 'clues' to guide him, precisely because he invents them once the fit is completed. So, again, we have roughly this pattern:

Solver: clues → clues + grid → grid only → determined final conditions

Compiler: determinable initial conditions → grid → grid + clues → clues only

Interestingly enough, we can make this 'circular' and interactive by taking the compiler's final term ('clues only') and assuming it to be identical with the solver's initial term ('clues'). For indeed, they are 'the same' clues.

But in another sense, they are not quite the same clues, as we can notice from Letter 5. The compiler always starts with a synonym or, as he calls it, a definition. He then builds up the clue mechanism ('secondary indication') by which the solver is supposed to find the synonym's other that is the answer. In doing so, he tries to hide the synonym (while observing the 'rule', which the solver also knows, of placing the synonym in the theme or rheme position in the clue). He does this by: (1) changing the part of speech of the synonym: so that, for example, TALISMAN (noun) → 'Charm' (verb); SHOEHORN (noun) → 'squeeze into tight space' (verb), and so on; (2) making the synonym 'semantically' related to the clue mechanism: 'Charm wild animals', 'engage associate', and so on; (3) using words that are cryptically ambiguous perhaps to have the solver do cryptic work on the *synonym* instead of the clue mechanism. Hence 'fashion residence' suggests an anagram of 'residence'; 'squeeze into' suggests a partial inclusion of one word in another, and so on.

This means, again, that the solver has to *begin* by trying to spot the synonym. The words 'this . . .' and 'for this . . .' sometimes help here – but they are few and far between. This is what our solver calls 'parsing': separating the synonym from the clue mechanism ('secondary indication') that will lead to its other, the answer. While the compiler has to disguise the two parts of the clue, the solver has to reveal them. But at the same time, each uses the same resources for the work:

- knowledge of how clue-types work; for example, that 'split' clues often refer to well-known phrases
- knowledge of letter-counting; such that the compiler might try to put in an anagram indicator and a word of a certain length in order to put the solver off the track of the synonym
- knowledge of certain abbreviations; V = 'against' or 'five,' CA = 'about' or 'circa', and so on
- knowledge of signals such as 'about' or 'around' to indicate words containing others
- knowledge of indicators; for example, anagram indicators

('doctor', 'wild', and 'made out'), and light-inclusive indicators ('hold' and 'contains')

- knowledge of how puns can be put on the agenda with 'we hear', 'for auditors' and the like
- knowledge of shorthand; 'mid-morning' → N; 'third of October' → T, and the rest

We can put this formally as follows, using superscripts to show we are dealing with *two* words that are synonymous, one of which goes into the clue and the other into the light.

Compiler: determinable synonym^1 in clue → clue mechanism → disguise tactics
Solver: parsing tactics → determined clue mechanism → synonym^2 in light

In addition, the ideal for solvers (which would be the worst scenario for compilers) is for their parsing tactics to work as the exact reverse of the compiler's disguise tactics. This shows that at least one sub-component of the game (the cluing part) has the same reversed procedure as the overall game (sketched above). If this is indeed what is going on, we can say that (again, almost but not quite): *compiler and solver competences are identical, but work counter-sequentially to each other.* This is extremely interesting, because it is one of the few instances we know where a fairly precise and symmetrical instance of *reflexivity* occurs (another might be when Hume and Miller, in our radio fragment, both know the stakes of membershipping or on-air silence – as does their audience). And we mean this term more in Sacks' sense than Garfinkel's. Garfinkel (1967) assumed that *accounts* and the *actions* they account for are reflexively constituted. Sacks was more interested in how a *culture* formed. He wanted to know the techniques people know, use, and share that establish a common culture, a common everyday order, which we think is displayed in our materials and the short analysis of them above.

Sacks conjectured that, for a culture to exist, its members must have methods for *producing* cultural objects (like promises and hammers) and methods for *recognizing* them as those cultural objects. In many cultural theories (all the ones we know) the theory consists of a conjecture about how production relates to recognition (or reception). Marxist theories of production and consumption, controlled by an economy of relations between them, are cases in point. Chomsky's positing of the 'wired in' grammatical competences of the 'ideal speaker-hearer' is another. Piaget's theory of a progressive equilibration between organism and environment is a third. Each relies on complex theorizations of the connections between two *different* parts of a culture: its production and recognition. Sacks does not offer another complex theoretical mechanism. Instead, he says, we think very boldly:

> A culture is an apparatus for generating *recognizable* actions; if the same procedures are used for generating as for detecting, that is perhaps as simple a solution to the problem of recognizability as is formulatable. (Sacks 1995a: 226)

This means, in effect, that if we look at everyday life closely enough, shifting our attention from content towards method and technique, we will begin to see that the *problem* of culture effectively disappears. We no longer have to conjecture about how production and reception (or generating and recognizing) are connected. At the level of everyday methods, they are no longer different entities. A culture is, in fact, where *we* recognize what *you* are doing because, for all of us, culturally, that is *how* we would do it. If there is a deep distinction between production and recognition, then there simply is not a culture. We are entitled to say only that there is a culture of participating in talk radio, viewing *The X-Files*, or doing crosswords, because the methods for the production and the methods for their consumption are identical. Practitioners in that culture must *assume* as much.

To put this another way, and returning to terms from our Preface, culture is only a 'problem' of connecting production ('generating') and consumption ('recognizing') when it is *speculatively* treated as a *spectacular* field in which cultural objects are always considered as *representing* something beyond them (such as gendered, economic, or racial 'patterns'). As we have seen from our investigations in this book, aspects of gender, economy, and race (to mention only three otherwise 'macro' concepts) are indeed important for understanding culture. But the crucial question is: how do these figure in *actual historical arrangements and in everyday events*? Looking at things this way, we begin to see the particularities and specificities of each case, and to see that how they might or might not be connected with wider issues has more to do with the actual case in question than it does with speculations about, for example, general and intangible socioeconomic patterns. Once culture becomes thoroughly ordinary (rather than spectacular), once it is inspected empirically (rather than speculatively), and once it is looked at in its own right (rather than as a secondary representation), it becomes a question of how people operate in everyday situations with particular devices – devices that turn out to be equally good for production and consumption (for generating and recognizing).

One recent definition of cultural studies runs as follows:

A new academic discipline dealing with a broad range of different types of texts for what they can tell us about the ways in which meanings, identities, and values are produced and reproduced in the world. Cultural studies is particularly interested in the political meaning of culture, dealing with issues such as gender, sexuality, ethnicity, class, technology, nationality, and so on. In contrast to the 'older' humanities, such as English studies, it is these theoretical and political issues that matter to cultural studies, rather than the value of the particular texts studied. (Fuery and Mansfield 1997: 200)

In this case, our EMICS-based approach is very much a contribution to the discipline as it stands and would want to retain some of what this definition contains. But at the same time, it also wants to remind students and professionals alike that everyday cultural 'texts' and 'macro' theories and politics do not always fit together seamlessly – in fact they rarely do on close inspection and, moreover, there is no reason why they *should*, for they exist in very different cultural fields from one another. In this case, it is our view that cultural studies can benefit most from beginning with actual cultural texts in their ordinary historical and everyday places *before* political and theoretical speculations are brought to bear upon them, *before* they are turned into mere artefacts of social criticism. And we even suspect that, once treated in this way, the value to them of critical speculations will often seem quite minimal in the light of their own complexities and peculiarities.

This concluding chapter, then, has involved several empirical demonstrations that (at least to a large extent) support Sacks' conjecture about the 'deviced' nature of everyday cultural 'texts' and about the complete *identity* between devices for their production and their recognition. As opposed to critical theorizing as a way of beginning any cultural study, then, we encourage readers to construct similar demonstrations from detailed step-by-step reconstructions of their own everyday activities to further test this conjecture. In each instance, we hope you'll try to use an EMICS-based approach by merging a thorough appreciation of relevant cultural theory and public discourse on cultural fields with precise inspections of local cultural practices and the devices that make them.

NOTES

1. Transcription conventions are as follows:

.hhh	audible exhalation
(hh)	audible inhalation
::	prolongation of sound
>word<	word spoken quickly
word	word stressed
wor-	word cut off
word – word	short pause between words
(.)	untimed pause
(0.0)	timed pause in seconds and tenths
[ ]	beginning and end of overlapped talk
= =	continuation points – no pause
( )	word(s) untranscribable
?	upward intonation

2. Here the term 'agent' covers what Sacks calls 'category members' and the term 'activities' covers what he calls 'category-bound activities.' (See Sacks 1972a, 1972b.)
3. For this section, we have simplified the transcript notation usually used in conversation analysis (see note 1) since speech-delivery features are not relevant to the current exercise. Most of the conventions should, therefore, be self-evident. Each transcript is labelled according to the following system: transcript 2.22.1 is the first transcript from episode 2.22. It is sequentially prior to transcript 2.22.2. The date of the original US broadcast is also given in the label.

Glossary: A Vocabulary for Popular Culture and Everyday Life

Cultural studies has borrowed its vocabulary from a diverse range of parent disciplines. In the list below, we have defined anything that looked to us as if it would appear as a specialist term to someone encountering cultural studies for the first time. For each entry, the term in question is followed by its principal discipline of origin, shown in square brackets. Where a term (for example 'discourse') has a number of possible definitions, we have opted to give the one most relevant to the way the term is used in the book, rather than aiming to be comprehensive. Cross-references appear in **bold italic** and foreign words and emphasis in *italics*.

a priori [philosophy]: before the fact. As an adjective, the term describes the fundamental grounds of a **discourse** – what it holds in place before any consideration of the empirical world of facts. A priori reasoning is reasoning on the basis of knowledge prior to experience.

accounting [ethnomethodology]: the ways in which everyday actors display what it is they are doing *in the very act* of doing it.

activity [EMICS]: what an **agent** does. Activities are described by **predicates**.

activity-description [EMICS]: see **predicates**.

agency [social theory]: technically, the capacity or scope for any social actor or group to act; often contrasted with structure (the formal limitations and constraints on any social actor or group in the performance of actions).

agent [EMICS]: one who does something (for example a participant in a drama). Cf. **activity**. Agents are, in effect, members in the technical ethnomethodological sense, and so the terms describing them can be collected in and as **MCDs**.

agent-description [EMICS]: a selection from an **MCD** to refer to a particular person as an instance of a set or group of persons. 'Quarterback' is an agent-description and 'football team' is the relevant MCD.

agoraphobia [psychology]: fear of public spaces; literally fear of the market-place.

alienology: a pseudo-science given to the investigation of an alien presence on this planet. Hence, an investigation of a non-existent object.

allo-regimentation [social theory]: discipline of the self from without; see *discipline*. Equivalent term: 'externalized inter-subjective government.' See also: *auto-regimentation*.

anomic [sociology]: adjective from *anomie*, a state of not being ruled, not being subject to laws or norms of social interaction.

auto-critique [social theory]: the capacity of a person to engage in correction through self-assessment and, eventually, self-discipline. See *discipline*; *auto-regimentation*.

auto-eroticism [psychology]: love of the self, self-arousal.

auto-regimentation [social theory]: discipline of the self by the self; see *discipline*. Equivalent term: 'internalized self-monitoring'. See also: *allo-regimentation*.

autotelic [philosophy]: adjective describing a situation in which the self achieves (or simply is) its own ends (from *telos*, an end or goal).

basic rules [ethnomethodology]: the formal rules of a game or sport which players must follow – by contrast with *preferential rules*.

behaviour modification [psychology]: a technique deriving from behaviourist psychology; here behaviour is modified through complex arrangements of rewards and punishments in order to induce 'correct' or desired responses in the subject.

bio-power [social theory]: the processes by which life (and in particular the body and its mechanisms) is brought under specific (often statistical) calculations and measurements.

bourgeois [social theory]: adjective describing the bourgeoisie, town or city dwellers (with connotations of at least moderate wealth and comfort, including those who own the means of economic production, such as shops and factories). Loosely, of the middle classes and their supposedly routine but pro-capitalist ideas and lifestyles.

bricolage [anthropology/cultural studies]: working in an ad hoc way with whatever comes to hand, as opposed to, for example, engineering, where plans, blueprints, and tools for a particular task are decided in advance. In cultural studies, *bricolage* (or 'improvisation') is thought to be an important process in the everyday use of commodities where, we sometimes hear, consumers are adept at assembling resistive 'meanings' from generically disparate commodities. Using Barbie and Ken dolls to simulate sado-masochistic sex would be one example; using empty supermarket carparks for roller-blading would be another.

canon [literary studies]: a valued collection of texts or art objects that exemplifies a particular tradition (for example, the course of English literature from *Beowulf* to Virginia Woolf). Originally the term referred to the approved collection of books in the Bible.

categorized pronouns (or categorials) [conversation analysis]: collective pronouns (you, we, they) which refer to a general sector of a population (for example men or women in general) and where an exhaustive list of those referred to cannot be drawn up – by contrast with *listed/summative pronouns*.

causation device [conversation analysis]: the division, in everyday language and action, of causes into two types. Type 1 causes are where the consequences flow directly from the activity (sticking your hand on a hot surface). Type 2 causes require the intervention of some agency before there is a result (being punished for under-age drinking).

ceteris paribus [law]: other things being equal. A point of law; a way of fudging irregular or disconfirmatory cases in the pseudo-sciences (such as economics); but also an everyday **orientational** that allows specific situations to be understood typically.

cognitive [philosophy/psychology]: adjective describing rational mental pro-cesses (as distinct from emotions).

collective unconscious [psychology]: Carl Jung's term for a pool of symbols and drives common to all human beings at all times and places.

commodification [social theory]: the process whereby natural materials (such as metal ores, trees, sand, and people) are turned into market goods (or commodities) with a particular exchange value (cars, books, window-panes and fashion models).

communicative rationality [social theory]: according to Jürgen Habermas, a form of rationality underpinning social relations when there is a genuine will to communicate between members; this is opposed to instrumental rationality, which is geared towards technical ends and outcomes.

confession [social theory]: initially a religious technique for bringing one's faults and sins to a priest in order to clear one's conscience and achieve absolution. Now any similar technique by which a *subject* narrates their internal states (usually, but not exclusively) to a professional authority.

connotation [semiotics]: see *denotation/connotation*.

continuity-system cinema [cinema studies]: associated with Hollywood fiction film, this model favours narratively motivated, cause-and-effect changes of camera angle or sound and editing, matching direction from shot to shot. This is designed to diminish the spectator's attention to the process of filmmaking in favour of spectacle, story, and plausibility.

cultural formation [cultural theory]: any cluster of cultural objects (and the cultural technologies that produce them) around particular events or practices that have their own identities and characteristics. Hence pop music, stamp-collecting, and rugby league are cultural formations. Going for a stroll, brushing one's teeth, and swearing are cultural, but they are not cultural formations, since they could each belong to any number of such cultural sets (or to none).

cultural materialism [cultural theory]: a theory associated with Raymond Williams in which cultural specifics (such as actual texts or objects) have primacy over theoretical generalizations about society, politics, or history.

culturalism [social theory]: an approach in the social sciences which holds culture to be central and primary rather than an *epiphenomenon* of a deeper and more 'real' order (such as the economy or climatic conditions).

cyber-pals [communication studies]: derivation from 'penpals'; persons who correspond regularly with one another using electronic means of communication such as e-mail.

decoding [cultural studies/semiotics]: at the level of cultural consumption, the attribution of cultural meaning to objects. See *encoding*.

demographic [social theory]: adjective describing the structural characteristics of a population: age, sex, class, race, income, place of residence, and so forth. The term is sometimes used as a noun: here 'a demographic' refers to a particular sector of a broader population in terms of one or more of the characteristics listed above. Hence, teenage girls constitute a demographic, as do the aged.

denotation/connotation [semiotics]: denotation is the (sometimes only apparently) literal meaning of a sign. 'It's cold in here' denotes the temperature, but it may actually mean 'Would you close the door?' This actual meaning is then the connotation.

determination [social theory]: effectively this means dependency. The concept crops up mostly in Marxist social theory where, in some cases, it is argued that economic conditions determine cultural production. This means that they cause the latter to happen in the form that they do.

diachronic [history/semiotics]: across periods of time or historical episodes.

dialectical sociology [social theory]: A synonym for some forms of Marxism – particularly those that rely on the philosopher Hegel's ideal of a dialectical pattern in historical change. Dialectical sociologists hold that *social formations* come about through the inevitable clash of contradictions in those that precede them. 'Dialectics', then, refers to the general law of development (usually of societies) based on the resolution of contradictions and antagonisms (theses and antitheses) at 'higher' levels (or syntheses).

diaspora [political science]: a dispersion or migration of whole peoples (or significant numbers of them) from one place, often a homeland, to another. Diasporic studies is now a major sub-branch of postcolonial studies.

diegesis/diegetic [literary and cinema studies]: diegesis is narration (originally the narration of facts in rhetoric); the term is now applied to features inside the narrative of a literary or film text. Hence diegetic space is roughly equivalent to *profilmic* space.

discipline [social theory]: any technique or set of techniques used to produce, police, or reform a particular kind of human subject *as* specifically that kind of subject. For example, medicinal dispensation used to regularize people as 'healthy' subjects; or punishments used to form children into schoolchildren. Discipline can arise from within the subject itself (*auto-regimentation*), or from external sites (*allo-regimentation*).

discourse [social theory]: a body of knowledge (particularly in the human sciences, but also elsewhere). Hence, the discourses of economics, biology, and linguistics.

dramaturgy [sociology]: a mode of social analysis associated with Erving Goffman in which dramatic concepts (performances, props, backdrops, scenery, scripts, scenarios, etc.) are used as models for describing and understanding everyday interaction.

effects model [media studies]: a model which assumes that media texts generate relatively automatic audience responses. (For example, the depiction of very thin models in magazines is supposed to lead young women to anorexia.)

encoding [cultural studies/semiotics]: at the level of cultural production, the imbuing of objects with cultural meanings. See: *decoding*.

epiphenomena [philosophy/social theory]: all things regarded (usually in a theory) as secondary to, or derived from, a more important and grounded reality. Singular: epiphenomenon.

epistemological break [history of ideas]: a term used by the social philosopher Louis Althusser to describe radical shifts in knowledge. The move from an earth-centred to a Copernican (heliocentric) view of the heavens is a good case in point because it involves (as did Althusser's original concept) a shift towards increased scientific status.

epistemological rupture [history of ideas]: see *epistemological break*.

epistemology [philosophy]: the branch of philosophy dealing with knowledge and the question of what can be known.

ethics of the self [social theory]: all the techniques of *discipline* by which a *subject* is formed and cares for itself.

ethnography [anthropology/sociology]: a method or technique for recording and describing particular cultural practices in as much lived detail as possible. This usually involves fieldnotes or, in some cases, audio, film, and video recordings.

existentialism [philosophy]: any philosophical position which assumes that human existence precedes its 'essence'. Strictly, a form of humanism. Any doctrine that holds human action and thought to be utterly in control of themselves and not subject to 'outside' (particularly divine) forces.

externalized intersubjective government [social theory]: see *allo-regimentation*.

figuration [sociology]: a concept used by Norbert Elias to describe how particular people come to inhabit generally available roles or social positions. It combines social structure (the **synchronic**) with historical change (the **diacronic**).

formulation [ethnomethodology/conversation analysis]: making explicit, in an everyday event, what that event is. For example saying 'Don't threaten me' marks the occasion, explicitly, as involving a threat.

functionalism [sociology]: the position, attributable to Émile Durkheim and, later, Talcott Parsons, in which any society can be viewed reductively in terms of its functions (for example its economic and cultural functions).

genre [literary/cinema studies]: strictly a type; usually referring to the classification of texts as novels, manuals, textbooks, diaries, handbooks, journals, dictionaries, and so forth. By extension, the term can apply to types of film, television, software, and other varieties of text.

Gestalt [psychology]: a school of psychology that reacts against atomism or reductionism (for example the reduction of mental states or behaviours to their basic components) by arguing that the whole (Gestalt) is greater than its parts. As a form of therapy, Gestalt psychology proposes self-discovery as the correct means of treatment. In this respect, it is aligned with **existentialism**.

governmentality/governmentalization [social theory]: terms coined by Roland Barthes and deployed by Michel Foucault to describe the whole of the arts and sciences of governing (from one's own bunch of keys to the world population). The term is, therefore, not restricted to national governments, but ranges more broadly to cover all cases of persons and equipment wherever and by whomever they are managed and regulated.

hegemony [political theory]: a concept, usually attributed to Antonio Gramsci, referring to processes by which people come to consent to the arbitrary social orders in which they find themselves because those arrangements are made to appear normal and natural.

hermeneutics [literary studies/philosophy]: a method of interpreting messages (from the name of Hermes, messenger of the gods) which assumes a relay (or recursive relation) between the details of a message's components and its overall meaning. Because of this recursion, meanings are not static but subject to historical change. This method had its initial foundations in biblical scholarship. More loosely, hermeneutics can mean any attempt at interpretation or decipherment.

heterosexism [political theory]: a moral and political belief in the inferiority of same-sex relationships.

hierarchy of needs [psychology]: Abraham Maslow's organization of human needs into seven main types, with an order of priority. The needs are associated with physiology, safety, belonging, esteem, knowledge, aesthetics, and self-actualization.

hippy movement [popular history]: a lifestyle, originating in the US in the 1960s but spreading in popularity across the world, embracing the mutually exclusive doctrines of 'universal love and peace' and 'doing one's own thing'. The movement is now almost defunct, or else displaced by New Age lifestyles.

homo-eroticism [psychology]: arousal of men by other men or their images.

homosocial [sociology]: adjective describing a group restricted to men – with connotations of possible sexual interest and attraction.

hypodermic model [media studies]: theorizes the interaction of the media and audiences as a case of direct, unmediated impact – texts enter and alter the brain much as a hypodermic enters and alters the bloodstream. See: *effects model*

indexical expressions [ethnomethodology]: expressions that indicate (from 'index', pointing, the pointing finger) something other than they literally express. A good example is 'It's cold in here' used to mean 'Close the window'.

infotainment [media studies]: a hybrid of information and entertainment used to describe texts (particularly television texts) that entertain by presenting (often quite low levels of) information on 'useful' topics such as gardening and cooking as well as celebrity news.

internalized self-monitoring [social theory]: see *auto-regimentation*.

light inclusive [cruciverbalism]: a type of crossword clue which has the answer embedded inside it.

lights [cruciverbalism]: the blank squares in a crossword grid; hence, by extension, the words that fit into them – the answers.

listed/summative pronouns [conversation analysis]: collective pronouns (you, we, they), where an exhaustive list of the persons referred to can be drawn up – by contrast with *categorized pronouns*.

marked/unmarked [linguistics]: a distinction (attributable to Nikolay Trubetzkoy) between members of linguistic pairs; between the 'normal' term in the pair and its 'other'. Hence in the pair 'duck/drake', 'duck' is unmarked because it is the usual term for that type of fowl (while 'drake' is marked for its difference because it refers only to the male of the species). By extension, the distinction has come into cultural studies to show political differences: hence, in horse racing, the male rider will be the unmarked form of the jockey, and the female rider the marked. In beauty contests, vice versa. Read 'unmarked' as 'the (culturally arbitrary) normal form'.

MCDs (Membership Categorization Devices) [conversation analysis]: devices used in ordinary language to collect ways of referring to persons. 'Football team' is such a device; it collects all the various playing positions on the football field. An MCD is effectively a set with members.

micro-object [EMICS]: a minute fragment or small empirical sample of everyday life such as somebody saying 'uh huh'.

micrological [EMICS]: a term describing any investigation of *micro-objects*.

mimetic [aesthetics]: closely resembling or imitating. In science, the term describes the mimetic tendencies of the animal kingdom (one species mimicking another; the lyre bird being a classical case in point). It also has status as part of an aesthetic doctrine that examines the arts as imitative of life.

MIRs (Membership Inference-rich Representatives) [conversation analysis]: a term coined by Harvey Sacks to draw attention to the ways in which certain expressions are 'rich' with inferences about those who use them and those they refer to. This is because some expressions are relative to particular persons or types of person (members). Their 'truth' depends on who applies them and to whom they are applied rather than on matters of logic or formal scientific inference.

modernity [history of ideas]: a period of time which is often thought of as lasting from the middle of the eighteenth century up to our own times. It is supposedly characterized by rationality, calculation, utilitarianism, humanism, and secularity, in keeping with its Enlightenment origins.

modes of subjectification [social theory]: see *subject*.

moral injunction(s) [social theory]: ideas about what should and should not be done.

myth [semiotics/anthropology]: originally, a tale of social and cultural origins. In current thinking, myths are not necessarily false ideas, but ideas by which cultural objects appear to become natural. The point of myth analysis (especially for Roland Barthes) was to make this process explicit and thereby to criticize some of the mystifications of cultural production (particularly in mass communications).

neoclassical [economics]: a return to the eighteenth- and nineteenth-century origins of economics, this model looks at fluctuations in the price of supply and the value of demand, favouring a model where the market fixes value at the margin, with the cost of supply and demand being mutually negotiable.

New Left [politics/history of ideas]: those on the Left in European and US politics during (and for some time after) the 1960s – a period when orthodox class-based Marxism was giving way to more fragmented forms of social liberation (feminism, gay liberation, black power). This political movement coincided with the formation of cultural studies.

oligarchy [political science]: rule by a select few.

ordinary language philosophy [philosophy]: the movement in philosophy (associated with Wittgenstein, Austin, Ryle and others) which argued that most philosophical problems were 'ills' that could be 'cured' by referring their uses of a specialized philosophical language to equivalent and ordinary uses of terms.

orientationals [ethnomethodology/conversation analysis]: an alternative to the idea of fixed rules of social interaction. While rules are binding, orientationals are broader templates, techniques that might or might not be taken up to bring about particular ends in particular situations.

orphaned initials [cruciverbalism]: in crossword puzzles, those answers (*lights*) whose first letter does not intersect with another.

paediatrics [medicine]: the branch of medicine specializing in diseases of, and other matters concerning, children.

pathologization [social theory]: the making of a subject or a population into a 'case' for treatment: medical pathologization is one example; psychological pathologization is another.

penology [social theory/criminology]: the study of prisons and incarceration, particularly with regard to their effectiveness in controlling populations.

performative [social theory]: those aspects of a social process, action, or event that are public and embodied; the audiovisual aspects of an ordinary scene that actors in them (members) must 'act out'. The term can be opposed to a variety of other possible descriptors: cognitive, formal, structural, semantic, and so on.

peristalsis [medicine/biology]: waves of contraction (in the alimentary canal and elsewhere) which are part of the digestion of food.

persona economica [economics]: the *subject* of economic theory; an idealized construction once known as the rational, calculating man in the market place.

phatic [anthropology/linguistics]: a descriptor for utterances performed mostly out of politeness (or for establishing some other 'mood') rather than for 'meaning what they say' or imparting information. For example 'How are you' is routinely phatic, since it's not always a request for details about somebody's health. Originally: phatic communion (Bronislaw Malinowski).

phenomenological bracketing [philosophy]: also known as the *epoché*, this technique deletes from a situation anything that cannot be directly attributed to consciousness.

plutocracy [political science]: rule by the wealthy.

Pollyanna(ish) [popular psychology]: a person exhibiting naive enthusiasm or optimism and who may be intolerable as a consequence. From the protagonist of *Pollyanna* by Eleanor Hodgman Porter.

power [social theory]: the capacity of bodies or populations to do things, and in particular to produce, control, or subject themselves (as bodies and populations). Power is not simple authority in the top-down sense, but a dispersion of force (in an almost physical or micro-physical sense) within and between bodies and populations.

predicates [conversation analysis]: descriptors used for persons' activities. 'Growing up' is a predicate, in this sense, and so are 'smoking' and 'having a sense of humour'.

preferential rules [ethnomethodology]: the loose rules of a game or sport that are open to the preferences of their players (for example, wearing or not wearing a cap for a cricket match – caps are allowed by the rules but are not obligatory). Preferential rules contrast with *basic rules*.

principle of epistemological humility [law]: a point of US law concerning the allowability of (marketing) claims; it considers scientific claims to truth to be nominalist. Nominalism is a doctrine that runs as follows: if terms (names) refer to objects, then the only connection between those actual objects is the terms (names) themselves and not any intrinsic or 'natural' relation. In effect, the doctrine reduces all truth claims to the status of mere (and temporary) beliefs.

profilmic [cinema studies]: adjective describing the inside of a film's space. Hence characters are profilmic (while actors are not) and cine-cameras are profilmic only if they actually appear in the film itself.

proprioceptive sense [physiology/psychology]: the sense a body has of its own musculature – sometimes extended to senses deriving from other bodily parts.

psy-complexes [history of ideas]: all those discourses and disciplines that investigate (and often propose therapies for) individual behaviour and thinking: psychology, psychoanalysis, psychotherapy, psychic healing, psychodrama, and so forth.

psy-discourse [history of ideas]: any one of the *psy-complexes*.

Rabelaisian [literary studies]: initially a follower of François Rabelais, a sixteenth-century French author who is held to have advanced the cause of extravagance in all things, including speaking and eating. Today, the adjectival form carries a sense of coarse manners and indecency.

reflexivity [ethnomethodology]: the theory or principle which holds that the methods which people use to go about their ordinary affairs are identical with the methods they use to make those affairs intelligible or accountable to one another.

representativity [conversation analysis]: the capacity for a speaker to 'authentically' represent the category of persons on behalf of whom they speak. Even if I am an Englishman, there may still be a problem of representivity when it comes to my speaking for that category of persons as such.

rheme position [linguistics/cruciverbalism]: at the end of an expression or clause. See *theme position*. In the area of text linguistics, themes are, strictly, clause-initial elements while rhemes are made up of the remainder of the clause.

scientific management [sociology]: the term is associated with F.W. Taylor, who worked towards a practical means of restructuring workplaces (at the end of the nineteenth century) so as to increase efficiency, output, and profit.

semiotics [history of ideas]: the discipline (sometimes science) which studies signs in terms of their formal properties, insisting on the arbitrariness of signs, as opposed to their 'motivation' or attachment to 'real' objects. (Hence the sign 'tree' does not have meaning by virtue of its attachment to a real leafy entity but through its formal location in an arrangement of other signs such as a sentence.)

sexology [history of ideas]: the study of sex and sexuality, particularly with regard to their control and maintenance within a population.

signification [semiotics]: the process of expressing as, or 'putting into', signs; the assignment of values and meanings through this process.

social formation [social theory]: a relatively broad-brush principle for describing the state of a society at a particular time. Hence modes of production (such as capitalism and socialism) are social formations while ideologies (such as Puritanism and liberalism) are not. The term can also be applied to smaller fractions than whole societies; hence, we can speak of the social formations of education, welfare, medicine, taxation, and so on – which brings the concept closer to that of **discourse**. The point of the concept is that it indicates the historical and material dynamics whereby societies are formed.

social phenomenology [social theory]: also known as phenomenological sociology; a school of sociology which (perhaps out of a mistaken reading of philosophical phenomenology) tries to show how everyday life (the life-world) is constructed in acts of consciousness.

solipsism [philosophy]: the mistaken belief that the only genuinely real thing in the world is oneself.

somatopsychic [history of ideas]: adjective describing **discourses** that operate, equally, to attribute causes to both the body and the mind.

specificity of struggle [political theory]: a term associated with the **New Left** to refer to local and particular forms of social struggle (for example for women's rights), as against the traditional Marxist notion of the centrality and universality of class-based struggles.

split clues [cruciverbalism]: clues with multiple-word answers.

subculture [social theory/cultural studies]: a fraction of a larger culture with its own practices, objects, and values (where these are often, but not always, in opposition to the larger culture).

subject [social theory]: the human person or, more strictly, a particular mode of being a human person (a mode of subjectification). Hence: the subject of medicalization, the incarcerated subject, the knowing subject, the speaking subject.

superstructure [social and political theory]: part of the Marxist distinction between base and superstructure (that is: between the economy and everything in a society other than the economy). Hence, the superstructure, on Marxist thinking, is typically where one finds all matters cultural, legal, religious, artistic, and so on.

surveillance [social theory]: control and management by the sheer fact of visibility – of oneself or another.

symbolic interactionism [sociology/social psychology]: a theory advanced by George Herbert Mead (in the 1930s) and closely related to **dramaturgy**. Everyday social events are inspected for their symbolic, communicational, and interpersonal contents – with particular regard to the relations between self and society, to actors' senses of themselves, and their capacities to understand one another and/or imaginatively take on others' roles.

synchresis [aesthetics]: when two or more parts of a cultural object (for example the sound and the image in a movie) achieve the effect of organic unity.

synchronic [history/semiotics]: during one period of time or historical episode. See **diachronic**.

synecdoche [literary studies]: a trope or figure of speech in which part stands for whole ('Fifty head of cattle', 'On behalf of the crown . . .'). In cultural studies, a synecdochal relation is where one cultural object comes to stand for a broader cultural entity: an oval ball stands for the game of rugby, a flag for a nation, and so on.

syntax [linguistics]: the rules for the horizontal arrangement of terms (especially in a language – word order in a sentence). By extension: the rules for any sequence of signs, objects, or events (such as the arrangement of goods for sale along a supermarket shelf).

tabula rasa [philosophy]: a blank slate; the state a person might be in prior to having any form of knowledge or experience.

teleology: any doctrine of ends or goals as necessary outcomes of particular actions and events; such that the particular actions and events appear to be determined by those outcomes (rather than by prior causes). Hence any doctrine of historical necessity.

theme position: at the beginning of an expression. See **rheme position** for a fuller treatment.

transactional analytic theory [psychology]: the theory informing transactional analysis – the therapy originated by Eric Berne which uses group settings in order to induce a 'mature' response in adults by overcoming their infantile impulses.

transhistorical [history of ideas]: adjective describing ideas that are believed to hold universally, at all times and in all places; not subject to historical change or variation.

transition relevance place [conversation analysis]: any point during one speaker's turn where another speaker can take the floor.

transubstantiation [theology]: Christian doctrine which holds that the bread and wine of the eucharist are actually converted into the body and blood of Christ. More broadly, any transmutation of one substance into another.

utilitarianism [philosophy]: an ethical doctrine which holds that the highest good is that which has most utility. Utility, in this case, means the production of happiness for the majority.

voluntarism [philosophy]: a doctrine in which the individual will is supreme and therefore controls, among other things, the intellect and the social environment.

Zeitgeist [history of ideas]: the spirit of the times; a worldview; any cultural totality as represented in the domain of ideas.

References

Abrams, Philip (1973) 'Television and Radio'. In *Discrimination and Popular Culture*, 2nd edn. Denys Thompson (ed.). Baltimore: Penguin. pp. 102–32.

Abu-Lughod, Lila (1990) 'Shifting Politics in Bedouin Love Poetry'. In *Language and the Politics of Emotion*. Catherine Lutz and Lila Abu-Lughod (eds). Cambridge: Cambridge University Press. pp. 24–45.

Adorno, Theodor W. (1991) 'Culture Industry Reconsidered'. In *Culture and Society: Contemporary Debates*. Jeffrey C. Alexander and Steven Seidman (eds). Cambridge: Cambridge University Press. pp. 275–82.

Adorno, Theodor W. and Max Horkheimer (1977) 'The Culture Industry: Enlightenment as Mass Deception'. In *Mass Communication and Society*. James Curran, Michael Gurevitch, and Janet Woollacott (eds). London: Edward Arnold. pp. 349–83.

Agnew, Robert and David M. Petersen (1989) 'Leisure and Delinquency'. *Social Problems* 36, 4: 332–50.

Albee, George W. (1977) 'The Protestant Ethic, Sex, and Psychotherapy'. *American Psychologist* 32, 2: 150–61.

Allison, Lincoln (1994) 'The Olympic Movement and the End of the Cold War'. *World Affairs* 157, 2: 92–97.

Alter, Joseph S. (1995) 'The Celibate Wrestler: Sexual Chaos, Embodied Balance and Competitive Politics in North India'. *Contributions to Indian Sociology* 29, 1–2: 109–31.

Altman, Rick (1992a) 'The Material Heterogeneity of Recorded Sound'. In *Sound Theory Sound Practice*. Rick Altman (ed.). New York: Routledge. pp. 15–34.

Altman, Rick (1992b) 'Sound Space'. In *Sound Theory Sound Practice*. Rick Altman (ed.). New York: Routledge. pp. 46–64.

Anderson, R.J., John A. Hughes, and W.W. Sharrock (1988) *Philosophy and the Human Sciences*. London: Routledge.

Ang, Ien (1991) *Desperately Seeking the Audience*. London: Routledge.

'Appendix: Episode Summary, 1993–1996' (1996) In *Deny All Knowledge: Reading the X-Files*. David Lavery, Angela Hague, and Marla Cartwright (eds). Syracuse, NY: Syracuse University Press. pp. 207–10.

Arbena, Joseph L. (1993) 'Sport and Social Change in Latin America'. In *Sport in Social Development: Traditions, Transitions, and Transformations*. Alan G. Ingham and John W. Loy (eds). Champaign, IL: Human Kinetics. pp. 97–117.

Arce, A. and T.K. Marsden (1993) 'The Social Construction of International Food: A New Research Agenda'. *Economic Geography* 69, 3: 293–311.

Arditi, Jorge (1996) 'The Feminization of Etiquette Literature: Foucault, Mechanisms of Social Change, and the Paradoxes of Empowerment'. *Sociological Perspectives* 39, 3: 417–34.

Aristotle (1962) *Nicomachean Ethics*, trans. Martin Ostwald. Indianapolis: Bobbs-Merrill.

Arminen, Ilkka (1996) 'On the Moral and Interactional Relevancy of Self-Repairs for Life Stories of Members of Alcoholics Anonymous'. *Text* 16, 4: 449–80.

Arnheim, Rudolf (1969) *Film as Art*. London: Faber & Faber.

Arnold, Peter J. (1994) 'Sport and Moral Education'. *Journal of Moral Education* 23, 1: 75–89.

Ashmore, Malcolm (1989) *The Reflexivity Thesis*. Chicago: University of Chicago Press.

Aycock, Alan (1992) 'The Confession of the Flesh: Disciplinary Gaze in Casual Bodybuilding'. *Play and Culture* 5, 4: 338–57.

Bakhtin, Mikhail (1994) 'The Banquet, the Body and the Underworld', trans. H. Iswolsky. In *The Bakhtin Reader: Selected Writings of Bakhtin, Medvedev, Voloshinov*. Pam Morris (ed.). London: Edward Arnold. pp. 227–44.

Barthel, Diane (1989) 'Modernism and Marketing: The Chocolate Box Revisited'. *Theory, Culture and Society* 6, 3: 429–38.

Barthes, Roland (1973) *Mythologies*, trans. Annette Lavers. St Albans: Paladin.

Beardsworth, Alan and Teresa Keil (1990) 'Putting the Menu on the Agenda'. *Sociology* 24, 1: 139–51.

Beardsworth, Alan and Teresa Keil (1997) *Putting Sociology on the Menu: An Invitation to the Study of Food and Society*. London: Routledge.

Bell, Philip and Theo van Leeuwen (1994) *The Media Interview: Confession, Contest, Conversation*. Sydney: University of New South Wales Press.

Bennett, Arnold (1957) *Mental Efficiency and Other Hints to Men and Women*. Kingswood: The World's Work (1913).

Bennett, Tony (1992) 'Putting Policy into Cultural Studies'. In *Cultural Studies*. Lawrence Grossberg, Cary Nelson, and Paula Treichler (eds). New York: Routledge. pp. 23–34.

Benthall, Jonathan (1995) *Disasters, Relief and the Media*. London: I.B. Tauris.

Beoku-Betts, Josephine A. (1995) 'We Got Our Own Way of Cooking Things: Women, Food, and Preservation of Cultural Identity among the Gullah'. *Gender and Society* 9, 5: 535–55.

Bergmann, Jörg R. (1992) 'Veiled Morality: Notes on Discretion in Psychiatry'. In *Talk at Work: Interaction in Institutional Settings*. Paul Drew and John Heritage (eds). Cambridge: Cambridge University Press. pp. 137–62.

Bernstein, Eldon and Fred Carstensen (1996) 'Rising to the Occasion: Lender's Bagels and the Frozen Food Revolution, 1927–1985'. *Business and Economic History* 25, 1: 165–75.

Biggart, Nicole Woolsey (1983) 'Rationality, Meaning, and Self-Management: Success Manuals, 1950–1980'. *Social Problems* 30, 3: 298–311.

Birch, David (1992) 'Talking Politics: Radio Singapore'. *Continuum* 6, 1: 75–101.

Bjelic, Dusan and Michael Lynch (1992) 'The Work of a (Scientific) Demonstration: Respecifying Newton's and Goethe's Theories of Prismatic Color'. In *Text in Context: Contributions to Ethnomethodology*. Graham Watson and Robert M. Seiler (eds). Newbury Park, CA: Sage. pp. 52–78.

Blinde, Elaine M. and Diane E. Taub (1992) 'Women Athletes as Falsely Accused Deviants: Managing the Lesbian Stigma'. *Sociological Quarterly* 33, 4: 521–33.

Boddy, William (1994) 'Archaeologies of Electronic Vision and the Gendered Spectator'. *Screen* 35, 2: 105–22.

Bolin, Anne (1992) 'Flex Appeal, Food, and Fat: Competitive Bodybuilding, Gender, and Diet'. *Play and Culture* 5, 4: 378–400.

Bonanno, Alessandro and Douglas Constance (1996) *Caught in the Net: The Global Tuna Industry, Environmentalism, and the State*. Lawrence: Kansas University Press.

Bordwell, David and Kristin Thompson (1996) *Film Art: An Introduction*, 5th edn. New York: McGraw-Hill.

Boscagli, Maurizia (1992–93) 'A Moving Story: Masculine Tears and the Humanity of Televized Emotions'. *Discourse* 15, 2: 64–79.

Bourdieu, Pierre (1994) *Distinction: A Social Critique of the Judgement of Taste*, trans. Richard Nice. Cambridge, MA: Harvard University Press.

Bracken, Peg (1960) *I Hate to Cook Book*. New York: HarcourtBrace.

Brodeur, Pierre (1988) 'Employee Fitness: Doctrines and Issues'. In *Not Just a Game: Essays in Canadian Sport Sociology*. Jean Harvey and Hart Cantelon (eds). Ottawa: University of Ottawa Press. pp. 227–42.

Brown, J. David (1991) 'The Professional Ex-: An Alternative for Exiting the Deviant Career'. *Sociological Quarterly* 32, 2: 219–30.

Brown, Richard Harvey (1992) *Society as Text: Essays on Rhetoric, Reason, and Reality*. Chicago: University of Chicago Press.

Brudnoy, David, Raoul Lowery Contreras, Blanquita Cullum, Marlin Maddoux, Jon Matthews, Mike Rosen, Mike Siegel, Errol Smith, and Armstrong Williams (1994) 'Gurus of Gab: Talk Radio Stars are Changing America'. *Policy Review* 69 (Summer): 60–67.

Budd, Joe (1989) 'A Tall Poppy Who Refuses to Bow'. *Sunday Mail* 26 February: 1–2, 21.

Burke, Peter (1995) 'Viewpoint: The Invention of Leisure in Early Modern Europe'. *Past and Present* 146 (February): 136–50.

Burroughs, Angela, Liz Ashburn, and Leonie Seebohm (1995) ' "Add Sex and Stir": Homophobic Coverage of Women's Cricket in Australia'. *Journal of Sport & Social Issues* 19, 3: 266–84.

Button, Graham (ed.) (1991) *Ethnomethodology and the Human Sciences*. Cambridge: Cambridge University Press.

Cahn, Susan K. (1994) *Coming on Strong: Gender and Sexuality in Twentieth-Century Women's Sport*. Cambridge, MA: Harvard University Press.

Cain, Carole (1991) 'Personal Stories: Identity Acquisition and Self-Understanding in Alcoholics Anonymous'. *Ethos* 19, 2: 210–53.

Callinan, E. (1906) *Look Up! Plain Talks with Working Boys*. London: The Religious Tract Society.

Cameron, Deborah and Deborah Hills (1990) ' "Listening In": Negotiating Relationships between Listeners and Presenters on Radio Phone-In Programmes'. In *Reception and Response: Hearer Creativity and the Analysis of Spoken and Written Texts*. Graham McGregor and R.S. White (eds). London: Routledge. pp. 52–68.

Cancian, Francesca M. (1986) 'The Feminization of Love'. *Signs* 11, 4: 692–709.

Cancian, Francesca M. (1987) *Love in America: Gender and Self-Development*. Cambridge: Cambridge University Press.

Cancian, Francesca M. and Steven L. Gordon (1988) 'Changing Emotion Norms in Marriage: Love and Anger in US Women's Magazines since 1900'. *Gender & Society* 2, 3: 308–42.

Cashmore, Ellis (1994) *. . . and then there was television*. London: Routledge.

Chion, Michel (1994) *Audio-Vision: Sound on Screen*, trans. and ed. Claudia Gorbman. New York: Columbia University Press.

Cicourel, Aaron V. (1964) *Method and Measurement in Sociology*. New York: Free Press.

Clarke, John and Chas Critcher (1985) *The Devil Makes Work: Leisure in Capitalist Britain*. London: Macmillan.

Cobb, Jean (1993) 'A Super Bowl-Battered Women Link?' *American Journalism Review* May: 33–38.

Collins, Randall (1992) 'Foreword'. In *The Classical Roots of Ethnomethodology: Durkheim, Weber, and Garfinkel*. Richard A. Hilbert. Chapel Hill: University of North Carolina Press. pp. ix–xiv.

Comfort, Alex (1978) *The Joy of Sex: A Gourmet Guide to Lovemaking*. Adelaide: Rigby.

'Congratulations John Gray!' (1997) *New York Times* 27 March: B30.

Cook, Ian and Philip Crang (1996) 'The World on a Plate: Culinary Culture, Displacement and Geographical Knowledge'. *Journal of Material Culture* 1, 2: 131–53.

Cooper, Pamela (1995) 'Marathon Women and the Corporation'. *Journal of Women's History* 7, 4: 62–81.

Cooper, Richard M., Richard L. Frank, and Michael J. O'Flaherty (1993) 'History of Health Claims Regulation'. In *America's Foods: Health Messages and Claims*. James E. Tillotson (ed.). Boca Raton, FL: CRC Press. pp. 45–84.

Coward, Rosalind (1987) *Female Desire: Women's Sexuality Today*. London: Paladin.

Cox, Tracey (1997) 'Living with Obsession: The Secret Disorder'. *Cosmopolitan* March: 22–26.

Crumley, James (1994) *The Mexican Tree Duck*. London: Picador.

Cuff, E. and G. Payne (1984) *Perspectives in Sociology*. London: Allen & Unwin.

Danto, Arthur C. (1992) *Beyond the Brillo Box: The Visual Arts in Post-Historical Perspective*. New York: Noonday Press.

Davidson, John (1992) 'Does Penis Size Really Matter? One Guy Gets Honest'. *Cleo* October: 68–70.

de Certeau, Michel (1988) *The Practice of Everyday Life*, trans. Steven Rendall. Berkeley: University of California Press.

DeLillo, Don (1986) *White Noise*. London: Picador.

DeLillo, Don (1987) *End Zone*. Harmondsworth: Penguin.

Derrida, Jacques with *Autrement* (1993) 'The Rhetoric of Drugs: An Interview', trans. Michael Israel. *Differences* 5, 1: 1–25.

Dessaix, Robert [with Joanne Finkelstein] (1990) 'Conversation on the Civility of Dining Out'. *Meanjin* 49, 2: 272–76.

de Swaan, Abram (1990) *The Management of Normality*. London: Routledge.

Dewar, Alison (1993) 'Sexual Oppression in Sport: Past, Present, and Future Alternatives'. In *Sport in Social Development: Traditions, Transitions, and*

Transformations. Alan G. Ingham and John W. Loy (eds). Champaign, IL: Human Kinetics. pp. 147–65.

Douglas, Mary (1979) *Purity and Danger: An Analysis of the Concepts of Pollution and Taboo.* London: Routledge & Kegan Paul.

Drew, Paul and John Heritage (1992) 'Analyzing Talk at Work: An Introduction'. In *Talk at Work: Interaction in Institutional Settings.* Paul Drew and John Heritage (eds). Cambridge: Cambridge University Press. pp. 3–65.

Duan, Changming and Clara E. Hill (1996) 'The Current State of Empathy Research'. *Journal of Counseling Psychology* 43, 3: 261–74.

Dyer, Richard (1992) *Only Entertainment.* London: Routledge.

Early, Gerald, Eric Solomon, and Loïc J.D. Wacquant (1996) *The Charisma of Sport and Race.* Berkeley, CA: Doreen B. Townsend Center for the Humanities Occasional Paper 8.

Eberts, Marjorie, Margaret Gisler, and Linda Brothers (1995) *Opportunities in Fast Food Careers.* Lincolnwood, NJ: VGM Career Horizons.

Eco, Umberto (1987) *Travels in Hyperreality,* trans. William Weaver. London: Paladin.

Egan, Timothy (1995a) 'Talk Radio or Hate Radio? Critics Assail Some Hosts'. *New York Times* 1 January: 22.

Egan, Timothy (1995b) 'Triumph Leaves Talk Radio Pondering Its Next Targets'. *New York Times* 1 January: 1, 22.

Eichberg, Henning (1986) 'The Enclosure of the Body – On the Historical Relativity of "Health", "Nature" and the Environment of Sport'. *Journal of Contemporary History* 21, 1: 99–121.

Elias, Norbert (1978a) *The Civilizing Process: The History of Manners,* trans. Edmund Jephcott. Oxford: Basil Blackwell.

Elias, Norbert (1978b) *The History of Manners.* New York: Pantheon.

Elias, Norbert (1986a) 'An Essay on Sport and Violence'. In *Quest for Excitement: Sport and Leisure in the Civilizing Process.* Norbert Elias and Eric Dunning. Oxford: Basil Blackwell. pp. 150–74.

Elias, Norbert (1986b) 'Introduction'. In *Quest for Excitement: Sport and Leisure in the Civilizing Process.* Norbert Elias and Eric Dunning. Oxford: Basil Blackwell. pp. 19–62.

Enloe, Cynthia (1990) *Bananas Beaches & Bases: Making Feminist Sense of International Politics.* Berkeley: University of California Press.

Evans, David T. (1993) *Sexual Citizenship: The Material Construction of Sexualities.* London: Routledge.

Falk, Pasi (1994) *The Consuming Body.* London: Sage.

Fantasia, Rick (1995) 'Fast Food in France'. *Theory and Society* 24, 2: 201–43.

Fiddes, Nick (1991) *Meat: A Natural Symbol.* London: Routledge.

Fine, Ben and Ellen Leopold (1993) *The World of Consumption.* London: Routledge.

Finkelstein, Joanne (1989) *Dining Out: A Sociology of Modern Manners.* New York: New York University Press.

Fiske, John (1988) *Television Culture.* London: Routledge.

Fiske, John (1989) *Understanding Popular Culture.* Boston: Unwin Hyman.

Fiske, John (1992) 'Audiencing: A Cultural Studies Approach'. *Poetics* 21, 4: 345–59.

Fiske, John (1993) *Power Plays, Power Works.* London: Verso.

Forbes, David (1994) *False Fixes: The Cultural Politics of Drugs, Alcohol, and Addictive Relations*. Albany: State University of New York Press.

Foucault, Michel (1977) 'Nietzsche, Genealogy, History'. In *Language, Counter-Memory, Practice: Selected Essays and Interviews*, trans. Donald F. Bouchard and Sherry Simon. Donald F. Bouchard (ed.). Ithaca, NY: Cornell University Press. pp. 139–64.

Foucault, Michel (1979a) *Discipline and Punish: The Birth of the Prison*, trans. Alan Sheridan. New York: Vintage.

Foucault, Michel (1979b) 'Interview with Lucette Finas', trans. Paul Foss and Meaghan Morris. In *Michel Foucault: Power, Truth, Strategy*. Meaghan Morris and Paul Patton (eds). Sydney: Feral. pp. 66–75.

Foucault, Michel (1980) 'Body/Power', trans. Colin Gordon. In *Power/Knowledge: Selected Interviews and Other Writings 1972–77. Michel Foucault*. Colin Gordon (ed.). New York: Pantheon. pp. 55–62.

Foucault, Michel (1982a) 'Grey Mornings of Tolerance', trans. Danielle Kormos. *Stanford Italian Review* 2, 2: 72–74.

Foucault, Michel (1982b) 'The Subject and Power', trans. Leslie Sawyer. *Critical Inquiry* 8, 4: 777–95.

Foucault, Michel (1983) 'How We Behave'. *Vanity Fair* November: 61–70.

Foucault, Michel (1984) *The History of Sexuality: An Introduction*, trans. Robert Hurley. Harmondsworth: Penguin.

Foucault, Michel (1986) *The Use of Pleasure: The History of Sexuality Volume Two*, trans. Robert Hurley. New York: Vintage.

Foucault, Michel (1987) *Mental Illness and Psychology*, trans. Alan Sheridan. Berkeley: University of California Press.

Foucault, Michel (1988a) *The Care of the Self: Volume 3 of The History of Sexuality*, trans. Robert Hurley. New York: Vintage.

Foucault, Michel (1988b) 'Histoire de la Médicalisation'. In *Masses et politique*. Dominique Wolton (ed.). Paris: Éditions du Centre National de la Recherche Scientifique. pp. 13–29.

Foucault, Michel (1988c) 'Technologies of the Self'. In *Technologies of the Self: A Seminar with Michel Foucault*. Luther H. Martin, Huck Gutman, and Patrick H. Hutton (eds). London: Tavistock. pp. 16–49.

Foucault, Michel (1995) 'Madness, the Absence of Work', trans. Peter Stastny and Deniz Sengel. *Critical Inquiry* 21, 2: 290–98.

Freadman, Anne (1988) 'Untitled (On Genre)'. *Cultural Studies*, 2, 1: 67–99.

Freud, Sigmund (1982) *Introductory Lectures on Psychoanalysis*, trans. James Strachey. Harmondsworth: Penguin.

Frith, Simon (1991) 'The Good, the Bad, and the Indifferent: Defending Popular Culture from the Populists'. *Diacritics* 21, 4: 102–15.

Frosh, Stephen (1989) *Psychoanalysis and Psychology: Minding the Gap*. New York: New York University Press.

Frow, John (1993) 'The Concept of the Popular'. *New Formations* 18 (Winter): 25–38.

Frow, John and Meaghan Morris (1993) 'Introduction'. In *Australian Cultural Studies: A Reader*. John Frow and Meaghan Morris (eds). Sydney: Allen & Unwin. pp. vii–xxxii.

Fuery, Patrick and Nick Mansfield (1997) *Cultural Studies and the New Humanities: Concepts and Controversies*. Melbourne: Oxford University Press.

Fussell, Sam (1993) 'Bodybuilder Americanus'. *Michigan Quarterly Review* 32, 4: 577–96.

Gans, Herbert J. (1993) 'Reopening the Black Box: Toward a Limited Effects Theory'. *Journal of Communication* 43, 4: 29–35.

Garfinkel, Harold (1963) 'A Conception of, and Experiments with, "Trust" as a Condition of Stable Concerted Actions'. In *Motivation and Social Interaction*. O.J. Harvey (ed.). New York: Ronald. pp. 183–238.

Garfinkel, Harold (1967) *Studies in Ethnomethodology*. Englewood Cliffs, NJ: Prentice-Hall.

Garfinkel, Harold and Harvey Sacks (1970) 'On Formal Structures of Practical Actions'. *Theoretical Sociology: Perspectives and Developments*. John C. McKinney and Edward Tiryakian (eds). New York: Appleton-Century-Crofts. pp. 338–66.

Gelder, Michael, Dennis Gath, and Richard Mayou (1994) *Concise Oxford Textbook of Psychiatry*. Oxford: Oxford University Press.

George, Richard J. and Russell G. Smith (1993) 'A Day in the Life of American and Irish Refrigerators: Implications for International Food Marketers'. *Journal of Food Products Marketing* 1, 2: 81–98.

Gerhards, Jürgen (1989) 'The Changing Culture of Emotions in Modern Society'. *Social Science Information* 28, 4: 737–54.

Gerhart, Julia and Charles Stinson (1994) 'The Nature of Therapeutic Discourse: Accounts of the Self'. *Journal of Narrative and Life History* 4, 3: 151–91.

Gibson, Ross (1992) *South of the West: Postcolonialism and the Narrative Construction of Australia*. Bloomington: Indiana University Press.

Gilligan, Carol (1997) 'A Therapist Examines the Hidden Problem of Male Depression'. *New York Times Book Review* 16 February: 24.

Given, Jock (1995) 'Red, Black, Gold to Australia: Cathy Freeman and the Flags'. *Media Information Australia* 75 (February): 46–56.

Goffman, Erving (1959) *The Presentation of Self in Everyday Life*. New York: Anchor.

Goffman, Erving (1981) *Forms of Talk*. Philadelphia: University of Pennsylvania Press.

Goldlust, John (1987) *Playing for Keeps: Sport, the Media and Society*. Melbourne: Longman Cheshire.

Goody, Jack (1978) *The Domestication of the Savage Mind*. Cambridge: Cambridge University Press.

Goody, Jack and Esther Goody (1995) 'Food and Identities: Changing Patterns of Consumption in Ghana'. *Cambridge Anthropology* 18, 3: 1–14.

Gopnik, Adam (1994) 'Read All About It'. *New Yorker* 70, 41: 84–102.

Gramsci, Antonio (1978) *Selections from the Prison Notebooks of Antonio Gramsci*, trans. and ed. Quintin Hoare and Geoffrey Nowell-Smith. New York: International Publishers.

Griffin, Christine (1993) *Representations of Youth: The Study of Youth and Adolescence in Britain and America*. Cambridge: Polity Press.

Groves, Ernest R., Gladys Hoagland Groves, and Catherine Groves (1945) *Sex Fulfillment in Marriage*. New York: Emerson.

Gruneau, Richard (1993) 'The Critique of Sport in Modernity: Theorising Power, Culture, and the Politics of the Body'. In *The Sports Process: A Comparative and*

Developmental Approach. Eric Dunning, Joseph A. Maguire, and Robert E. Pearton (eds). Champaign, IL: Human Kinetics. pp. 85–109.

Gruneau, Richard and David Whitson (1993) *Hockey Night in Canada: Sport, Identities and Cultural Politics*. Toronto: Garamond Press.

Guttmann, Allen (1994) *Games and Empires: Modern Sports and Cultural Imperialism*. New York: Columbia University Press.

Hacking, Ian (1992) 'Multiple Personality Disorder and its Hosts'. *History of the Human Sciences* 5, 2: 3–31.

Hall, M. Ann (1993) 'Gender and Sport in the 1990s: Feminism, Culture, and Politics'. *Sport Science Review* 2, 1: 48–68.

Hall, Stuart (1980) 'Encoding/Decoding'. In *Culture, Media, Language: Working Papers in Cultural Studies, 1972–79*. Stuart Hall, Dorothy Hobson, Andrew Lowe, and Paul Willis (eds). London: Hutchinson. pp. 128–38.

Hall, Stuart (1988) 'The Rediscovery of "Ideology"'. In *Culture, Society and the Media*. Michael Gurevitch, Tony Bennett, James Curran, and Janet Woollacott (eds). London: Routledge. pp. 56–90.

Hall, Stuart (1993) 'Deviance, Politics, and the Media'. In *The Lesbian and Gay Studies Reader*. Henry Abelove, Michèle Aina Barale, and David M. Halperin (eds). New York: Routledge. pp. 62–90.

Hanke, Robert (1989) 'Mass Media and Lifestyle Differentiation: An Analysis of the Public Discourse About Food'. *Communication* 11, 3: 221–38.

Harari, Fiona (1993) 'The New Face of Beauty'. *Australian* 18 June: 15.

'Hardcover Bestsellers' (1997) *Publishers Weekly* 244, 3: n. p.

Hargreaves, John (1986) *Sport, Power and Culture: A Social and Historical Analysis of Popular Sports in Britain*. Cambridge: Polity Press.

Hartley, John (1992a) *The Politics of Pictures: The Creation of the Public in the Age of Popular Media*. London: Routledge.

Hartley, John (1992b) *Tele-ology: Studies in Television*. London: Routledge.

Harvey, Jean, Lucie Thibault, and Geneviève Rail (1995) 'Neo-Corporatism: The Political Management System in Canadian Amateur Sport and Fitness'. *Journal of Sport & Social Issues* 19, 3: 249–65.

Hatt, Michael (1993) 'Muscles, Morals, Mind: The Male Body in Thomas Eakins' *Salutat*'. In *The Body Imaged: The Human Form and Visual Culture since the Renaissance*. Kathleen Adler and Marcia Pointon (eds). Cambridge: Cambridge University Press. pp. 57–69.

Haug, W.F. (1986) *Critique of Commodity Aesthetics: Appearance, Sexuality and Advertising in Capitalist Society*, trans. Robert Bock. Cambridge: Polity Press.

Hay, James (1992) 'Afterword'. In *Channels of Discourse, Reassembled: Television and Contemporary Criticism*, 2nd edn. Robert C. Allen (ed.). Chapel Hill: University of North Carolina Press. pp. 354–85.

Hearn, Jeff (1992) *Men in the Public Eye*. London: Routledge.

Hebdige, Dick (1994) 'Foreword'. In *Bad Aboriginal Art: Tradition, Media, and Technological Horizons*. Eric Michaels. Minneapolis: University of Minnesota Press. pp. ix–xxv.

Heidegger, Martin (1962) *Being and Time*, trans. John Macquarrie and Edward Robinson. New York: Harper & Row.

Heller, Agnes (1984) *Everyday Life*, trans. G.L. Campbell. London: Routledge & Kegan Paul.

Henneberry, Shida R. and Barbara Charlet (1992) 'A Profile of Food Consumption Trends in the United States'. *Journal of Food Products Marketing* 1, 1: 3–23.

Heritage, John and Rodney Watson (1979) 'Formulations as Conversational Objects'. In *Everyday Language: Studies in Ethnomethodology*. George Psathas (ed.). New York: Wiley. pp. 123–62.

Heritage, John and Rodney Watson (1980) 'Aspects of the Properties of Formulations in Natural Conversations: Some Instances Analysed'. *Semiotica* 30, 3–4: 245–62.

Higgins, C.S. and P.D. Moss (1982) *Sounds Real: Radio in Everyday Life*. St Lucia: University of Queensland Press.

Hill, Richard J. and Kathleen Stones Crittenden (eds) (1968) *Proceedings of the Purdue Symposium on Ethnomethodology*. Purdue, IN: Institute for the Study of Social Change, Dept. of Sociology, Purdue University (Institute Monograph Series 1).

Hillis, Marjorie (1936) *Live Alone and Like It: A Guide for the Extra Woman*. New York: Sun Dial Press.

Hoberman, John (1993) 'Sport and Ideology in the Post-Communist Age'. *The Changing Politics of Sport*. Lincoln Allison (ed.). Manchester: Manchester University Press. pp. 15–36.

Hochschild, Arlie Russell (1994) 'The Commercial Spirit of Intimate Life and the Abduction of Feminism: Signs from Women's Advice Books'. *Theory, Culture & Society* 11, 2: 1–24.

Hoggart, Richard (1971) *The Uses of Literacy: Aspects of Working-Class Life with Special Reference to Publications and Entertainments*. Harmondsworth: Penguin.

Houlihan, Barrie (1994) *Sport and International Politics*. London: Harvester Wheatsheaf.

Hunter, Ian (1984) 'Laughter and Warmth: Sex Education in Victorian Secondary Schools'. In *Sex, Politics, Representation*. Peter Botsman and Ross Harley (eds). Sydney: Local Consumption. pp. 55–81.

Hunter, Ian (1988) 'Providence and Profit: Speculations in the Genre Market'. *Southern Review* 22, 3: 211–23.

Husch, Jerri A. (1992) 'Culture and US Drug Policy: Toward a New Conceptual Framework'. *Daedalus* 121, 3: 293–304.

Huyssen, Andreas (1988) *After the Great Divide: Modernism, Mass Culture and Postmodernism*. London: Macmillan.

Irvine, Leslie J (1995). 'Codependency and Recovery: Gender, Self, and Emotions in Popular Self-Help'. *Symbolic Interaction* 18, 2: 145–63.

Ivory, Kimberley (1998) 'Australia's Vegemite'. *Hemispheres* (January): 83–85.

Jarvie, Grant and Joseph Maguire (1994) *Sport and Leisure in Social Thought*. London: Routledge.

Jayyusi, Lena (1991) 'Values and Moral Judgement: Communicative Praxis as a Moral Order'. In *Ethnomethodology and the Human Sciences*. Graham Button (ed.). Cambridge: Cambridge University Press. pp. 227–51.

Jayyusi, Lena (1993) 'The Reflexive Nexus: Photo-Practice and Natural History'. *Continuum* 6, 2: 25–52.

Jenks, Chris (1993) 'Introduction: The Analytic Bases of Cultural Reproduction Theory'. In *Cultural Reproduction*. Chris Jenks (ed.). London: Routledge. pp. 1–16.

Jerome, Jerome K. (1938) *Three Men In a Boat (To Say Nothing of the Dog)*. Bristol: Arrowsmith.

Jessop, Noel (1994) *Crossword Puzzles without Tears*. Springwood: Butterfly.

Jiminez, Mary Ann and Susan Rice (1990) 'Popular Advice to Women: A Feminist Perspective'. *Affilia* 5, 3: 8–26.

Johnson, Lesley (1987) 'Raymond Williams: A Marxist View of Culture'. In *Creating Culture: Profiles in the Study of Culture*. Diane Austin-Broos (ed.). Sydney: Allen & Unwin. pp. 163–77.

Kang, Joon-Mann (1988) 'Sports, Media and Cultural Dependency'. *Journal of Contemporary Asia* 18, 4: 430–43.

Kessler, Suzanne J. and Wendy McKenna (1978) *Gender: An Ethnomethodological Approach*. New York: Wiley.

Klein, Alan M. (1991) 'Sport and Culture as Contested Terrain: Americanization in the Caribbean'. *Sociology of Sport Journal* 8, 1: 79–85.

Klein, Alan M. (1995) 'Life's Too Short to Die Small: Steroid Use among Male Bodybuilders'. In *Men's Health and Illness: Gender, Power, and the Body*. Donald Sabo and David Frederick Gordon (eds). Thousand Oaks, CA: Sage. pp. 105–20.

Kline-Graber, Georgia and Benjamin Graber (1975) *Woman's Orgasm: A Guide to Sexual Satisfaction*. Indianapolis: Bobbs-Merrill.

Kohut, Andrew and Carol Bowman (1995) 'The Vocal Minority in U.S. Politics'. In *Radio – The Forgotten Medium*. Edward C. Pease and Everette E. Dennis (eds). New Brunswick, NJ: Transaction. pp. 45–57.

Kort, Michelle (1988) 'Go, Jackie, Go'. *Ms* 17, 4: 30–33.

Lasch, Christopher (1979) *The Culture of Narcissism: American Life in an Age of Diminishing Expectations*. New York: Warner.

Lavery, David, Angela Hague, and Marla Cartwright (eds) (1996) *Deny All Knowledge: Reading the X-Files*. Syracuse, NY: Syracuse University Press.

Lawrence, Geoffrey (1995) 'Futures for Rural Australia from Agricultural Productivism to Community Sustainability'. Inaugural Address, Central Queensland University.

Lears, Jackson (1994) *Fables of Abundance: A Cultural History of Advertising in America*. New York: Basic Books.

Lee, Chun Wah (1997) 'Relocating Coca-Cola's Cultural Space in Singapore'. Paper presented at the 47th annual conference of the International Communication Association, Montreal, 22–26 May.

Lefebvre, Henri (1987) 'The Everyday and Everydayness', trans. Christine Levich, Alice Kaplan, and Kristin Ross. *Yale French Studies* 73: 7–11.

Lenskyj, Helen (1991) 'Combating Homophobia in Sport and Physical Education'. *Sociology of Sport Journal* 8, 1: 61–69.

Leong, Laurence Wei-Teng (1992) 'Cultural Resistance: The Cultural Terrorism of British Male Working-Class Youth'. *Current Perspectives in Social Theory* 12: 29–58.

Lévi-Strauss, Claude (1987) *Anthropology and Myth: Lectures 1951–82*. Oxford: Basil Blackwell.

Lewis, P. (1985) 'Men on Pedestals'. *Ten-8* 17: 22–29.

Lewis, Peter M. and Jerry Booth (1989) *The Invisible Medium: Public, Commercial and Community Radio*. London: Macmillan.

Lewis, Tom (1995) 'Triumph of the Idol – Rush Limbaugh and a Hot Medium'. In

Radio – The Forgotten Medium. Edward C. Pease and Everette E. Dennis (eds). New Brunswick, NJ: Transaction. pp. 59–68.

Lichterman, Paul (1992) 'Self-Help Reading as a Thin Culture'. *Media, Culture & Society* 14, 4: 421–47.

Liddicoat, Anthony, Susanne Döpke, Kristina Love, and Anne Brown (1994) 'Presenting a Point of View: Callers' Contributions to Talkback Radio in Australia'. *Journal of Pragmatics* 22, 2: 139–56.

Limbaugh, Rush (1994) 'Voice of America: Why Liberals Fear Me'. *Policy Review* 70 (Fall): 4–10.

Livingston, Eric (1986) *The Ethnomethodological Foundations of Mathematics*. London: Routledge & Kegan Paul.

Lueschen, Guenther (1993) 'Doping in Sport: The Social Structure of a Deviant Subculture'. *Sport Science Review* 2, 1: 92–106.

Lunt, Peter K. and Sonia M. Livingstone (1992) *Mass Consumption and Personal Identity: Everyday Economic Experience*. Buckingham: Open University Press.

Lupton, Deborah (1994) 'Food, Memory and Meaning: The Symbolic and Social Nature of Food Events'. *Sociological Review* 42, 4: 664–85.

Lurie, Rachel (1994) 'Martina and Me: A Trilogy'. *SportsDykes: Stories from On and Off the Field*. Susan Fox Rogers (ed.). New York: St Martin's Press. pp. 120–29.

Lutz, Catherine A. and Jane L. Collins (1993) *Reading 'National Geographic'*. Chicago: University of Chicago Press.

Lutz, Catherine and Geoffrey M. White (1986) 'The Anthropology of Emotions'. *Annual Review of Anthropology* 15: 405–36.

Lynch, Michael (1993) *Scientific Practice and Ordinary Action: Ethnomethodology and Social Studies of Science*. Cambridge: Cambridge University Press.

Lynch, Michael and David Bogen (1991) 'The Primacy of Mundane Conversation: An Ethnomethodological Critique of Foundationalist Conversation Analysis'. Paper presented at conference on Current Work in Ethnomethodology and Conversation Analysis, Amsterdam, 15–19 July.

Lynch, Michael and David Bogen (1994) 'Harvey Sacks's Primitive Natural Science'. *Theory Culture and Society* 11, 4: 65–104.

Lynd, Robert S. and Helen Merrell Lynd (1956) *Middletown: A Study in Modern American Culture*. New York: Harcourt, Brace.

Lynd, Robert S. and Helen Merrell Lynd (1965) *Middletown in Transition: A Study in Cultural Conflicts*. New York: Harcourt Brace Jovanovich.

MacAloon, John (1987) 'Missing Stories: American Politics and Olympic Discourse'. *Gannett Center Journal* 1, 2: 111–42.

Macdonald, Dwight (1978) 'A Theory of Mass Culture'. In *Culture and Mass Culture*. Peter Davison, Rolf Meyersohn, and Edward Shils (eds). Cambridge: Chadwyck-Healy. pp. 167–83.

Maguire, Edward R. and Jeffrey B. Snipes (1994) 'Reassessing the Link between Country Music and Suicide'. *Social Forces* 72, 4: 1239–43.

Maguire, Joseph (1993a) 'Bodies, Sportscultures and Societies: A Critical Review of Some Theories in the Sociology of the Body'. *International Review of the Sociology of Sport* 28, 1: 33–52.

Maguire, Joseph (1993b) 'Globalisation, Sport and National Identities: "The Empire Strikes Back"?' *Loisir et société* 16, 2: 293–322.

Mäkelä, Klaus, Ilkka Arminen, Kim Bloomfield, Irmgard Eisenbach-Stangl, Karin Helmersson Bergmark, Noriko Kurube, Nicoletta Marilini, Hildigunnur Olafsdóttir, John H. Peterson, Mary Phillips, Jürgen Rehm, Robin Room, Pia Rosenqvist, Haydée Rosovsky, Kerstin Stenius, Grazyna Swiatkiewicz, Bohdan Woronowicz, and Antoni Zielinski (1996) *Alcoholics Anonymous as a Mutual-Help Movement*. Madison: University of Wisconsin Press.

Mancini, Marc (1985) 'The Sound Designer'. In *Film and Sound: Theory and Practice*. Elisabeth Weis and John Belton (eds). New York: Columbia University Press. pp. 361–68.

Marling, Karal Ann (1992) 'Betty Crocker's Picture Cook Book: The Aesthetics of American Food in the 1950s'. *Prospects: An Annual of American Cultural Studies* 17: 79–103.

Marqusee, Mike (1994) *Anyone but England: Cricket and the National Malaise*. London: Verso.

Marshall, D.W. and G. Cook (1992) 'The Corporate (Sports) Sponsor'. *International Journal of Advertising* 11, 4: 307–24.

Maryles, Daisy (1997) 'How the Winners Made it to the Top'. *Publishers Weekly* 244, 1: 46–49.

Mason, Tony (1995) *Passion of the People? Football in South America*. London: Verso.

Mattelart, Michèle (1986) 'Women and the Cultural Industries', trans. Keith Reader. In *Media, Culture and Society: A Critical Reader*. Richard Collins, James Curran, Nicholas Garnham, Philip Schlesinger, and Colin Sparks (eds). London: Sage. pp. 63–81.

McCloskey, Donald N. (1985) *The Applied Theory of Price*, 2nd edn. New York: Macmillan.

McHoul, Alec (1994) 'Towards a Critical Ethnomethodology'. *Theory, Culture & Society* 11, 4: 105–26.

McHoul, Alec and Wendy Grace (1993) *A Foucault Primer: Discourse, Power and the Subject*. Melbourne: Melbourne University Press.

McHoul, Alec and Tom O'Regan (1992) 'Towards a Paralogics of Textual Technologies: Batman, Glasnost and Relativism in Cultural Studies'. *Southern Review* 25, 1: 5–26.

McLuhan, Marshall (1974) *Understanding Media: The Extensions of Man*. London: Abacus.

McMurtry, Roy (1993) 'Sport and the Commonwealth Heads of Government'. *The Round Table* 328: 419–26.

McQueen, Humphrey (1992) 'The Essence of Modernity'. *Island* 52: 15–19.

Media Studies Center (1996) 'Talk Radio: Not for Everybody'. *The Media and Campaign 96 Briefing* 2 (July): 7–10.

Mennell, Stephen (1985) *All Manners of Food: Eating and Taste in England and France from the Middle Ages to the Present*. Oxford: Basil Blackwell.

'The Messiah of Taipei's Taxis' (1994) *Economist* 332, 7874: 32.

Michaels, Eric (1990) 'A Model of Teleported Texts (with Reference to Aboriginal Television)'. *Continuum* 3, 2: 8–31.

Mickler, Steve (1992) *Gambling on the First Race: A Comment on Racism and Talk-back Radio – 6PR, the TAB, and the WA Government*. Perth: Centre for Research in Culture and Communication, Murdoch University on behalf of the Louis St John Johnson Memorial Trust Fund.

Miller, Toby (1990) 'Sport, Media and Masculinity'. In *Sport and Leisure: Trends in Australian Popular Culture*. David Rowe and Geoff Lawrence (eds). Sydney: Harcourt Brace Jovanovich. pp. 74–95.

Millman, Dan (1979) *The Warrior Athlete: Body, Mind and Spirit: Self-Transformation through Total Training*. Walpole, MA: Stillpoint.

Mills, C. Wright (1970) *Power, Politics and People: The Collected Essays of C. Wright Mills*. Irving Louis Horowitz (ed.). New York: Oxford University Press.

Mills, Sara (1989) 'Corporate Karma Beats Burn-Out'. *Australian Financial Review* 30 August: 36.

Mintz, Sidney W. (1993) 'Feeding, Eating, and Grazing: Some Speculations on Modern Food Habits'. *Journal of Gastronomy* 7, 1: 46–57.

Mintz, Sidney W. (1996) *Tasting Food, Tasting Freedom: Excursions into Eating, Culture, and the Past*. Boston, MA: Beacon Press.

Mitchell, Susan and Ken Dyer (1985) *Winning Women: Challenging the Norms in Australian Sport*. Ringwood: Penguin.

Moerman, Michael (1988) *Talking Culture: Ethnography and Conversation Analysis*. Philadelphia: University of Pennsylvania Press.

Montemayor, Gail (1995) 'FOX Sets New Marketing Goals for Football Season'. *Marketing Society News* 6, 2: 5.

Moore, Robert and Douglas Gillette (1992) *The King Within: Accessing the King in the Male Psyche*. New York: Avon.

Morse, Margaret (1983) 'Sport on Television: Replay and Display'. In *Regarding Television*. E. Ann Kaplan (ed.). Los Angeles: American Film Institute. pp. 44–66.

Moskowitz, Eva (1996) ' "It's Good to Blow Your Top": Women's Magazines and a Discourse of Discontent, 1945–1965'. *Journal of Women's History* 8, 3: 66–98.

Moss, Howard B., George L. Panzak, and Ralph E. Tarter (1993) 'Sexual Functioning of Male Anabolic Steroid Users'. *Archives of Sexual Behavior* 22, 1: 1–12.

Munson, Wayne (1993) *All Talk: The Talkshow in Media Culture*. Philadelphia: Temple University Press.

Murch, Walter (1994) 'Foreword'. In *Audio-Vision: Sound on Screen*. Michel Chion, trans. and ed. Claudia Gorbman. New York: Columbia University Press. pp. vii–xxiv.

Musto, David (1995) 'No Cure but Care'. *Times Literary Supplement* 4800 (31 March): 6.

Myers, Fred R. (1991) *Pintupi Country, Pintupi Self: Sentiment, Place, and Politics among Western Desert Aborigines*. Berkeley: University of California Press.

Myers, Fred R. and Donald Lawrence Brenneis (1984) 'Introduction: Language and Politics in the Pacific'. In *Dangerous Words: Language and Politics in the Pacific*. Donald Lawrence Brenneis and Fred R. Myers (eds). New York: New York University Press. pp. 1–29.

Nafziger, James A.R. (1992) 'International Sports Law: A Replay of Characteristics and Trends'. *American Journal of International Law* 86, 3: 489–518.

Nathan, Debbie (1994) 'Dividing to Conquer? Women, Men, and the Making of Multiple Personality Disorder'. *Social Text* 40 (Fall): 77–114.

Newcomb, Horace (1994a) 'Overviews'. In *Television: The Critical View*, 5th edn. Horace Newcomb (ed.). New York: Oxford University Press. pp. 499–502.

Newcomb, Horace (1994b) 'Television and the Present Climate of Criticism'. In

Television: The Critical View, 5th edn. Horace Newcomb (ed.). New York: Oxford University Press. pp. 3–13.

'Now That We Have Your Attention . . .' (1997) *New York Times* 26 January: 13.

Nye, Peter (1994) 'Talk Radio – Electronic Democracy or Just Noisy Harrumphing?' *Public Citizen* 14, 5: 10–14.

Ochs, Elinor, Clotilde Pontecorvo, and Alessandra Fasulo (1996) 'Socializing Taste'. *Ethnos* 61, 1–2: 7–46.

Osfield, Stephanie (1997) 'Don't Underestimate the Power of Intuition'. *New Woman* March: 58–61.

Page, Benjamin I. and Jason Tannenbaum (1996) 'Populistic Deliberation and Talk Radio'. *Journal of Communication* 46, 2: 33–54.

'Paperback Bestsellers' (1997) *Publishers Weekly* 244, 4: n. p.

Park, Roberta J. (1994) 'A Decade of the Body: Researching and Writing about the History of Health, Fitness, Exercise, and Sport, 1983–1993'. *Journal of Sport History* 21, 1: 59–82.

Patton, Cindy (1993) 'Embodying Subaltern Memory: Kinesthesia & the Problematics of Gender & Race'. In *The Madonna Connection: Representational Politics, Subcultural Identities, and Cultural Theory*. Cathy Schwichtenberg (ed.). Sydney: Allen & Unwin. pp. 81–105.

Paulson-Box, Elaine and Peter Williamson (1990) 'The Development of the Ethnic Food Market in the UK'. *British Food Journal* 92, 2: 10–15.

Pener, Degen (1994) 'The Games Men Play'. *Gay Games IV Official Souvenir Program*: 26–30.

People Weekly (1996) *Entertainment Almanac*. New York: Cader.

Pettavino, Paula J. and Geralyn Pye (1994) *Sport in Cuba: The Diamond in the Rough*. Pittsburgh: University of Pittsburgh Press.

Pinch, Adela (1995) 'Emotion and History: A Review Article'. *Comparative Studies in Society and History* 37, 1: 100–9.

Polanyi, Livia (1997) 'Interview with Deirdre McCloskey'. *Challenge* 40, 1: 16–29.

Potts, John (1989) *Radio in Australia*. Sydney: University of New South Wales Press.

Prilleltensky, Isaac (1989) 'Psychology and the Status Quo'. *American Psychologist* 44, 5: 795–802.

Pronger, Brian (1990) *The Arena of Masculinity: Sports, Homosexuality, and the Meaning of Sex*. New York: St Martin's Press.

Pynchon, Thomas (1973) *Gravity's Rainbow*. New York: Viking Press.

Quinn, Judy (1996) ' "The Rules" Gets a Male Response'. *Publishers Weekly* 243, 45: 19.

Real, Michael R. (1996) 'The Postmodern Olympics: Technology and the Commodification of the Olympic Movement'. *Quest* 48, 1: 9–24.

Redish, Martin H. (1993) 'Product Health Claims and the First Amendment: Scientific Expression and the Twilight Zone of Commercial Speech'. In *America's Foods: Health Messages and Claims*. James E. Tillotson (ed.). Boca Raton, FL: CRC Press. pp. 17–44.

Reed, Susan (1994) 'Unlevel Playing Fields'. *Gay Games IV Official Souvenir Program*: 20–24.

Reiter, Ester (1996) *Making Fast Food: From the Frying Pan into the Fryer*, 2nd edn. Montreal: McGill-Queen's University Press.

Remnick, David (1996) 'Inside-Out Olympics'. *New Yorker* 72, 22: 26–28.

Renne, Elisha P. (1993) 'All Right, Vegemite! The Everyday Constitution of an Australian National Identity'. *Visual Anthropology* 6, 2: 139–55.

Rensi, Edward H. (1995) 'Foreword'. In *Opportunities in Fast Food Careers*. Marjorie Eberts, Margaret Gisler, and Linda Brothers. Lincolnwood, FL: VGM Career Horizons. pp. xi–xiii.

Rice, John Steadman (1992) 'Discursive Formation, Life Stories, and the Emergence of Co-Dependency: "Power/Knowledge" and the Search for Identity'. *Sociological Quarterly* 33, 3: 337–64.

Rich, Frank (1995) 'AIDS on the Air'. *New York Times* 2 April: E15.

Ridgeway, James (1994) 'Rightward Ho! Talk Radio's Journey to the End of Night'. *Village Voice* 14 June: 27–29.

Riessman, Frank and David Carroll (1995) *Redefining Self-Help: Policy and Practice*. San Francisco: Jossey-Bass.

Rind, Bruce and Prashant Bordia (1996) 'Effect on Restaurant Tipping of Male and Female Servers Drawing a Happy, Smiling Face on the Backs of Customers' Checks'. *Journal of Applied Social Psychology* 26, 3: 218–25.

Ritzer, George (1993) *The McDonaldization of Society: An Investigation into the Changing Character of Contemporary Social Life*. Thousand Oaks, CA: Pine Forge Press.

Rodger, Ian (1982) *Radio Drama*. London: Macmillan.

Rogers, Carl R. (1977) *On Becoming a Person: A Therapist's View of Psychotherapy*. London: Constable.

Rombauer, Irma S. and Marion R. Becker (1973) *Joy of Cooking*. New York: NAL Dutton.

Ross, Andrew (1992) 'New Age Technoculture'. *Cultural Studies*. Lawrence Grossberg, Cary Nelson, and Paula A. Treichler (eds). London: Routledge. pp. 531–48.

Ross, Ellen (1980) ' "The Love Crisis": Couples Advice Books of the Late 1970s'. *Signs* 6, 1: 109–22.

Rowe, David (1995) *Popular Cultures: Rock Music, Sport and the Politics of Pleasure*. London: Sage.

Russell, James A. (1991) 'Culture and the Categorization of Emotions'. *Psychological Bulletin* 110, 3: 426–50.

Russell, James A. and Kaori Sato (1995) 'Comparing Emotion Words between Languages'. *Journal of Cross-Cultural Psychology* 26, 4: 384–91.

Russo, Vito (1987) *The Celluloid Closet: Homosexuality in the Movies*, rev. edn. New York: Harper & Row.

Ryle, Gilbert (1984) *The Concept of Mind*. Chicago: University of Chicago Press.

Sabo, Donald (1993) 'Sociology of Sport and New World Disorder'. *Sport Science Review* 2, 1: 1–9.

Sabo, Donald and Sue Curry Jansen (1992) 'Images of Men in Sport Media: The Social Reproduction of Gender Order'. In *Men, Masculinity, and the Media*. Steve Craig (ed.). Newbury Park, CA: Sage. pp. 169–84.

Sacks, Harvey (1972a) 'An Initial Investigation of the Usability of Conversation for Doing Sociology'. In *Studies in Social Interaction*. David Sudnow (ed.). New York: Free Press. pp. 31–74.

Sacks, Harvey (1972b) 'On the Analyzability of Stories by Children'. In *Directions in Sociolinguistics*. J.J. Gumperz and D. Hymes (eds). New York: Holt, Rinehart & Winston. pp. 325–45.

Sacks, Harvey (1995a) *Lectures on Conversation Volume I*. Gail Jefferson (ed.). Oxford: Blackwell.

Sacks, Harvey (1995b) *Lectures on Conversation Volume II*. Gail Jefferson (ed.). Oxford: Blackwell.

Sacks, Harvey, Emanuel A. Schegloff, and Gail Jefferson (1974) 'A Simplest Systematics for the Organization of Turn-Taking for Conversation'. *Language* 50, 4: 696–735.

Savan, Leslie (1994) *The Sponsored Life: Ads, TV, and American Culture*. Philadelphia: Temple University Press.

Schegloff, Emanuel (1978) 'On Some Questions and Ambiguities in Conversation'. In *Current Trends in Textlinguistics*. Wolfgang U. Dressler (ed.). Berlin: Walter de Gruyter. pp. 81–102.

Schegloff, Emanuel (1992) 'On Talk and its Institutional Occasions'. In *Talk at Work: Interaction in Institutional Settings*. Paul Drew and John Heritage (eds). Cambridge: Cambridge University Press. pp. 101–34.

Schegloff, Emanuel and Harvey Sacks (1973) 'Opening up Closings'. *Semiotica* 8, 4: 289–327.

Schieffelin, Bambi B. (1993) *The Give and Take of Everyday Life: Language Socialization of Kaluli Children*. Cambridge: Cambridge University Press.

Schoenfeld, Bruce (1996) 'The Waiting Game'. *Golf Journal* 49, 7: 32–39.

Schreier, Barbara A. (1989) 'Sporting Wear'. In *Men and Women: Dressing the Part*. Claudia Brush Kidwell and Valerie Steele (eds). Washington: Smithsonian Institution Press. pp. 92–123.

Scraton, Sheila (1987) ' "Boys Muscle in Where Angels Fear to Tread" – Girls' Sub-Cultures and Physical Activities'. In *Sport, Leisure and Social Relations*. John Horne, David Jary, and Alan Tomlinson (eds). London: Routledge & Kegan Paul. pp. 160–86.

Segal, Lynne (1990) *Slow Motion: Changing Masculinities, Changing Men*. London: Virago.

Sen, Amartya (1996) 'Freedom Favors Development'. *New Perspectives Quarterly* 13, 4: 23–27.

Serrano, Isagani R. (1994) 'Civil Society in the Asia-Pacific Region'. In *Citizens: Strengthening Global Civil Society*. Civicus (ed.). Washington: Civicus. pp. 271–317.

Shapiro, Michael J. (1989) 'Representing World Politics: The Sport/War Intertext'. In *International/Intertextual Relations: Postmodern Readings of World Politics*. James Der Derian and Michael J. Shapiro (eds). Lexington, MA: Lexington Books. pp. 69–96.

Sharrock, W.W. (1987) 'Individual and Society'. In *Classic Disputes in Sociology*. R.J. Anderson, J.A. Hughes, and W.W. Sharrock (eds). London: Allen & Unwin. pp. 126–56.

Sharrock, W.W. (1995) 'Ethnographic Work'. *Discourse Analysis Research Group Newsletter* 11, 1: 3–8.

Shattuc, Jane M. (1997) *The Talking Cure: TV Talk Shows and Women*. New York: Routledge.

Shilling, Chris (1994) 'Review of *Body Matters*'. *Sociological Review* 42, 1: 143–45.

Shils, Edward (1966) 'Mass Society and its Culture'. In *Reader in Public Opinion and Communication*, 2nd edn. Bernard Berelson and Morris Janowitz (eds). New York: Free Press. pp. 505–28.

Silverstone, Roger (1994) *Television and Everyday Life*. London: Routledge.

Sims, Calvin (1996) 'Loony Radio's Not So Crazy. It's Great Therapy'. *New York Times* 14 May.

Skillen, Anthony (1993) 'Sport: An Historical Phenomenology'. *Philosophy* 68, 265: 343–68.

Smith, Dorothy E. (1987) *The Everyday World as Problematic: A Feminist Sociology*. Boston: Northeastern University Press.

'Sport from the Settee' (1995) *Spectrum* 18 (Summer): 24.

Stauber, John C. and Sheldon Rampton (1995) *Toxic Sludge is Good for You: Lies, Damn Lies and the Public Relations Industry*. Monroe, NY: Common Courage Press.

Stavitsky, Al (1995) 'Ear on America'. In *Radio – The Forgotten Medium*. Edward C. Pease and Everette E. Dennis (eds). New Brunswick, NJ: Transaction. pp. 81–93.

Stearns, Peter N. (1994) *American Cool: Constructing a Twentieth-Century Emotional Style*. New York: New York University Press.

Steele, Paula, Annette Dobson, Hilary Alexander, and Anne Russell (1991) 'Who Eats What? A Comparison of Dietary Patterns among Men and Women in Different Occupational Groups'. *Australian Journal of Public Health* 15, 4: 286–95.

Stenson, Kevin (1993) 'Social Work Discourse and the Social Work Interview'. *Economy and Society* 22, 1: 42–75.

Stephenson, Peter H. (1989) 'Going to McDonald's in Leiden: Reflections on the Concept of Self and Society in the Netherlands'. *Ethos* 17, 2: 226–47.

Streibel, Dan (1989) 'A History of the Boxing Film, 1894–1915: Social Control and Social Reform in the Progressive Era'. *Film History* 3, 3: 235–57.

Susman, Warren I. (1984) *Culture as History: The Transformation of American Society in the Twentieth Century*. New York: Pantheon.

Synnott, Anthony (1993) *The Body Social: Symbolism, Self and Society*. London: Routledge.

Taylor, Lynne (1996) 'Food Riots Revisited'. *Journal of Social History* 30, 2: 483–96.

Tomlinson, John (1991) *Cultural Imperialism: A Critical Introduction*. London: Pinter.

Trepp, Anne-Charlott (1994) 'The Private Lives of Men in Eighteenth-Century Central Europe: The Emotional Side of Men in Late Eighteenth-Century Germany (Theory and Example)', trans. Ursula Marcum. *Central European History* 27, 2: 127–52.

Turner, Bryan S. (1982) 'The Discourse of Diet'. *Theory, Culture & Society* 1, 1: 23–32.

Turner, Patricia A. (1993) *I Heard It Through the Grapevine: Rumor in African-American Culture*. Berkeley: University of California Press.

Van Otterloo, Anneke H. (1987) 'Foreign Immigrants and the Dutch at Table, 1945–1985. Bridging or Widening the Gap'. *Netherlands Journal of Sociology* 23, 2: 126–43.

Verhovek, Sam Howe (1995) 'In Texas, the "Inner Child" Has Finger on the Trigger'. *New York Times* 8 November: A1, D25.

Vines, Gail (1988) 'Is Sport Good for Children?' *New Scientist* 119, 1622: 46–51.

Vogel, Harold L. (1995) *Entertainment Industry Economics: A Guide for Financial Analysis*, 3rd edn. Cambridge: Cambridge University Press.

Volkerling, Michael (1994) 'Death or Transfiguration: The Future for Cultural Policy in New Zealand'. *Culture and Policy* 6, 1: 7–28.

Walsh, Thomas (1994) 'Hundt Blasts Talk Radio at NY Feed'. *Variety* 24–30 October: 44.

Warde, Alan and Kevin Hetherington (1994) 'English Households and Routine Food Practices: A Research Note'. *Sociological Review* 42, 4: 758–78.

Warner, Michael (1993) 'Introduction'. In *Fear of a Queer Planet: Social Politics and Social Theory*. Michael Warner (ed.). Minneapolis: University of Minnesota Press. pp. vii–xxxi.

Watson, Rod (1973) 'The Public Announcement of Fatality'. *Working Papers in Cultural Studies* 4 (Spring): 5–20.

Watson, Rod (1992) 'The Understanding of Language Use in Everyday Life: Is There a Common Ground?' In *Text in Context: Contributions to Ethnomethodology*. Graham Watson and Robert M. Seiler (eds). Newbury Park, CA: Sage. pp. 1–19.

Weber, Bruce (1997) 'Taking the Stage to Help Mars and Venus Kiss and Make Up'. *New York Times* 26 January: 29–30.

Weinberg, Martin S., Rochelle Ganz Swensson, and Sue Kiefer Hammersmith (1983) 'Sexual Autonomy and the Status of Women: Models of Female Sexuality in US Sex Manuals from 1950 to 1980'. *Social Problems* 30, 3: 312–24.

Weis, Elisabeth (1995) 'Sync Tanks: The Art and Technique of Postproduction Sound'. *Cineaste* 21, 1–2: 56–61.

'What the World is Reading' (1997) *Economist* 342, 8004 (15 February): 18.

Wieder, D. Lawrence (1974) *Language and Social Reality: The Case of Telling the Convict Code*. The Hague: Mouton.

Wiedermann, Michael W. (1996) 'Women, Sex, and Food: A Review of Research on Eating Disorders and Sexuality'. *Journal of Sex Research* 33, 4: 301–11.

Williams, Eric (1964) *Capitalism and Slavery*. London: André Deutsch.

Williams, Raymond (1975) *The Long Revolution*. Harmondsworth: Pelican.

Williams, Raymond (1977) *Marxism and Literature*. Oxford: Oxford University Press.

Williams, Raymond (1989) *The Politics of Modernism: Against the New Conformists*. Tony Pinkney (ed.). London: Verso.

Willis, Susan (1991) *A Primer for Daily Life*. London: Routledge.

Wilson, Caroline (1994) 'Cricket's Battle of the Sexes'. *Sunday Age* 23 January: 13.

Wolff, Janet (1992) 'Excess and Inhibition: Interdisciplinarity in the Study of Art'. In *Cultural Studies*. Lawrence Grossberg, Cary Nelson, and Paula Treichler (eds). London: Routledge. pp. 706–18.

Wouters, Cas (1995) 'Etiquette Books and Emotion Management in the 20th Century: Part One – The Integration of Social Classes'. *Journal of Social History* 29, 1: 107–24.

Wuthnow, Robert (1994) *Sharing the Journey: Support Groups and America's New Quest for Community*. New York: Free Press.

Index

Note: a letter 'g' after an entry in this index cross-references an entry in the Glossary, pp. 183–97.